IT LOOKS AT YOU

THE SUNY SERIES IN
POSTMODERN CULTURE

IT LOOKS AT YOU

The Returned Gaze
of Cinema

WHEELER
WINSTON
DIXON

STATE UNIVERSITY OF NEW YORK PRESS

Published by
State University of New York Press, Albany

For information, address State University of New York Press,
State University Plaza, Albany, N.Y., 12246

Production by Marilyn P. Semerad
Marketing by Nancy Farrell

Library of Congress Cataloging-in-Publication Data

Dixon, Wheeler W., 1950-
    It looks at you : the returned gaze of cinema / Wheeler Winston
Dixon.
        p.   cm. — (SUNY series, postmodern culture)
    Includes bibliographical references and index.
    ISBN 0-7914-2339-5 (alk. paper). — ISBN 0-7914-2340-9 (pbk. :
alk. paper)
    1. Motion picture audiences. 2. Motion pictures—Influence.
3. Motion pictures—Social aspects. I. Title. II. Series: SUNY
series in postmodern culture.
PN1995.9.A8D58 1995
302.23'43—dc20   94-13343
                                                                   CIP

10 9 8 7 6 5 4 3 2 1

For Gwen

CONTENTS

LIST OF
ILLUSTRATIONS

■■

ACKNOWLEDGMENTS

■■

This book was originally inspired by the work of Marc Vernet and Paul Willemen (see bibliography) on the question of the "returned gaze" in cinema; I freely acknowledge my intellectual debt to them as the originators of this current line of inquiry. Nevertheless, "the look back" is an underestimated and insidious coefficient of the cinema/video production/reception process that is certainly worthy of more attention, and indeed, my research uncovered a great deal of additional material on this concept, as indicated in the list or resource materials at the end of this volume. Much recent cinema theory has focused on the viewer as voyeur, as a scopophilic construct of cinema discourse, and yet this seems to cover only a portion of the process of seeing/being seen by the film/video image. The reciprocal gaze of surveillance, admonition, guidance, instruction—whether relatively benign or a labor of panopticonic control—is at the center, it seems to me, of all sign/image/suture systems employed in cinema/video discourse, although the conditions of cinema/video text reception differ greatly, one involving a shared public space, the other generally taking place in the domestic sphere (although, as I will document, there are numerous "crossover" instances of discursive reinscription employed by both media).

Then, too, there are the questions of cinema texts "translated" to a video image; of video as a surveillance tool in the most liberal sense; of trans/genderal address by the camera's gaze of video texts reconfigured as "cinema" images and projected on the theatre screen; and of the nature of the film/video image as it is procedurally constructed (one being the result of plastics, dyes, and light, essentially a "magic lantern" process; while the video image is composed of a series of lines and pixels continually reconfiguring themselves on the video screen. In the cinema, we see light thrown on a screen; with video, the image *is* the light source, projected *at us*. These are just some of the questions and functions of the reciprocal gaze in cinema/video examined in this text; undoubtedly much more remains to be written.

On a more "technical" yet deeply appreciated level of acknowledgment, portions of Chapter 1 originally appeared in a slightly different form as "It Looks At You: Notes on the 'Look Back' in Cinema" in *Post Script*; my thanks to Stephen Prince and Gerald Duchovnay for permission to reprint this material as part of this volume. My notes on the workings of the Warhol Factory and the films of Montgomery Tully first appeared in the journal *Classic Images*; my thanks to Robert King, editor, for permission to use this material here. Sections of Chapter 1, on the films of Alice Guy Blaché, and sections of Chapter 3, on the use of the first-person camera, originally appeared in *New Orleans Review*; my thanks to John Biguenet, editor, for permission to reprint this material. My writing on the Dystopian science fiction film first appeared in the April 1992 issue of *NFT Monthly*, the magazine of the British Film Institute, on the occasion of a season of Dystopian films I programmed at the National Film Theatre, London; thanks to Mark Adams, head of Programme Planning, for permission to reprint this work here. My comments on *Bus Riley's Back in Town* originally appeared in *Literature/Film Quarterly*; my thanks to Jim Welsh, editor, for permission to reprint this text. Portions of Chapter 5 originally appeared in *Thousand Oaks Journal* 1.1; my thanks to editor Ken Anderson for permission to reprint these materials.

In all these writings, it is clear to me now that I was moving toward the issues considered in this volume; these texts serve as manifestations of this concern as expressed in the work of many differing film artists. My sincere appreciation goes as well to Joseph Natoli, Carola Sautter, William D. Eastman, and Marilyn Semerad of SUNY Press for their support of this project, and to Gwendolyn Foster for her continued and insightful criticism.

My thanks, too, to Roma Rector, for her excellent job in preparing the manuscript for publication, and to my colleagues at the University of Nebraska, Lincoln, for providing a congenial and stimulating work environment over the past several years.

Finally, I wish to express my sincere appreciation to a number of scholars and theorists whose work has inspired me (either directly or indirectly) over the past several years, including Arthur Nolletti, David Desser, Brian Coe, Brian McIlroy, Mas'ud Zavarzadeh, Brian McFarlane, Antonia Lant, Caroline Merz, Deac Rossell, Janet Staiger, Barry Keith Grant, Elaine Scarry, Patrick Clancy, Barton Weiss, David Pirie, and many other influential writers on cinema theory practice. Numerous additional works that inspired this text appear in the bibliography as recommendations for further reading, and the interested reader is directed to these studies, as well as others, as potential sites of discourse for new research on the phenomenon of the reciprocal gaze in cinema/video. Hopefully, as Mas'ud Zavarzadeh might say, this brief text "gestures" in the direction of further work in a relatively unexplored area of film studies, and I look forward with anticipation as further critical writing appears on this crucial site of cinema/video reception discourse.

CHAPTER ONE

∷

It Looks at You: The Returned Gaze of Cinema/Video Reception

What is most significant is . . . the confluence of the two distinct formal developments, of movie technology on the one hand, and a certain type of modernist or protomodernist language on the other, both of which seem to offer some space, some third term, between the subject and the object alike.

—Jameson

What is at stake here is the 'fourth look' . . . that is to say, any articulation of images and looks which brings into play the position and activity of the viewer also destabilizes that position and puts it at risk. . . . When the scopic drive is brought into focus, then the viewer also runs the risk of becoming the object of the look.

—Willemen

Near the beginning of George Landow's short film *Remedial Reading Comprehension* (1970), there is a shot of a group of moviegoers ostensibly waiting for the projection of a film to begin. Landow's camera adopts the point-of-view of the film screen, staring out at the audience it seeks to possess. This shot thus accomplishes at least two functions. It valorizes the audience (Landow later asserts, "This is a film about you, not about its maker," in a textual intertitle within the body of the film), and it also directly expresses the gaze of the projection surface, impassively "looking back" at the faces of the spectators. As a function of this "look back," we (the viewers) are, "in a sense . . . more aware of our own reactions [to the film] than we are of the film itself" (Camper 76-77). The film acts upon us, addressing us, viewing us as we view it, until the film itself *becomes* a gaze, rather than an object to be gazed upon. This "gaze of the screen" in Landow's film resembles the look of the Gorgon, because the screen's gaze transfixes the audience into a state of willing immobility just as the viewers within Landow's films are rendered immobile. Cinema audience members may, at times, verbally or gesturally respond to the spectacle they bear witness to on the screen, but for the most part, audience reception of the cinematic process involves a reciprocity of "looks:" the gaze of the spectator, and the concomitant gaze of the screen looking out into the darkness.

There has been much discussion of the viewer as voyeur or omniscient auditor of the cinematic spectacle, and recent reception theory has aggressively investigated the crucial role of the audience in interpreting the film it visually apprehends, usually along sociological or psychoanalytic lines of interpretation. Marc Vernet's pioneer 1983 essay "The Look at the Camera" discusses the "look back" from the screen to the viewer, but centers much of its argument in the "gaze" of the performers within the film out into the audience. This is indeed a part of the "look back" in cinema, but one should also take into account the returned gaze of the cinematic apparatus itself, or as Sobchack puts it, the fact that "the film can look at and make visible to itself and to us an array of filmmaking apparatus presently connected to and enabling its very look, its present perception and *perceptive presence*" (emphasis mine) (224). What I may call "the gaze of the screen," or "the look back" (of the cinema/body) deserves further examination, and should not be narrowly categorized within genres. This widening of the "scopic scope," the function of the "returned gaze," is the work this volume seeks to accomplish.

Practitioners of "the look back" range from the reflexively sophisticated Landow to such commercially and/or artificially diverse filmmakers as Ernst Lubitsch, Wesley E. Barry, Andy Warhol, Robert Montgomery, Laurel and Hardy (as directed by James Parrott), Jean-Luc Godard, and many other artists—all of whom employ the reciprocal gaze of the screen to mesmerize or entrance their intended audiences. Godard's *Masculine/Feminine* (1966), *La Chinoise* (1967), and *Contempt* (1963) both incorporate direct declarations of the power of the gaze of the camera out *into* the audience. In *La Chinoise*, one of the actors refers to the fact that he is being filmed and then we see the camera filming *us*, (as well as the actor); *Contempt* begins with a long tracking shot that culminates with cinematographer Raoul Coutard composing a shot into the void beyond the periphery of the screen that directly "looks back" at the film's audience. Ernst Lubitsch's *One Hour With You* (1932) includes numerous instances of Maurice Chevalier and Jeanette McDonald "breaking through the frame" to directly address and gaze upon the spectator.

Laurel and Hardy used "the look back" to express frustration or disbelief, directly "viewing" the audience in such films as *Brats* (1930) and *Hog Wild* (1929). Buster Keaton also directly acknowledged his audience with a solemn stare. All of these instances of reflexive film practice incorporate the audience *into* the work—not as a by-product of exhibition and reception, but an essential part of the entire apparatus of cinema. For one of the key tenets of "the look back" is the supposition that an audience for the film will someday exist, and that inversely, the film itself will *not* exist until it is actually projected on a screen. Films that employ "the look back" are thus considerably diminished in their visual resonance when translated to video, inasmuch as screen size, and thus the scope of the screen's gaze out into the viewing space, is greatly reduced.

But what I wish to stress here above all other considerations is my notion that the "look back" is an integral function of all cinema, whether this responsive "look of the screen" is foregrounded by the work or not. It is not so much the returned gaze of the actors within a film, or the intensity of subject matter (as Willemen suggests) that introduces this phenomenon, but rather the combined, cohesive act of the entire cinematic apparatus in

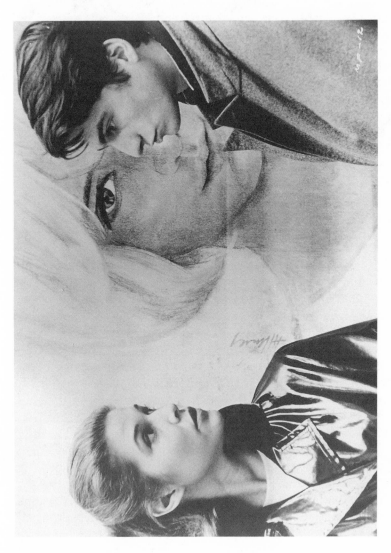

FIGURE 1. The look of the advertisement in Godard's *Masculine/Feminine*. (Courtesy of Jerry Ohlinger.)

FIGURE 2. Maurice Chevalier and Jeanette McDonald contemplate the viewer in *One Hour with You*. (Courtesy of Jerry Ohlinger.)

FIGURE 3. Laurel and Hardy acknowledge the spectator in *Brats*. (Courtesy of Jerry Ohlinger.)

operation: the production, presentation, and ultimate reception of a film. If there is a finite background to every shot in the cinema (or even if there is not, as in John Ford's spatially infinite elegies to Monument Valley, or the many science-fiction films set in interstellar space), there is still a look that is *returned* by the frame, by a force deep within the field it embraces, a force focussed by the rectangular dimensions of the screen—a window, a portal, an emitter of light into the audience.

This "gaze of the screen," or "look back," has the power to transform our existences, to substantially change our view of our lives, and of the world we inhabit. The violent "gaze" of Jonathan Demme's *The Silence of the Lambs* (1991), or of its low-budget predecessors such as *I Spit On Your Grave* (1977) or *Last House on the Left* (1972), as positioned within the body of the film (as shown between characters in varying shot strategies encompassing point-of-view, over-shoulder, extreme close-up, and seemingly benign establishing shots) or experienced as an external function by audiences (when the characters, or the shots themselves, extend their collective or separate gaze out into the auditorium) has a profound and problematic visual hold on viewers, conversely inciting or desensitizing patrons to acts of violence, misandry, misogyny, and/or calculated cruelty.

It has often been remarked that films of extreme violence adopt point-of-view shots to encourage audiences to identify with either the victim or the tormentor within the narrative structure of the work, particularly at crucial points during the film when scenes of risk or retribution are played out upon the screen. But these films also possess a gaze that projects out into the audience, a gaze that transfixes and collectivizes individual auditors into a momentarily cohesive group, stunned by the reflection of light thrown on the screen. In the same way, many "pornographic" films such as *Teenage Fantasies* (1970) include sequences in which the protagonists speak directly to the audience, even enticing the presumably male spectator of the film to engage in simulated sexual intercourse with one of the film's actors during the final ten minutes of the work.

Willemen argued that "the look back" (what he called "the fourth look") operated most aggressively in the reception/production of pornography, describing it as "a look 'imagined by me in the field of the other which surprises me in the act of voyeurism and causes a felling of shame,' as J[acques] Lacan put it . . . in simpler terms: the fourth look gains in force when the viewer is looking at something he or she is not suppose to look at" (56). But this seems to me a limited and "lack" driven defini- tion of the returned gaze. For me, the "look back" gathers force from shot duration, composition, and editorial patterning; it can also gain power from the gender origins of its address. As Stephen Prince (27-39) and others have demonstrated, however, deter- mining the origin of the gender/production in pornography is an inherently reflexive process that also looks back on itself, and many of our presuppositions as to exactly what audience is being addressed (or catered to) in pornographic representation are open to sustained additional discussion.

The idealized bearer of the gaze of the screen in *First Comes Courage* (1943) and *La Fée aux Choux* (1896) is female, as these two films (directed by Dorothy Arzner and Alice Guy, respec- tively), turn the gaze of feminist film practice back into an audi- ence expecting the confines of patriarchal narrative. In Arzner's film, the returned gaze is that of the lone practitioner of feminist film practice in 1940s Hollywood, excoriating the audience for her marginalization from then-contemporary commercial film production. Much has been written on Dorothy Arzner's work, particularly *Dance, Girl, Dance* (1940). Although that film con- tains effective and deeply felt testimony in the marginalization of women within the twentieth-century American patriarchy, one might prefer the countertestimonial example of Merle Oberon's Nikki in *Fast Comes Courage*, a Norwegian freedom fighter who effectively operates undercover during the Nazi occupation of Norway to bring down the fascist hierarchy. Nikki rejects the boring patriarchal domesticity offered in the "generically required" love interest (Brian Aherne) to continue her disruptive fight against the conquering dictatorship beyond the boundaries of her intended espionage assignment. Throughout the film, Oberon's Nikki is continually framed by Arzner in striking close- ups, looking directly at the audience. Much of the film's action is seen through her eyes; indeed, the opening sequences of the film is a staged optometrist's examination. All the viewer can see is Nikki's eyes, and the eyes of the doctor who examines her (the doctor is actually her underground "contact" for espionage operations). Framed in the surrounding darkness, Nikki gazes beyond the camera, out into the auditorium, alerting us to the fact that the power of the "*look at controls*" is central to Arzner's conception of the film. This strategy of the returned gaze continues throughout *First Comes Courage*, climaxing in a crushingly gothic Nazi wedding ceremony that Nikki is forced to endure. Arzner frames the sequence in a series of near-Bressionian wide shots, bordered by groups of SS "honor guards" in attendance, emphasizing the panopticonic surveillance implicit in the hierarchy of the Nazi regime.

In Alice Guy's work, the look back is imbued with wonder and amazement, as one of the first filmic narratives unspools (within a single shot) before our entranced eyes. The "look back" in the cinema films can either enlighten or degrade us; it is, it seems to me, a mistake to say that we are not possessed by the body of the film during the period in which its visual presence and control defines the perimeters of our existence. Although only a handful of Alice Guy's films survive, in those films that do still exist, we can see Guy exploring a number of interesting visual and syntactical strategies. *His Double*, a tale of romance and mistaken identity, is typical of the surviving Solax films, and because the film is difficult to obtain for viewing, it is analyzed here in some detail.

Grace Burleston, a young woman, wishes to marry the man she loves, but is temporarily thwarted in this ambition by her father, who wishes her to marry "Count Laking Coyne" ("lacking coin"). However, the Count's moustache makes him easy to impersonate, and Grace's true love, Jack, does exactly this. No split-screen work of any kind is used to carry off this "duplication of identity"; two actors with similar features are employed to stage the scenes. The highlight of the film is a pantomime sequence in the hallway of the Burleston home, as Jack, standing in for a conveniently missing mirror, copies the Count's actions perfectly. At the conclusion of the film, Jack, in disguise as the Count, is married to Grace.

Immediately after the wedding ceremony, Grace's father discovers the deception, and is furious. The minister, however, admonishes him, and points to the "Eleventh Commandment" in a Bible he has used to conduct the ceremony: "thou shalt not swear when thou are outwitted." At length, the father relents and agrees to the duplicitous marriage. Most of the action in *His Double* is staged in a single set, the living room of the Burleston home. A wide angle lens is used, and close-ups are almost nonexistent, except in the mirror sequence discussed above. Exteriors are photographed with natural light; interiors are obvious stage sets. In these strategies, Alice Guy mirrors the work of her contemporaries, particularly D. W. Griffith, who intercut obvious studio sets with near neo-realist exteriors in many of his early films.

In *A House Divided*, the best known of the Solax films, similar visual strategies are employed, with the only significant difference being the number of sets that are used. In the latter film, there are at least four major sets that are intercut to tell the story, that of a young couple who, due to a series of misunderstandings, refuse to speak to each other except through notes. The film also offers a caustic commentary on the place of attorneys in the marital contract, as the couple's jointly shared lawyer enthusiastically approves of this domestic rupture, as long as he is paid to draw up the documents to enforce it. There are a few more close-ups used in the film, but on the whole, the direction is straightforward and unadorned. The camera stays approximately twelve feet from the subjects, photographing them head on in a conventional master-shot.

However, even with the confines of such traditional visual choreography, Solax films often display a flair for deep-focus staging and the use of simultaneous planes of action. In *The Girl in the Arm Chair*, which has been preserved in its original color tints (these tints were accomplished by a machine process, and not by hand), the main set of the film is the drawing room of a well-to-do suburban home. Much of the action of the film takes place in the foreground of the shot, but exits, entrances, and instances of eavesdropping are often confined to a staircase that dominates the rear of the set. This main set is seen for more than two-thirds of the completed film; in view of this strategy, it is a tribute to the ingenuity of the director that the film still holds audience interest.

In *The Girl in the Arm Chair*, Frank, a young man who is betrothed to Peggy Wilson, is "forced into stealing $500 from his father-in-law-to-be's safe. Frank's descent from respectability begins when he falls in with a group of card sharps, who swindle him during a crooked game. The direction here is particularly astute, as the card sharps (in the foreground, left) contemplate Frank, their victim (to the right of the shot), while a sleazy bartender (in the extreme rear of the set) chuckles with obvious amusement at Frank's naïveté. These dubious companions then induce Frank to borrow money from a loan shark to cover his losses. When the loan shark's note falls due, "at 500% interest," Frank, in desperation, steals the money. As he does so, Peggy watches him, unobserved, from the armchair mentioned in the film's title, to the extreme right of the frame. In the wake of his crime, Frank endures a horrible nightmare, effectively suggested with blue tints and swirling superimposed cards which hover over his bed. The next morning, Peggy covers for him, but Frank makes a clean breast of it and is forgiven. In the final red-tinted scene, Peggy and Frank contemplate matrimony, as Peggy's parents look on approvingly.

The performances in *The Girl in the Arm Chair* are rather exaggerated, a trait paradoxically typical of Alice Guy's films. While she strove to get "natural" performances out of her actors, Alice Guy often let them play scenes in the broadest possible manner, with the result that some sections of Guy's shorts have much in common with episodes of the television series *I Love Lucy*, or other contemporary situation comedies. The subject matter in *The Girl in the Arm Chair* is much more serious, however, and as a consequence, the film verges on the melodramatic. The loan shark, in particular, is a caricature rather than a genuine creation, rubbing his hands together in glee at the amount of money he will realize on his short-term loan, and conducting his business dealings in the manner of a conventional nineteenth-century stage villain. Of all of the surviving Solax shorts, *The Girl in the Arm Chair* is easily the most stagebound, using the minimum number of camera set-ups possible to realize the narrative, with most of its action confined to a single set, and one camera set-up. Still, with the added enhancement of the color tints, the film effectively captures our imagination, and for a project realized in one or two days of shooting, it is certainly an admirable effort.

Other surviving Solax productions, such as *Officer Henderson* (a comedy involving two undercover cops who dress in women's clothing to catch purse-snatchers), *Burstup Homes' Murder Case* (a parody of the Sherlock Homes stories), *Matrimony's Speed Limit* (in which a young man must marry by noon of a certain day in order to gain an inheritance) *The Detective's Dog* (in which the detective himself is tied to a log in a sawmill for the film's climax, thus neatly inverting the generic requirements of conventional melodrama), *A House Divided* (a brief domestic comedy in which a young wife and husband refuse to speak to each other because of a misunderstanding), and *Canned Harmony* (a young man pretends to play the violin, with the aid of a hidden phonograph, to win the hand of the girl he loves over the objections of her father), display an engaging sense of relaxed character development, and an air of cheerful haste in their often improvised construction.

Nevertheless, in these brief films, Guy demonstrates a level of daring and sophistication absent from other American shorts of the period. In *Officer Henderson*, the cross-dressing policemen adapt easily to their roles as "women": after arresting several criminals, the two men return to the police station, where they amuse their comrades with demonstrations of "womanly" hand gesture, bearing, and manner. The other policemen laugh uproariously, but the scene is still a sharply observed comment upon the role of dress and presentation in the creation of one's sexual identity. It is one of the structural conceits of the film that when the two policemen wear wigs and skirts, their true gender is effectively concealed; even though their faces are clearly masculine, the other characters refuse to recognize them as men, as long as they wear traditional "feminine" clothing.

One of the policemen is married; Guy inserts a subplot in which the detective's wife, sure that her husband is being unfaithful, returns home to her mother with some of the clothing her husband is using to realize his disguise. The other policemen spends time in an up-scale restaurant, attracting the attentions of a Fatty Arbuckle-like admirer, with whom he makes a date for a rendezvous for the following day. Both of these situations are developed in an innocent fashion, neatly skirting any serious issues of gender identification and sexual placement the two subplots might have raised. Yet one still gets the feeling that Alice Guy knew precisely what she was exploring in *Officer Henderson*, even if she chose not to develop her material in more serious directions. Solax films were primarily popular entertainments, and strove to satisfy the American appetite for primitive comedy; this does not mean, however, that Guy was any less adventurous in her choice of the material for these films.

Matrimony is a persistent theme in the surviving Solax films; often the heroine must overcome the objections of either her husband-to-be or a doltish patriarch to effect the requisite happy ending. In *Canned Harmony* and *His Double*, it is the father who objects to the proposed match; in both cases, the woman refuses to marry anyone but the desired object of her affection. Through a combination of aural and visual deception (the wig and moustache in *Double*; the same disguise, with the addition of a prop violin and the aid of an off-screen photography, in *Harmony*), the woman is at last able to marry the man of her choice. In *Matrimony's Speed Limit* it is the husband-to-be who objects to the match, but only because of his comparative poverty. Realizing this, the young woman concocts a flimsy ruse, inventing a mysterious relative who will leave the young man a fortune, but only if he marries by noon of that day.

Much of *Matrimony's Speed Limit* is taken up with the man's desperate search for a mate, any mate, in order to beat the twelve o'clock deadline. (There is one unfortunate racist "joke" used here: one of the young women the young man accosts is heavily veiled. When she removes her hat, we see that she is black. The young man reacts with horror and runs away. The "joke" is all the more distressing because of its inclusion in a film created under the supervision of a woman who knew first-hand of the deleterious effects of sexism.) Predictably, the man meets his true beloved in time, and the two are married just before the stroke of noon. The new bride then reveals her deception and is immediately "forgiven" by her new husband. One of the titles in *His Double* assures the viewer that "everything is fair in love and war"; this theme is repeated again and again in the Solax comedies. In many respects, the heroines of Solax films are far more individual than those offered by Griffith during the same period. In all of these films, the "returned gaze" of the performer is an integral part of Guy's performative and syntactical structure.

WATCHING THE VIEWER IN
COMMERCIAL CINEMA

Perhaps no "commercial film" carries the visual strategy of "watching the viewer" to the limits explored by Wesley E. Barry's *Creation of the Humanoids* (1962). The film consists of a series of metronomically timed, unhurried, seemingly unemotional shots that proceed from establishing wide-shots to lengthy, minimalist close-ups, in which an actor often addresses the camera (and thus the audience) for minutes at a time, all the while ostensibly speaking to another performer within the film, supposedly viewing the speaker through the perceptual filter of her/his point-of-view. This "fragmentation of the look" is made all the more intense by Barry's studious avoidance of "standardized" rules of editorial structure governing sequences of expository dialogue; that is, that the camera should, for the most part, gaze upon the face of the speaker, with occasional glimpses of the face of the person being addressed. In Barry's film, once the simultaneous, bipolar point-of-view of character/audience is established, we (the audience) are never deprived of the gaze of the speaker. Conversely, we are seldom allowed to see the face of the person whose point-of-view the camera has adopted, although we can *hear* (from time to time) the off-screen responses made by the bearer of the protagonist's gaze. This oracular vision results in a pronounced distanciation from normative rules of cinematic practice and recalls Foucault's description of Jeremy Bentham's panopticon, in which one is continually subjected to external (as well as internal) surveillance as an ineluctable process of penal existence (216). Barry's radical film structure watches *us*, and when his characters gaze at each other, they gaze at us as well. Even in the wide-shots of the film, we feel the look of the image being turned against us, surveilling us, subjecting us to the "look back" of the screen. Entombed in darkness, enmeshed in the eye-matches of Barry's protagonists, we cannot extricate ourselves

FIGURE 4. The gaze of the machine melts the gaze of "human" inquiry in Wesley E. Barry's *The Creation of the Humanoids*. (Courtesy of Jerry Ohlinger.)

from either the gaze of the screen, or of the actors within the fictive construct the film documents.

The informing mechanism of Barry's look at the audience is
revealed in the final shot of the film. All of the actors in the film,
whether human or "humanoid" (robotic) are revealed, in fact, to
be "humanoids" (thus, there are no humans left alive). In a final
perverse twist, we are informed (by an actor who speaks directly
to us) that we too are "humanoids," the progeny of the protagonists of the film we have just witnessed and which has just "witnessed" us. While Barry's use of the "look back" is an extreme
example of this phenomenon (recalling, as an inverse example,
the perpetual point-of-view shots employed by Robert Montgomery's "famously unsuccessful" (Levinson 76) Lady in the
Lake (1946), Barry's film seems ultimately more aesthetically
successful (i.e., pleasurable) than Montgomery's work, precisely
because it delivers to the viewer exactly that which it implicitly
promises: the controlling power of the "look back" at the audience.

As Vivian Sobchack notes of Lady in the Lake's mono-
mythic visual structure, "the desperately felt self-consciousness
of incarnate existence that Lady in the Lake belabors as the film's
body strives to convince us of its bodily authenticity as human"
(246), but the illusion is never convincing. A punch is never con-
cretized, a kiss never resonates; we are perpetually locked outside
the spectacle, no matter how desperately Montgomery tries to
drag us in with his endless series of P.O.V. shots. Barry, on the
other hand, promises to subject us to the omniscient gaze of a
panopticon universe, and we can feel the power, oppression, and
scrutiny of this "look back."

Barry's film failed to recoup its investment at the box office;
however, Andy Warhol cited Creation of the Humanoids as one
of the most interesting films of the year. Shortly after seeing (and
being seen by) the film, Warhol purchased a 16mm Bolex with an
electric motor and commenced production of his own "reciprocal
gaze" films. Tellingly, Warhol's filmic practice began with a series
of three-minute "screen tests," in which a person would gaze
directly into the camera, while the camera gazed intently into the
eyes of its subject. These filmic constructs remain the purest and
most direct confirmations of Warhol's interest in the "look back."

The subject matter of these films is nothing more or less than the returned, or reflected, gaze. Yet beyond the audience-subject eye-match interlock inherent in Warhol's and Barry's projects, I would argue that the film itself constitutes a body, a living being (however animated), that throughout the duration of its existence (i.e., screening time), views its potential audience, holds them in its gaze, subjects them to the same sort of reciprocal surveillance that is experienced between prisoners and guards, a state that leads the viewer, inevitably, to look within her/himself.

RISK AND PLAY: WARHOL'S FACTORY

While many film historians have chronicled Andy Warhol's substantial career as a filmmaker in New York in the 1960s, the precise details of Warhol's working methods during this period are worthy of sustained examination. Later "Warhol" films (such as *Trash* and *Flesh*, which will be discussed later), actually directed by Paul Morrissey, have obscured Warhol's own achievement as a filmmaker. Thus a brief "redaction" of Warhol's genesis as a filmmaker seems appropriate at this juncture. Warhol's film style was an individual and highly idiosyncratic affair, but at his best, he created films of real intellectual interest, quickly and cheaply, using whatever materials were readily available.

Warhol was born in Pittsburgh, and attended what was then known as Carnegie Tech (it is now Carnegie-Mellon University) for training in commercial art. Moving to New York City in the 1950s, he began a long period of work as a commercial artist and steadily rose in prominence and influence in the Manhattan commercial art world. However, although the window displays, advertisements, and jobs illustrating cookbooks had all been extremely lucrative, Andy longed for a different kind of fame. He saw others around him, particularly Jasper Johns and Roy Lichtenstein, appropriating "found" imagery—newspaper ads, comics, and stock photographs—and incorporating these images in their paintings.

Warhol began fooling around with comic strip assemblages, in which he would cut panels out of comic strips and paste them onto canvas or paper, then add some paint to highlight certain portions of the strip. This gave way to the "S&H Green Stamp" paintings, for which Andy would sometimes paint each stamp individually and later use rubber stamps to create the multiple image effect of a large "block" of the trading stamps. Robert Rauschenberg showed Andy how to use a photo silkscreen, directly transferring a photograph to canvas with a single stroke, to create much the same effect. Immediately, Andy had silkscreens made up of many of the images he'd been most interested in, and began turning out paintings by the dozen at home. He still had no studio to work in. During a telephone interview with me in 1991, Gerard Malanga recalled,

> On visiting Bob Rauschenberg's studio sometime in 1962, Warhol was both fascinated and intrigued by the silkscreens that he saw being applied to the canvases and that he soon afterward ordered screens of his own to emulate Bob Rauschenberg's technique.

Using silkscreens, which could create a "finished" painting in a matter of seconds, Andy created his first major series of paintings starting in 1962, including the *Campbell's Soup Can* series, the *Disaster* series, and the *Marilyn, Elvis,* and *Troy Donahue* paintings. He later used these same images over and over to create "new" canvases to pay the rent and living expenses.

> I remember we were like little kids when we first met Marcel Duchamp out at Pasadena, whose retro coincided with Andy's LA exhibit of *Liz* and *Elvis* portraits. Duchamp was the spiritual father and role model, suggesting ways to "embrace the mistakes" that ultimately became the style of Andy's paintings and movies in the early to mid-sixties.

The first paintings sold well but weren't valued very highly. One could buy a Warhol painting for a hundred dollars, less if you purchased a group of paintings at once. Andy simply had to pay for his living expenses, and during this period, he even gave his paintings away to curry favor with influential art world figures. Sometimes, Andy would invite prospective buyers up to his house to select a group of paintings for purchase.

FIGURE 5. The gaze of the voyeur: Andy Warhol. (Courtesy of Jerry Ohlinger.)

In June 1963, Andy met Gerard Malanga at a party hosted by Willard Maas. Maas, a well-known experimental filmmaker who often collaborated with his wife, Marie Menken, had offered Gerard a place to live in New York, at their penthouse in Brooklyn Heights.

> I first met Andy at a party at Willard and Marie's. However, it wasn't until several months later that I met Andy again through an introduction orchestrated by Charles Henri Ford. Andy let it be known to Charles that he was in need of an assistant, and Charles, aware that I had previous silkscreen experience, arranged to have us meet at a reception for a Sunday afternoon poetry reading at the New School. In a matter of minutes Andy asked me to come to work for him. The pay was $1.25 an hour. Somehow the work appealed to me. The money obviously was not at issue, otherwise I would have moved on.

Gerard's first day on the job took place at an old abandoned firehouse on East 87th Street, which was the prototype of the first real Warhol "Factory," or studio. Warhol rented the entire building for $150 a year, but could only use the top floor for a studio. The rest of the building was practically falling down around him.

> I went to work for Andy in June of '63. It was warm weather, and so we got a lot of work done. But in the Fall, when we were still working there, and we were also in the process of looking for a new loft, there was no heat in the building, or even running water, and so we could only work there a few hours a day, because it got too cold. The building had electricity, but that was it. There was no heat. We set up a few lights to work with, but it was completely primitive as a work space.
>   He had the whole building. No one else was on the other two floors. But he used the top floor for his first studio. It was an actual firehouse that the City of New York owned. Andy rented it through some city agency for nothing. And then eventually we had to vacate because someone bought the building at an auction from the city.

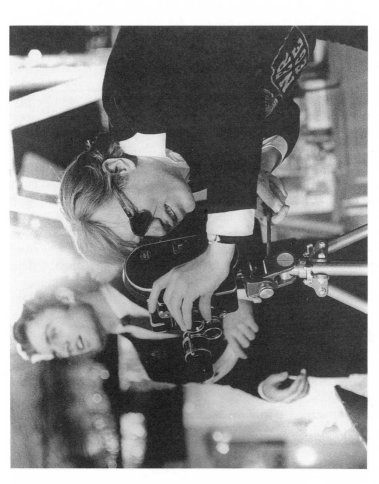

FIGURE 6. Gerard Malanga (rear) and Andy Warhol at work at The Factory. (Courtesy of Jerry Ohlinger.)

Almost immediately, Andy began turning to Gerard and others for ideas for his paintings. Although Warhol maintained a file of images early in his career, he soon gave this up and began simply using whatever came to hand. Gerard was already proficient with the silkscreen process, and even when he used too much ink or too little, Andy liked the end result. Gerard accelerated Andy's production assembly line, turning out numerous paintings and sculptures every day.

In July of 1963, Gerard Malanga and the poet Charles Henri Ford took Warhol to buy his first 16mm camera, a Bolex. Andy, who knew nothing about cameras, relied on Gerard to pick out a suitable machine. They went to Peerless Camera on 47th Street, where Andy paid $500 for the camera, which could hold only a 100-foot spool of film at a time, good for about three minutes running time on the screen. Malanga advised Warhol to purchase an electric motor for the camera, capable of powering through an entire roll of film in one burst. As always, Andy wanted everything to be as simple as possible. The object in all his work was mass production with minimal effort. Andy wanted everything to be "Easyville," as if the work would magically appear almost by itself, without any help from him: "The whole reason for getting the Bolex with a motordrive in the first place was so Andy could manage to work the equipment by a mere flick of the switch: On/Off, Off/On."

In November 1963, Andy and Gerard moved into the most famous of the Warhol Factory studios, located in a loft at 231 East 47th Street. There was only one way to get up to the Factory, an old freight elevator that took forever to get to the fourth floor, where the studio was located. All day long at the Factory, rock and roll and opera blasted out of a cheap portable phonograph, as Andy, always the first to arrive and the last to leave, continued to crank out paintings, graphics and sculptures at an incredible pace. Malanga assisted him in turning out the silkscreen canvases that supported the Factory's decidedly chaotic lifestyle. People drifted in and out at will. Andy welcomed nearly everyone who came, putting them to work on various projects, although Malanga always remained his principal collaborator.

The Factory was a turning point in American gay culture. The whole situation became more lax, although no one really "came out." But within the subculture itself, every-body was completely uninhibited. People like Ondine, Fred-die Herko or Frank O'Hara were all quite obviously gay, and didn't care who knew it. So that was refreshing. The artistic milieu had always been heavily dominated by homosexu-als anyway, and this certainly filtered down into the Fac-tory scene.

Under Warhol's direction, Billy Name (Billy Linich) began covering everything in sight in the new Factory—the walls, the doors, the ceiling, even the toilet—with silver paint and alu-minum foil. Andy was lionized by Hollywood and New York pop society, and the Factory became an endless party zone. There was always time to dance to rock and roll, or invite a visiting celebrity over for a "screen test." Dennis Hopper, Peter Fonda, Jane Fonda, Troy Donahue, and other young pop celebrities of the period would drop in unannounced. Warhol filmed each new visitor with his Bolex.

Film was cheap. A 100-foot spool of black-and-white film cost $4; processing was another $6. Color film cost roughly twice that. Warhol bought film in bulk and shot anything that seemed of interest. Fascinated with the Hollywood star system, Warhol began his major period of work as a filmmaker. For the time being, the painting supported the film work, which showed no immediate sign of making any profit. Andy started an aggressive campaign to "re-invent" the history of the cinema, beginning with a series of 100-foot 16mm portraits of the famous and near-famous, including Allen Ginsberg, Donovan, Lou Reed, and Bob Dylan.

Barbara Rubin brought Bob Dylan to the Factory. She knew Bob through her association with Allen Ginsberg. Barbara was a great catalyst. She loved to bring people together to share ideas, collaborate with each other, and so she thought that Bob should meet Andy. Andy was all excited; he thought, "maybe we can get Bob to be in one of our movies." Dylan and Bob Neuwirth came to the Factory, and Andy shot a screen test of him. Then Andy gave Dylan a gift of one of his Elvis Presley paintings. At one point, I gave the Bolex camera to Barbara, and she shot 100 feet of color film of Bob and me together, which I still have.

Sleep was followed by a number of Warhol films composed of 100-foot reels strung together, including *The Thirteen Most Beautiful Boys*, *Kiss* (originally presented as a serial), *Eat*, and others. The first Factory "superstars" appeared: Ondine, Baby Jane Holzer, Bridget Berlin, and Malanga, who stepped into *Kiss* as a substitute player at the last minute, when a scheduled "actor" failed to show.

However, the Bolex camera was a problem. It was simply too small, and didn't hold enough film. Also, it couldn't record dialogue during the shooting, and Andy was becoming more interested in doing "staged" movies. After shooting his eight-hour homage to the Empire State Building, *Empire*, in 1964 with a rented Auricon camera, Warhol was struck with the ease of using the machine. The Auricon could shoot 35 minutes of film in a single take. The sound was recorded directly on the film, eliminating the need for editing, titles, or post-production. The sound quality was terrible, but Andy didn't care. It was fast, cheap, and above all, easy to use. Warhol decided to buy an Auricon, and once again, Gerard went around to the various rental houses with Andy, looking for a used model for a reasonable cost. They finally found a machine at F&B Ceco on 43rd Street for $1200, and Andy was truly launched as an independent feature filmmaker.

Almost immediately, Andy began turning out an enormous number of feature films. The average cost of a Warhol production was $200 for a seventy-minute black-and-white film.

Andy shot a feature film roughly every ten days from 1964 through 1966. The first sound film we made was *Harlot* (1964). After that, we didn't make a film for about a month. Then we started making them on a regular schedule, as fast as Ronnie could write scripts. Sometimes, there was no script, as in *Poor Little Rich Girl* (1965) or *Suicide* (1965).

Other Warhol films during this period included *Camp* (1965), which Warhol gleefully publicized as "my first film to use bad camera work, zooming, panning, and acting" (*FMC Catalogue No. 4*, 153). Best described as a broken-down variety show, *Camp* features "performances" by Jack Smith, transvestite Mario Montez, and Malanga as master of ceremonies. *The Life of Juanita Castro* (1965) starred Marie Menken as Juanita and consisted of a long series of monologues, in which, according to Warhol's press release, "Juanita criticizes her brother's regime, and condemns the infiltration of homosexuality into their lives." All of those films were shot rapidly and cheaply. Since Andy released practically everything he shot, he was never at a loss for willing participants to appear in his films.

THE RETURNED GAZE OF WARHOL'S *VINYL*

One of the most famous of Warhol's films during this period is his production of *Vinyl*, written by Ron Tavel. The film was originally titled *Leather*, but Warhol changed it at the last minute, "because *Vinyl* is more plastic." Gerard Malanga played the lead role of a juvenile delinquent who goes through forced "reconditioning" after a crime spree; Tavel named Malanga's character "Victor, the Victor." The other actors were cast very quickly from the usual crew of Factory regulars.

> The script was given to me by Ronnie [Tavel] about a week before the shooting. I was so bad at memorizing lines that I literally had the script by my side during the filming. During the shoot, the script got thrown on the floor, and a glass of water spilled on it. At that point, utter chaos broke out, because there were parts of the script I hadn't memorized. The film became totally improvised after that point. My lifestyle was so busy, so intense during this period—going to parties, openings, whatever—that there was literally no *time* to rehearse. I was kidding myself. There simply wasn't time to prepare for the role.

At the last minute, Edie Sedgwick, who had just arrived at the Factory a few days before, was put in the film as an extra. Edie sits on a steamer truck to the right of the frame, idly smoking a cigarette. John MacDermott appears as the cop, who busts Victor after a brief crime spree. The doctor who "reforms" Victor was played by Tosh Carillo. Rounding out the cast, Bob Olivo (Ondine), later famous for his portrayal of the Pope in *The Chelsea Girls* (1966), appeared as Victor's sidekick, Scum Baby.

> When Andy threw Edie into the shooting of *Vinyl*, at first I was upset, because Edie wasn't part of the script. She was put there as a human prop. I was nervous, because I thought Andy was using her to upstage my part, since the film was written especially for me. But then Edie and I became friends, and I didn't feel there was any threat involved.

Vinyl was shot during April 1965, just before Andy's departure for Europe, where he had a show at the Sonnabend Gallery in Paris. The film was photographed in front of a large group of people. Contrary to what has been reported elsewhere, the filming was not done late at night. Gerard remembers that filming

> started around noon, and lasted until 3 o'clock. There was no direction. Basically, the film was supposed to be locked into place by the structure of the script. We did do a couple of rehearsals at the Factory with Ronnie and John MacDermott, but not everybody in the cast was present during rehearsals, so there was never a formal run-through before filming.

Warhol shot the film so quickly that none of the actors had adequate time to rehearse, but this gave Andy the rough look he was aiming for. As usual, the filming became yet another excuse for a party. A number of art world insiders were invited to witness the shoot, turning the atmosphere around the production into an astutely staged media event. Both the *Herald Tribune* and Fred McDarrah of *The Village Voice* were ready with cameras in hand.

As 1965 continued, Andy hit his stride, turning out *Horse, Space, The Life of Juanita Castro, Drunk, My Hustler, Screen Tests No. 1 and 2, Poor Little Rich Girl, Kitchen* (also known as *Kitchenette*), and many other films.

FIGURE 7. Gerard Malanga and Edie Sedgwick in a two-frame enlargement from Warhol's *Vinyl*. (Courtesy of Museum of Modern Art Film Stills Archive.)

In mid-1965, Andy made a movie of the Velvet Underground and Nico rehearsing at the Factory. The cops were coming up and bothering us all the time, and during the shooting of the film, the police busted into the Factory because we were making too much noise. It's in the film. Andy panned the camera away from the Velvets and on to the policemen, and then after a minute or so pans back to the Velvets. But it was just a noise complaint, so we turned it down, and they left.

The films were mostly seventy minutes long, or 2400 feet of 16mm film. Lighting, sound, and technical facilities were primitive; Warhol didn't care about details. Most of the films were in black-and-white; occasionally, for a particular project, Warhol might splurge on a reel of color film. Technicians on the films included Malanga and Paul Morrissey, introduced to the Factory scene by Malanga. Malanga emerged as the official press spokesperson for the Factory, writing all publicity materials for Warhol's films through 1966. Warhol ended 1965 with the announcement that he had "retired" from painting (although this was certainly not true).

Turning all his attention to film work, Warhol began the production of what was to be later known as *The Chelsea Girls*, the 3 1/2 hour split-screen feature film that was his first real commercial success as a filmmaker. Warhol shot various reels of Eric Emerson doing a striptease, Nico playing with her son, Ari, and Bridget Berlin talking on the phone in various rooms of New York's Chelsea Hotel. Some reels were shot in color; most were black-and-white. The shooting continued through the summer of 1966, and Andy picked up the pace of production, shooting a 35-minute reel of film nearly every other day. The filmmaking process appealed to Warhol because of its ease and immediacy. As soon as a good reel of film had been shot, Warhol would screen it at the Filmmakers' Cinematheque, then located in the basement of the now-demolished Wurlitzer Building on 41st Street.

The Chelsea Girls is a good example of this. Warhol was still shooting the film as late as September 9, 1966, yet the first public performance of the film took place only a few days later on September 15. Production at the Factory was still a haphazard affair. During the shooting of Ondine's sequences as the "Pope" hearing the confessions of some Factory regulars, Andy failed to notice that the microphone wasn't plugged in properly; as a result, the initial ten minutes of the first reel are completely silent. Warhol printed the reel anyway, incorporating it near the end of the film. In addition to production difficulties, Andy was also rather lax in preparing his films for exhibition. The day before *The Chelsea Girls* premiered, Andy was still getting the reels printed up for the first screening.

Less than a month after *The Chelsea Girls* opened (the film would eventually generate more than a million dollars in rentals), Warhol shot one of his most unusual and mysterious projects, a film on the assassination of John F. Kennedy. The film was made in a single night, on October 12, 1966, and was far longer than the usual Warhol sync-sound feature, clocking in at 140 minutes. Although the film was never shown publicly, or even named, the originals exist in the archives of the Andy Warhol Foundation for the Visual Arts. With typical aplomb, Warhol cast Mary Woronov as John F. Kennedy, and used both Malanga and Ronnie Cutrone (who would assist Warhol in the 1980s as a silkscreen technician) interchangeably in the role of Lee Harvey Oswald. Yet the resultant film was surprisingly uninteresting, and Andy decided against releasing the finished product.

Warhol's films have been unavailable for decades, but now film scholars can rent prints of some of his best early films, including *Vinyl* and *The Chelsea Girls*, from the Museum of Modern Art. Later films released under the Warhol banner, such as *Flesh* and *Trash*, were actually directed by Paul Morrissey, and come nowhere near the power of Warhol's early work. When Warhol was shot by Valerie Solanas on June 3, 1968, his filmmaking and screenpainting activity were drastically curtailed. Yet his first films, made under primitive conditions and nonexistent budgets, are as resonant today as when they were first produced and deserve to be viewed, and re-viewed, as some of the finest film work created during the turbulent 1960s, and an index of the social, political and sexual concerns of the era. And Warhol's films retain this power only when they are projected, released from the prison of their film cans, and shown in theatrical dimensions on a large screen. Only then does *Vinyl* return the gaze of the viewer for which it was intended—creating a spectatorial zone that is concomitantly seeing and seen.

A frame enlargement from *Vinyl* carries little, if any, of the power of the projected image of the film, and gives no sense of the *duration* of the gaze of the film back at the audience, a central issue in the establishment of "the look back." Warhol's *Vinyl* (1965) consists of three long takes: one of thirty-five minutes duration, one twenty minutes long, and a final shot running fifteen minutes long, for a total of seventy minutes running time. The film begins with a tight close-up of the protagonist, Gerard Malanga, lifting weights, and slowly zooms back to reveal a wide-angle shot of the film's entire performance space, populated by various members of the Warhol entourage.

Much has been written about the impassive and, some have argued, conscienceless and clinical gaze of Warhol's camera, which simultaneously entraps and paradoxically enshrines his chosen subjects. What seems to have been overlooked is the reciprocal effect: the fact that the film, as an inverse function of its "gaze inward," looks back at the spectator. The production of this returned look from the screen is an integral part of Warhol's vision in the creation of his early "fixed gaze" films. This "look back" becomes, then, considerably less intense in such later Warhol films as *The Chelsea Girls* (1966), which employs a good deal of camera movement that valorizes the viewer/camera operator over the reciprocal gaze of the performers, and the returned gaze of the Proscenium Arch performing area they inhabit. For "the look back" is not only a function of the gaze of the performers, or of the settings they use. Rather, it is a result of the power of the screen *framed by the gaze of the cinematic apparatus,* and the resultant *reflection of this gaze upon the viewer.*

The fact that we are witnessing, through the agency of *Vinyl,* a gay sadomasochistic variation on Anthony Burgess's *A Clockwork Orange,* lays some claim to our attention in the area of "forbidden spectacle," as Willemen suggests. But I would argue that it is not so much the subject matter but rather the intense stylization, which produces the "returned gaze" in the film—certainly there is an abundancy of graphic sadomasochistic material on film, but for most of these films, questions of style are not paramount. In Warhol's film, it is the style that informs the creation of the work, not the ritualistic sex-play documented within the highly reflexive narrative of the film. When watching *Vinyl* one gets the continual and uneasy feeling that one is being watched, being *judged*, by Warhol's returned gaze, a gaze that is almost solely a product of the performance space of the film, rather than the "look" of the actors (most of whom are staring offscreen at cue-cards, desperately trying to decipher their lines). *Vinyl* is spatial response above all else; the viewer viewed, the gaze returned (see also Bourdon 202-203; Michelson 57-62; McShine 408-409).

Michelson notes that Warhol's films operated within the scope of the Bakhtinian carnivalesque; a zone where "time is indeed expended, not clocked or measured . . . the spectator is positioned within an hallucinated *now*. Warhol's films generate another kind of temporality, for they take, as it were, their time, the distended time of contemplation and expectation" (60). But as Katerina Clark and Michael Holquist observe in their study of Bakhtinian poetics, "such a poetics [of carnivalesque time and space disruption] must assume a Januslike gaze in two directions at once" (202). The gaze inward is matched by a look outward; we see into a space of distended time, but this space returns our gaze with a look of its own.

THE MEDITATIONAL GAZE: ROSSELLINI'S HISTORICAL EPICS

Roberto Rossellini's late historical epics for RAI (the Italian television network) employ a strategy of long takes and a robotically controlled camera (reminiscent of the passive gaze of Warhol's camera or, as discussed next, the camera as employed by Jean-Marie Straub and Daniele Huillet) to confront the viewer with the recreation of a time and place long past, making the remote *immediate* through the uninterrupted scopic drive of the motion picture camera as recording instrument. Partly because of economic constraints, or partly because of the verisimilitude of the "unbroken" image, Rossellini in *The Rise to Power of Louis XIV* (1966), *Blaise Pascal* (1975), and *Socrates* (1970), began to use a constantly moving camera without the editorial syntax found in more conventional films to convey the physical and emotional reality of his protagonists experiences.

In an interview with Victoria Schultz, Rossellini admitted:

> I was pushed to discover other kinds of techniques in order to make films more quickly and with less money, because the resistance against the films was very great. In order to win I had to work with very little money. So we developed a lot of techniques, for example, [in] the use of the zoom. All the movements in these films are made with a zoom, nothing else. We have a remote control with a little bit of transformation inside the zoom lens to reduce the optical effect. When the zoom stops it always trembles, and even in motion it is never totally smooth. The remote control allows us to do all the movements that we want, back and forth, back and forth all the time. . . . If the actor is a little bit too weak when he does a scene, you can look at him more carefully. Very smooth, very small movements just toward the image of the actor playing underline really what he is doing and give him a certain kind of strength and force. This Panicor camera speeds work tremendously. I made *Louis XIV* in 23 days, *Socrates* in 24. You see, we have big pieces of film to put together, so in three days we can cut the film. . . . When you conceive that way you conceive by sequence, by plans, no longer by cut. You have everything tied together, you can have a scene of a thousand feet, or six hundred feet and everything is inside with the movements of the actors and the zooms. . . . I have always done the editing, and I do it now too, it is nothing at all. I have a Moviola at home and in two, three nights I cut the film. It is a very simple thing. (Schultz 16-17)

And yet in the purity of the uninterrupted shot, the event viewed from one angle alone, Rossellini found a kind of clarity, a release from the artificial constructs of preordained narrative imposed upon conventional cinema. In *Socrates*, the philosopher's death is recorded in one long take, recorded

> from a single angle, no more. Why have more angles? It means confusion, you must go straight into the thing. . . . I knew very well that when I was doing the shooting I was

tempted to do close-ups and a lot of different things. But I thought, no, I must take a risk, it is much more fun to take a risk. If the rhythm of the scene is right the scene will be alive. So I have done a single shot, a single time. . . . In the beginning the montage was essential, but today it is much less important because it is no more a language, it is a choice of things. And one thing that is too often forgotten is the fact that film is a microscope that magnifies everything. A magnificent tool, I think. (Schultz 18)

The death scene in Rossellini's *Blaise Pascal* is also photographed from one angle, although there are two long takes used, one directly following the other. Together, however, these two shots comprise nearly twenty uninterrupted minutes of screen time and are the final two shots we see in the film. In directing our gaze ineluctably toward the image of the dying Pascal in his bed, his labored breathing overwhelming the soundtrack, Rossellini forces us to gaze at one of the most feared and private moments in life—the moment of death. Impassively and clinically viewing Pascal's suffering, Rossellini forces us into identification with the image of the human body in extremity, the look of he who is about to die, the image of imminent departure from life, the gaze returned from the screen that will be terminated only through death. Appropriately enough, only when Pascal breathes his last are we, the audience, released from the countersurveillance of the lushlyappointed death chamber, and confronted with a single end title, "Fin." The reciprocal gaze in both *Blaise Pascal* and *Socrates* begins in birth and ends in death: for Rossellini's visual strategy to succeed, it could not be otherwise.

THE RETURNED GAZE: STRAUB/HUILLET

Jean-Marie Straub's *The Chronicle of Anna Magdalena Bach* (1968) uses a series of thirty-two minimalist tableaux to advance its narrative of Bach's life, incorporating:

1. Actual instrumentation of the period (Straub went to the considerable trouble of locating musical instruments from Bach's time in various museums and using them in the film).

FIGURE 8. *The Chronicle of Anna Magdalena Bach.* (Courtesy of Jerry Ohlinger.)

FIGURE 9. Gustav Leonhardt as Bach in Straub's *The Chronicle of Anna Magdalena Bach*. (Courtesy of Museum of Modern Art Film Stills Archive.)

2. Actual costuming of the period (again, obtained from various archives).
3. The use of musicians rather than actors to represent Bach (Gustav Leonhardt), Anna Magdalena (Christiane Lang), and the other members of the cast.
4. Shooting on the locations in which the events documented in Bach's life occurred.
5. A syntactical structure involving a series of lengthy takes that allow us to enter Bach's world as a participant in his (recreated) existence.

This pervasive sense of verisimilitude, the result of scrupulous control over the film's mise-en-scène by the director has, however, the perverse and precisely designated result of "erasing" Straub's presence within the film, and allowing Bach's presence to flow out from the screen as a function of the interlocked gaze between spectator/performer. The protagonists of Straub's film, and the various sunlit chambers they inhabit, return our inquisitorial "look" with a gaze of their own; the "look back" of a reconstituted reality so all-encompassing that it seems to transcend not only the "fourth wall" of the screen, but the boundaries of time (which seems suspended) and space (which appears to be infinitely extended beyond the screen, out into the auditorium).

Again, however, it is important to note that the reciprocal gaze derives its authority not so much from the look of Straub's performers but rather from the force of Straub's cinematic gaze upon them, in shots that last up to seven minutes duration without a single cut. It is the reflected power of Straub's "look" into Bach's world that holds us in thrall above all other considerations; Straub's film acknowledges its theatricality, while simultaneously providing us with a window to the eighteenth century, through which one may gaze in either direction. In his landmark monograph on Straub, the late Richard Roud commented on the director's rigorously graceful techniques as well as Straub's careful editorial structure for the film as a whole:

Each of [Straub's] 32 scenes, each of his 113 shots, is cunningly composed, making the most of small changes of angle and slight movements of the camera. Many of the sequences find an imaginative equivalent to the baroque quality of the music by employing certain of the principles of baroque painting, notably what one might call the oppressive diagonal. (77)

Still more complicated is the distribution of the shots and their lengths. The briefest . . . lasts for one second; the longest runs to seven and a half minutes. Of the 113 shots in the film, 47 run for less than 10 seconds; 26 from 10 to 15 seconds; and 50 last longer than 15 seconds. Thus 80 per cent of the playing time if accounted for by 20 per cent of the number of shots, and vice versa. Before making the film, Straub had planned to have the shots become briefer and briefer as Bach approached death, so as to give an impression of that acceleration of time when a man knows his days are numbered. (82)

Straub utilizes this "reciprocal gaze" in many of his other films, most notably *Class Relations* (1983), *The Bridegroom, the Comedienne and the Pimp* (1968) and *En Rachachant* (1982). In each case the "look back" valorizes the audience, and seeks to minimize (as Warhol did) the "gaze inward," that is, the "voyeur spectator" often invoked as the implicit visual auditor of minimalist or structuralist cinema practice. Reflexive films such as Michael Snow's *La Région centrale* (1970-71) (see Snow, 58-63, for details on the shooting of this film) or Hollis Frampton's *Poetic Justice* (1972), in which an endlessly tumbling panorama of sky and snow (Snow's film) or a page-by-page breakdown of a proposed script (Frampton's work) stare back at the viewer, also carry forward the concept of the returned gaze of the object, as do the films of Ernie Gehr, Morgan Fisher, and other independent practitioners of postmodernist cinema practice. This is the gaze of the object returned—of the frame that possesses the object—of the projected image that possesses the viewer. But what of characters, personages within the confines of the reflexive film—a film that regards its viewer? When actors within a film look at the camera, do they look at us? Do we imagine that they do? Or are the visions of audience/actor fused within the structure of a point-of-view shot?

In Landow's film, and Straub's works, and in Warhol's *Vinyl*, we have discussed three highly stylized (and it may be argued, aberrant) filmic structures that employ the reciprocal gaze between viewer and the projected image on the screen. What of these questions of reciprocity in more commercial, mainstream cinema? When *do* we identify with the characters we see on the screen, and if so, does this identification work against (or with) what Willemen terms "the fourth look"?

This identification, or mutual recognition of the spectatorial bond between viewer and performer (or, as I am arguing, between the viewer and the filmic text itself, regardless of whether the text presents an "inhabited" frame or not) is present materialist or "reflexive" film practice (as defined by Gidal, 1-11) and also penetrates the fabric of commercial film structure and suture, as Marc Vernet (48-63) and Willemen (53-66), among others, have persuasively argued. "If we now put ourselves in the position of the spectator," Vernet notes in *The Look Back at the Camera*, "We are forced to admit that it is not always easy to judge the direction of a look and to know if this look is entirely 'contained' within the frame, whether because the look seems to fluctuate towards the edges of the frame or because the actor is too far from the camera for us to know if the look is being directed towards the lens or to the side of it," (49) or as I would posit, out into the audience beyond the lens of the camera.

As one possible example of this "uncontained look" in commercial film practice, David L. Hewitt's *The Wizard of Mars* (1964) features a metaphysical dialogue between a group of interstellar travelers and the last survivor of an extinct culture, who has projected his being into a zone beyond temporal spatiality in order to survive. In this sequence, the survivor directly addresses the viewer and, it seems almost tangentially, the astronauts who have sought him out. Yet again, it is the *duration* of each individual take, as well as the trance-like tempo of the editing, in *conjunction* with the composition of the frame (the survivor is seen in an extremely tight close-up which enhances his dominance over the spectator, and hence the power of his "look back" into the audience) which together combine to create the viewer's sense of being watched *by* the film—a film. Hewitt's film exists not to lull the viewer into a state of narrative stupor through the usual strategies of intensely structured editorial syntax, point-of-view shots that directly link various actors to their "looks" within the film, music cues, and other more conventional strategies of cinematic structure. Rather, it seeks to reaffirm the power of the reciprocal gaze from both sides of the cinematic apparatus; the gaze from without (that of the viewer), and the gaze from within (the "look back" of the film itself).

THE CASE OF *WHAT CAN I DO?*

My own film, *What Can I Do?* (1993) constitutes a further exploration of this reciprocal discourse between spectator, image, and performer. In the film, an old woman (Anna Lee) gathers a group of paid dinner guests in her New York apartment for an evening of dinner and drinks. The film's narrative begins at the conclusion of the dinner, as the woman opens a bottle of Scotch and attempts, in the manner of Scheherezade, to beguile her "guests" into staying the night. Though the film was shot on a sound-stage in Los Angeles, and compresses an entire evening into eighty minutes of performance duration, *What Can I Do?* directly addresses the politics of verisimilitude within fictive constructs through the agency of the woman's direct address to the spectator, which forms the central informing structure of the work. As the film progresses, we see that the woman is not only looking at us; she is also looking at her five guests, who directly return her gaze in a series of precise eye-matches. Intercut with the woman's monologue are extreme close-ups of the listeners smoking, pouring coffee with cream, drinking wine, and blocks of written text from the woman's diatribe, presented in long scrolling sections *against* the flow of the narrative.

The construction of the film thus operates on a number of intentionally conflicting levels. On one level, it is an oral history of fictitious events, events that are, incidentally, called into question by the narrator herself, who reminds her listeners (and the audience) that her entire narrative may well be "a lie." On another plane, the film is a staged fictive meditation on the power of the look in all its manifestations: the look of the viewer, the diegetic eye-matches between the protagonists of the film, and

FIGURE 10. Anna Lee in Wheeler Winston Dixon's *What Can I Do?* (Photo by Andrew Taylor.)

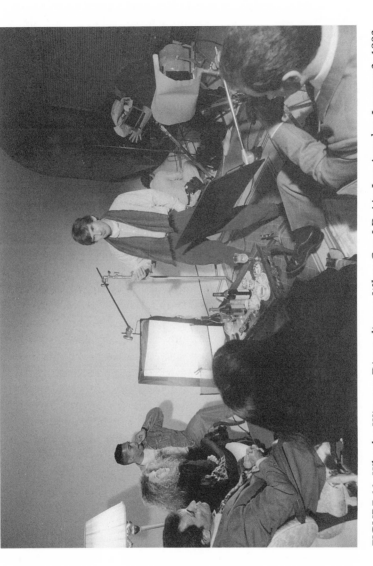

FIGURE 11. Wheeler Winston Dixon directs *What Can I Do?* in Los Angeles, January 2, 1993. (Photograph by Andrew Taylor.)

the "look back" of the woman, her guests, and the reflected gaze of the camera itself. Viewed from another perspective, the film emerges as a self-reflexive consideration of the fictive act, in which staging, lighting, props, and sets are all acknowledged as the emblems of the iconic support system employed by more conventional, "nonmaterialist" film practice. Foregrounding the power of the gaze, the film contains only eighty-nine cuts in its entire eighty-minute running time, allowing the identity of the viewer in the theatre to merge with that of the guests, and reinforcing the reciprocal interlock of eye-matches between the teller of the tale, and the auditor of the cinematic apparatus attendant to the production representation/reception of the film. Finally, the relentless oral sweep of the protagonist's voice becomes a voice of the living film/body itself, holding the double audience of the film (the listeners, and the audience) prisoners in the scopic thrall of the work.

Writing to me in a letter dated July 12, 1993, Mas'ud Zavarzadeh said of *What Can I Do?*:

> Like Molly Bloom's long monologue which closes Joyce's *Ulysses* and in its "excess"ive realism puts an end to conventional realist narrative, *What Can I Do?* critiques and gestures toward the emergence of a new post-story film. [Your] contribution to the Postfilm, however, exceeds mere formal questionings. It is, above all, a postmodern political meditation on the cultural discontinuities of late capitalism, and the place of woman in it. It is a rigorous Foucauldian genealogy of femininity, the female desire and the question of "other"ness in the commodity culture. Although formally it is radically different from such postmodern neopedagogical films as *Boyz N the Hood* (1992), *What Can I Do?* is a resistance film on counter-memory and a protest against a world that no longer has a place for collectivity, and regards itself to be post-historical [that is, post-narrative].

When *What Can I Do?* was screened at the Museum of Modern Art in New York on January 18, 1994, the reception was predictably mixed; the film calls into question the entire process of narrative identification and reception, to say nothing of the "all-encompassing" phenomenon of reciprocal suspension of disbelief within/from the spectator, a required (and desired) function of most feature-length narratives.

In the structure of the Postfilm, there is a certain "phantasmatic" air noted by Mary Ann Doane, which seems specifically tailored to *What Can I Do?*. Doane finds, "The body reconstituted by the technology and practices of the cinema is a *phantasmatic* body. . . . This phantasmatic body acts as a pivot for certain cinematic practices of representation and authorizes and sustains a limited number of relationships between voice and image" (335-336). In the case of *What Can I Do?*, one of the "limited number of relationships between voice and image" is the rendering of the protagonist as oracle, of an endless string of worlds to complement a seemingly endless succession of frames, of the scopic interlock between speaker, audience, and "the watchers" (Anna Lee's own, and rather telling, term) within the expanded boundaries of the film. This project, however, is a decidedly experimental enterprise, and not emblematic of commercial film discourse.

Since the very act of seeing a film is an act of submission—and the darkened auditorium, our mostly unidentified companions, the secrecy and individuality of our responses, the enormous size of the screen, the rapidly shifting (for the most part) image sizings all contribute to this willing subservience to "the gaze that controls"—it seems odd that most reception theory continues to center upon the viewer as giver of the gaze, and the screen as the bearer of the viewer's look. The viewer, it seems to me, is instead the subject/object of the gaze of the cinematic image. Landow's film, the starting point in this chapter, may seem to valorize the viewer in its introductory sequence, but as we have seen, the scene in question has more sinister implications. Rather than being viewers of an external phenomenon, we are being acted upon by a mechanism possessing a gaze that stuns and transfixes us, like rabbits caught in the glare of a set of headlights, unable to move, to leave, to act unless given permission to do so. Deconstruction of the syntactical structure that makes up the apparatus of the cinema may give us the illusion of control, but it is simply that—an illusion. The film looks at us, not we at it, and as long as the body of the film remains alive, we remain enthralled. Only when the lights come up does the "look back" cease to exist, until the next time we enter the darkened cinema auditorium, and again experience the power of the screen looking at us, gazing into our eyes, subjecting us to the look that controls and defines our spectatorial experience.

CHAPTER TWO

■■

Surveillance in the Cinema:
The Black Box

The movie theatre is above all a zone of surveillance, as are most other public locations in our lives. The Bentham/Foucault panopticon model of self-surveillance/external surveillance is hardly a new concept, and yet it is never more present than it is today. At the same time, it is also masked beneath layers of deception. Surveillance cameras hide behind one-way glass; every multiplex theatre now includes as part of its construction a bank of video monitors in the manager's office that assists the supervisory staff in its surveillance of the theatre's patrons. The same is true of department stores, shopping malls, gas stations, art galleries, post offices, supermarkets, public parks, and other areas of shared space. Yet even in the cinema theatre itself—inside the "black box" of the cinematographic apparatus, this surveillance does not cease, even when the lights dim. In the darkness, infrared surveillance cameras continually scan the auditorium; heat-sensing devices remain alert to changes in temperature that might be caused by a patron's smoking of a cigarette; motion-sensing devices prevent a viewer from coming too close to the screen; ushers patrol the aisles. Short generic "trailers" admonish members of the audience to "be considerate of others around you, and do not talk during the movie." In short, every aspect of the reception experience in the cinema is monitored, seen by the unseen, a space of fabulation that masquerades as semiprivate, when it is, in fact, part of the public sphere.

In this respect, the returned gaze from the screen within the black box of the cinema is one additional coefficient of the reflected scopic process. As Truffaut posited, we become one with the characters when they address us directly from the screen, although Truffaut saw this as a form of first-person camera, in which the gaze of the spectator is merged with that of the doubly removed fictive signifier of the narrative within the construct of the film. The character within the machine gazes out into the darkness, addressing the audience—either as an actor, inhabiting a role, or directly as the person her/himself. As Norma Desmond acknowledges at the end of *Sunset Boulevard* (1950), cinema *exists* for all the people in the dark who will view each "finished" film—and the film is only complete when the gaze of, in this instance, Norma Desmond meets that of the spectator. It can be persuasively argued that we are becoming more sophisticated in our presentation of self to the camera, and at first glance, this consciousness of bodily/facial display would seem to confirm the more traditional model of voyeurism/scopophilia as the governing force in the cinematic apparatus.

If, however, we regard the camera as the transmitter of the gaze from the performer/character from personal interiority out into the depth of the audience, it becomes apparent that the cinema gaze functions most pronouncedly from the zone of recorded space *outward*, and that each pose, each facial expression, each glance and gesture of the performer/character is an *address* of the audience, a gaze that challenges the viewer to return the gaze of the supposed "object" of the camera's scrutiny. In certain instances, where the subject of the apparatus gaze is entirely passive, we might argue that the "Fourth Look" (what Willemen calls the "look back" from the screen) is not in effect, that the process is one of external acting upon a subject/object, which does not involve any reciprocal negotiation. And yet, the more furtive the performer's gaze, or the more disengaged, the more we strive to meet it—the more unconcerned the performer sees with the mechanics of representation/reproduction, the more conscious that person actually is. Robert Indiana in Warhol's *Eat* (1963) munches studiously on a mushroom while seemingly avoiding the camera's gaze, yet this very "lack of address" confirms the lack of the reciprocal returned gaze we expect in conventional filmic practice, and reinforces the power of the construct of the "look back." To look, then, is to address the audience; not to look is *also* to address the audience through studied distanciation.

THE RETURNED GAZE OF THE DOCUMENTARY SUBJECT

The documentary art of Frederick Wiseman, for example, is based almost entirely on an acknowledgment of the eternal reciprocity of camera/subject/object gaze, linked with the viewer's barely masked scopophilic desire to inhabit the world being documented without seemingly being at risk. The participants in Wiseman's documentaries, though manipulated through incident selection, editorial constructs and sutures, the mechanics of sound recording and image illumination, shot duration and other mitigating factors, retain a degree of control over the image they present because they are, at all times, aware of the presence of the cinematographic recording device within their field of vision.

Wiseman has argued (in a lecture in my class at the University of Nebraska, Lincoln) that after a time, as in the filming of *The Store* (1983), the participants within Wiseman's zone of surveillance cease to be consciously, or at least overpoweringly aware of the presence of the camera's gaze, and fall back into more natural, less surveilled modes of bodily discourse. I would argue that Wiseman's subjects gradually adjust to the new form of surveillance Wiseman subjects them to, after an initial period of adjustment, and embrace the camera as yet another auditor/visitor within the sphere of their gaze and social influence. In his monograph on Wiseman's work as a documentarist, Barry Keith Grant notes:

> Exploring in a visual medium the cultural construction of visual images (in a sense, advertising is also a "natural history of the way we live"), Wiseman also logically deconstructs his own work in *Model* and *The Store* through

a consistent self-reflexivity. These are Wiseman's most overtly Brechtian films, and like Godard, in them he is more interested in the illusion of reality than in the reality of the illusion. In this sense, the title of *Model* expresses a significant double entendre, suggesting not only the film's ostensible subject but also a blueprint for a kind of documentary cinema that seeks to situate itself outside the dominant tradition of unproblematic observational empiricism.

Most obviously, *Model* is filled with cameras, more so than any of Wiseman's other films (most of which contain someone with a camera). The ubiquitous presence of cameras, light reflectors, boom mikes, and other cinematographic and photographic equipment in the film makes the viewer aware of the apparatus and methods of its own production. There are numerous fashion photo sessions, a tourist taking pictures of the production of a commercial, and the documentary being shot with Warhol and the two male models. Another of the film's self-reflexive strategies is to present images within images, as in the opening montage of magazine cover photos. All of the prospective models' portfolio shots are shown as images, their edges clearly visible rather than filling the entire frame. Similarly, in the improvised busstop seduction scene for the Brut commercial, we see auditions both "live" and on a video monitor, the difference inviting us to compare the two kinds of images. (Grant 188-189)

Thus, the protagonists within Wiseman's films grow to accept Wiseman's camera as yet another viewer of their lives, and yet concomitantly they return the camera's gaze with a look of their own, as they would with any other field of vision that surveils their existence, and project themselves into the audience through the medium exchange of the cinematographic device. The camera is never the "end," the final receptor in the apparatus of film/video. It is rather the vehicle that makes the exchanges of gaze possible, and it is this fabric of congruent eye-matches that forms the basis of the cinema/video construct/contract. When a character in one of Wiseman's or Warhol's films looks at the camera, she/he is looking at us, as the ultimate receptors of their gaze; when a person portraying a fictive character looks at the camera within the confines of a narrative construct, they also seek an engagement with our visual track. As it has been argued that effective performance within a fictive construct depends upon the ability of the performer to make the audience "forget" that they are watching the creation of an artificial construct, so may it be argued that a coefficient of this process of immersion is present in the "look back" at the audience, where the gaze of the actor challenges the spectator to detect any indirection of the shared eye-match.

THE "LOOK BACK" AS A DARE

John Malkovich in *In the Line of Fire* (1993) bases his performance as an assassin almost entirely on the "coldness" of his confrontational glare. Robert De Niro's most memorable moments in *Taxi Driver* (1976) occur when he directly addresses the camera in his ruined apartment, merging the camera and viewer into a single apparatus of reception. Kurtwood Smith's baleful gaze as an archetype of the visual referent of the "heavy" informs such disparate films as *Heart and Souls* (1993), *Robo-Cop* (1987), *Dead Poets Society* (1989) and particularly Stuart Gordon's ultrapanopticonic *Fortress* (1993), in which Smith portrays the warden of a futuristic prison capable of surveilling even a prisoner's dreams. In each of these films, Smith intimidates both the audience and those who participate in the fictive construct of the film's narrative through the power of his inflexible surveillance. This results in the projection of the self into the auditorium culminating in the moment when the apparatus fusing the actor/viewer and the receptor/viewer becomes transparent, the transcendent instant in which we are controlled by the gaze of the screen, and of the personages (real or constructed) inhabiting it. We can find this acknowledgment of the reciprocal gaze in the late Derek Jarman's *Wittgenstein* (1993) and *Edward II* (1992); in the haunted eyes of Maria Casares in Robert Bresson's *Les Dames du Bois de Boulogne* (1945) as she stalks her prey; in the all-seeing yet seemingly blind orbs of Darby Jones, leader of the zombies in Jacques Tourneur's *I Walked With a Zombie* (1943); in

Godard's mid to late 1960s films such as *Masculine/Feminine* (1966) and *Weekend* (1968); and in Fritz Lang's *The 1,000 Eyes of Dr. Mabuse* (1960) in which Mabuse wires up an entire hotel (the "Luxor") with video monitors to surveil the inhabitants of the establishment. In this last case, however, there is one mitigating factor not present in the other examples cited. Peter Van Eyck, Dawn Addams, and the other actors in Lang's film must act as if they are being surveilled without their knowledge or consent. They must pretend, in short, that they have no knowledge of the scopophiliac project pursued by Mabuse.

At the same time, the characters in *The 1,000 Eyes of Dr. Mabuse* inhabit a world of disorienting rapidity and change. Lotte Eisner notes:

> The film is constantly kept on the move by Lang's characteristic overlapping, ellipsis, rapid cutting. If someone mentions a person, an object or an event, the next shot will show us something about this person, object or event. (392)

Thus the protagonists of Lang's nightmare world live in a doubly confining prison of continual internal/external surveillance, coupled with perpetual uncertainty as to the solidity of the events they witness; they are forced to operate in a landscape of unrelenting mutability. The same theme has been recently reworked in *Sliver* (1993), in which Alec Baldwin presents himself to the audience as an eccentric multimillionaire, who secretly wires up the apartment building he owns with thousands of video surveillance cameras. In Lang's film, we are told at the conclusion of the film that the Luxor's panopticon system was originally installed by the Nazis, and later appropriated by Mabuse; a telling comment on one of the most intently self-surveilled political regimes in recent geopolitical history (Eisner 396).

In *The 1,000 Eyes of Dr. Mabuse*, Lang plays with the ontological trope of the unintentional gaze into the camera, as the customers of the hotel gaze directly into the lenses of various surveilling surfaces without being aware of their engagement with the video apparatus. But whether or not the personage/character within any given film directly confronts the audience with her/his gaze, or concentrates the power of that gaze onto the other characters who share the fictive construct or documentary project being produced, every act of the surveilled personages is in fact a projected act, one which confronts the audience, an actor look that challenges and meets the gaze of the receptor. Elena Dagrada argues that, during the evolution of early filmic narrative,

> at some point in the teens (there is no specific date), the look at the camera became, in the fiction film, a universally acknowledged ban. It is, in fact, a look turned to the only point impracticable for the action, the point occupied by the camera. To address this point means to unmask it and reveal the artificial nature of cinematic fiction. In early cinema, however, this prohibition did not exist, and the look at the camera was commonplace, not because of naïveté—as has long been held—but because the conditions motivating its banishment did not yet exist: the diegetic conception of camera position. (97)

Dagrada then characterizes "three different types" of the look at the camera in early cinema, the first being

> the furtive glance of the absent-minded or curious passersby—for example, the look of the voyager who gets off the train at La Ciotat station in *L'Arrivée d'un train* (Lumière, 1895). It is a casual glance, either uncertain or insisting, which transgresses nothing but good manners, as it was presumably considered rude, then as today, to stare at strangers. . . . Then there is [the second look], the brazen look of those actors who, in the middle of a scene, ask the director (or a fellow actor) for instructions about what to do. (97)

Most interesting for Dagrada, however, is

> the third look, the look of the actor in a scene who expressly addresses the audience in the theater. He greets the spectators, comments on the events together with them, and dedicates the performance to them. It is a look that, unlike what would happen today, does not break any diegetic illusions; there were, in fact, no diegetic illusions to break. It

does not evoke any hypothetical "off-screen" of the fiction but rather evokes the look of the spectator, whose presence and participation was intended to be an integral part of the performance. (98)

This "third look," which Willemen dubs "the fourth look," is important to Dagrada "because it is the means of assigning the spectator a place *in* the film" (98). What I find of great interest here is the fact that such early practitioners of narrative cinema as Alice Guy used this "look at the camera" with (it seems to me) more aggressive insistence than D. W. Griffith or Edwin S. Porter, who strove to create an insular world populated by visual archetypal icons who studiously sought to avoid the gaze of the cinematographic apparatus. Dagrada contends that: "Early cinema audiences were accustomed to this look because it was the same one that vaudeville actors addressed to them form popular stages," (98) and while this point of structural origin seems entirely credible, I would argue that no matter what the origin of the practice of the returned gaze within the cinema is, the incorporation of this gaze into the language of cinema constitutes a revolutionary and subversive act.

Such early Alice Guy films as *His Double* (1912), *Matrimony's Speed Limit* (1912), and *The Detective's Dog* (1912) incorporate "the look back" as an integral part of their staging. Part of this "naturalism" embraced the freedom to directly address the members of the audience, and as a result, the vitality of Guy's vision reaches out from the screen into the auditorium, meeting the gaze of the spectator directly, using the camera as a conduit for reciprocity of vision. And yet, beyond any requirements of predilections of staging in early cinema, the "look back" of the apparatus itself looms as the largest factor to be examined. In Edwin S. Porter's *Uncle Josh at the Moving Picture Show* (1902), Uncle Josh is finally enraged by the spectacle he witnesses, and tears down the theatre screen in a frenzy, thinking that to attack the screen is to attack the photographic phantoms inhabiting it (see Charles Keil, 63-76, for a full discussion of this interesting film). As he tears the screen to shreds, the image being projected upon it abruptly vanishes, and Josh becomes involved in a fight with (ostensibly) the cinematograph operator, who has been hiding behind the screen.

Most interesting to me is what happens when the screen goes "blank," and the shared reciprocity of gazes is interrupted. In most theatres, the actual projection surface (the screen) is hidden behind a curtain until the projection of the film is about to commence. As the house lights dim, the curtains swing open to reveal the beaded-glass projection surface, and almost immediately, the screen is filled with the reflected/refracted light of the projector beam, which passes through the celluloid base of the film stock and its attendant dyes, binding materials, and other physical/representational properties. It seems to me that the empty screen resembles nothing so much as a corpse—the tabula rasa of reception, something that we do not wish to view unless it is involved in the process of projection/reception. Otherwise, why is it hidden from our eyes, as if it were a potentially forbidden site of cultural discourse?

Similarly, there is nothing quite so disturbing within the confines of the contemporary household as television set projecting only "snow" into the shared family space. Although the power is on, no signal exists to be received, and the transient comfort of the modern electronic hearth becomes instead a site of intense unease, as witness the *Poltergeist* films ("They're *here*," the young girl warns her parents, staring at the seemingly blank, "snow"-filled screen) or David Cronenberg's *Videodrome*, an extremely complex and disturbing film in which the images transmitted onto the screen not only surveil the viewer, they also physically transform her/him. In medical slang, the phrase "to snow" someone means to bury the patient in a blizzard of painkillers until they overdose, drift into a coma and die. This "snowing" is used most often in connection with patients who possess no hope of recovery, and is sometimes openly, sometimes clandestinely performed by those attending. In either sense, the "snow" presents the death of the figurative or transmitted body, the corpse as uninvited guest in the home.

BRAKHAGE

In his early 1970s films *Eyes* (1970), *Deus Ex* (1971) and *The Act of Seeing With One's Own Eyes* (1971), Stan Brakhage took it upon himself to gaze into the world of the police, the hospital, and the autopsy room, thus investigating with typically silent rigor these "forbidden, terrific locations of our culture" (Frampton, *FMC Catalogue No. 7*, 48). Stripped of any sort of sound, either "actual" or "constructed," and mediated by the intensity of Brakhage's hand-held investigating gaze, these films are among the most powerful of those works that project a "look back" at the audience precisely because, as Willemen suggests (see previous citations), we are viewing here that which is partitioned off from general public view, withheld from the gaze of all but a few. We are witness, here, to the taboo—that which we should not be "allowed" to examine. The contract of shared silence reinforces the power of Brakhage's gaze, and yet the insistent visual rhythm of viewing the unviewable, calls our attention to the unreality of the construct we are witnessing, even as its returned scopic drive overwhelms us.

In his discussion of *Eyes*, the late Jerome Hill noted:

What Brakhage has come up with here is a small masterpiece of dispassionate compassion. Armed with his lightweight 15-inch lens and shooting on extra sensitive stock, he was able to take an inconspicuous, if not actually invisible place in the squad car, or behind it; or in ill-lit corners of station houses and jail corridors. For several days he accompanied the members of the Pittsburgh Police Force on their rounds of duty. The main events that he treats are in critical focus. Each subject that the police deals with is a complete figure, screen size, —a bleeding corpse in a gutter, a battered bum, an annoyed prostitute, traffic violators, young vagrants. The emotional impact of each "mission" is intensely felt. The I—Thou relationship is total, —the "I" being Brakhage—and consequently the viewing public, the "Thou" being suffering humanity. . . . Structurally monolithic, *Eyes* is set in a parenthesis of clouds and waves, —sky at the start, sea at the finish.

There are admittedly less than thirty splices in the whole film. Many scenes begin with the tell-tale single overexposed frame that signifies that the entire shot has been used. Leaving these in is illustrative of Brakhage's stated intention to downgrade the role of the editor, —"that man with the green eyeshade who makes everything look OK later at the cutting table," as he puts it. The material rolls out on the screen ostensibly, as it passed through the camera. Selection was made mostly at the time of shooting. The scenes of an airplane taking off at the beginning and the Atlantic wave sequences that sandwiches into the city nocturne at the end, were admittedly already on one of the reels from which Brakhage was to make his film. He did not eliminate them. His film has been "assembled," he writes, "rather than edited, and is thus the surest track I could make of what it was given me to see." (Hill 46-47)

In his sojourn into the nightime metropolis, Brakhage has confronted the gaze of surveillance and authority present in the "look" of the police and directed that gaze (one usually reserved for the eyes of "alleged suspects") directly to *us* through the filter of his camera. The entire project of the constabulary being one of "looking for trouble," Brakhage has taken this inquisitorial vision and framed it for us, and *to* us, thus inflicting upon the viewer the forbidding and impersonal "look" of those whom we (as a society) have designated to "look" for us. It is a world of details, fragments, sections of vision. As Hill comments:

> Brakhage has prepared us, through many of his films (especially the *Songs*) for a rich matrix of initially unrecognizable details, which ultimately, through reiteration and emphasis, crystallize into identification and meaning. The most unforgettable of these visual accents [in *Eyes*] is the revolving red light on the roof of the squad car. A night sequence of a frightened man showing his identification papers is swept by this lurid will-of-the-wisp with the rhythm of a bloody whiplash. (Hill 46-47)

In his own notes on *Eyes*, Brakhage commented that

> As to the film itself: 'Polis is eyes,' said Charles Olson, having found the archeological root of the word-end (thus beginning) of, say, 'metropolis,' etc. 'Police is a clear etymo-

logical derivative of "polis."' . . . The Police, then, are the public eyes; and they are, thus, expected to be Specialists of that ability to respond which most of the rest of the society has lost. (Brakhage, *FMC Catalogue No. 7*, 47-48)

And of Brakhage's "autopsy film," *The Act of Seeing With One's Own Eyes* (1971), Hollis Frampton continued his consideration of Brakhage's visuals by stating that the autopsy room is

> a place wherein, inversely, life is cherished, for it exists to affirm that no one of us may die without our knowing exactly why. All of us, in the person of the coroner, must see that, for ourselves, with our own eyes. It is a room full of appalling particular intimacies, the last ditch of individuation. Here our vague nightmare of mortality acquires the names and faces of *others*.
>
> This last is a process that requires a *witness*; and what 'idea' may finally have inserted itself into the sensible world we can still scarcely guess, for the *camera* would seem the perfect Eidetic Witness, staring with perfect compassion where we can scarcely bear to glance. (Frampton, *Catalogue No. 7*, 48)

Frampton is right—"we can scarcely bear to glance" at that which we are being confronted with, but as Willemen suggests, the very scopic power of this "forbidden" imagery *compels* our gaze, defies our visual comprehension, seeks to brand its look upon our collective visual ontological/anthropological unconscious.

Returning to the discussion of *Remedial Reading Comprehension*, Fred Camper notes:

> *Remedial Reading Comprehension* works [because of] the degree of filmic distance which each image has in the film. Distance here refers to the degree of awareness on the part of the viewer that the image he is watching is a film image, rather than "reality." Landow's film does not try to build up an illusion of reality, to combine the images together with the kind of spatial or rhythmic continuity that would

suggest that one is watching "real" people or objects. It works rather toward the opposite end, to make one aware of the unreality, the created and mechanical nature, of film. (74)

Similarly, I would argue that the three Brakhage films cited above (as with much of the filmmaker's other work) does not attempt to abrogate the inherent unreality of the filmic production/reception process, but rather, through an intensity of reciprocal gaze and the embrace of potentially forbidden subject matter, focus our attention on the internal fabric of the spectacle we are confronted with.

TO "LOOK AT" THE CAMERA

Similarly, in Jean-Luc Godard's *Tout va bien* (codirected with Jean-Pierre Gorin), the artist, in the words of Robin Bates "metaphorically rips the cover off society, showing power relationships through the cross section of [a] seized factory" (Bates 29). As Gilbert Klein observes, Godard achieves a directness here not found in earlier films. In *Contempt*, for instance, Klein notes "depths of mystery, multiple levels behind the main action taking place before the camera. . . ." By contrast, in *Tout va bien*, "The aim of the camera is to demystify, to expose social reality in the clear light of day, even as the outer wall of the factory set is stripped down. . . . The space is simple, flat, planimetric" (Bates 29; Klein 39). Godard and Gorin's camera movements in the film amplify and foreground this "stripped down" effect through a series of coolly impersonal lateral dollies past the stylized neon-encased factory set, a set that Gorin and Godard admitted on several occasions was inspired by the gigantic breakaway hotel set used in Jerry Lewis's *The Bellboy* (1960). *The Bellboy* also returns the viewer's gaze of surveillance as Lewis's camera sweeps from room to room in an upscale Florida hotel, showing us the daily interior existence of a group of vacationers whom we would otherwise remain unacquainted with.

In both Godard/Gorin's and Lewis's films, we are impersonally swept along with the camera's gaze as it invades the "privacy" of its chosen subjects. This majestic sweep has force, power, and arrogant grace as a hallmark of its presence, recalling the ineluctable sweep of the camera down the hallways of the luxurious hotel in *Last Year at Marienbad* (1961). We read these texts, but these texts also read us, checking our responses to the staged spectacle we bear witness to, willingly or unwillingly. One gets the uncomfortable sense that the protagonists of these films, existing in a world where the peripheries of surveillance are constantly mutating spend much of their time anticipating the surveillance-to-be of the perpetually moving camera, that moment when the gaze of the lens as transmitter will rest upon their images, their corporeal reality. As the camera sweeps on past them, is there not a perceptible moment of relief on the part of the actors that the scrutiny of the camera was, for the moment, ceased to be operative?

This brings us to the question of bodily and facial display within the cinema, of the feigned verisimilitude of "natural" performance within the domain of the recorded object/being. In her essay on the construction of narrative continuity in home movies of the 1960s (a series of rules, incidentally, which have been abrogated by the rise of the camcorder, which has replaced the once-omnipresent Super 8mm camera as the universal tool of familial surveillance), Patricia R. Zimmerman states:

> Home movies were again aligned with a photographic naturalism that displayed an uninterrupted surveillance and objectification of subjects. . . . This ideology of naturalism and uninhabited action as a more accurate record of family activities and emotion was elevated to a set of strategies designed to manipulate spontaneity, as shown in the following list of directives published in a 1960 *Better Homes and Gardens* article:
>
> (1) Shine the lights in the direction of the subject for several seconds before actually beginning to shoot the scene.
> (2) Don't encourage your subjects to look at the camera. They will look much more natural if they simply continue to do what they were doing before you started to shoot.

(3) Grown-ups will be much less self-conscious if they are engaged in some activity with a child while you are shooting. (Zimmerman 34; *Better Homes* 26)

Thus "to look at the camera" becomes one of the forbidden acts of cultural transgression in the site of discourse for the home movie; the subjects being surveilled must continue to pretend that no such act of intrusion is occurring. What Zimmerman terms "the ideology of naturalism" thus becomes a contract for both the Hollywood narrative and the domain of the real, transgressed upon by the instrumentation of "the recording zone operator," in reference to Gerard Malanga's 1968 "lost" film of the same title (*FMC Catalogue No. 6*, 172).

The inherent aspect of surveillance in the cinema is doubled when those who are confronted with the product of the cinematographic apparatus are themselves truly "captives" of the societal structure that informed the creation of Hollywood narrative film practice. In *Captive Light*, Robert Gerson, a projectionist of 16mm films within the walls of a state prison (and himself a prisoner there), describes this process of double-monitoring in precise and unsettling terms:

> Have you ever decided against going to a particular movie theater, though it was featuring a film you wanted to see, on account of an apprehension of being accosted by street criminals either within the theater or the neighborhood in which it was located? What if the only movie theater you had access to was frequented exclusively by criminals? Such an unwelcome and seemingly improbably scenario in fact exists—in prison, where movies have long been utilized as a management and recreation tool. . . .
>
> The prison very recently switched from a 16mm film format to a video system wired to each cell and dayroom of every housing unit . . . but we used to present approximately sixty-five films per year, one per weekend and on state holidays, in the prison's 536-seat auditorium. To ensure that every prisoner had the opportunity to attend each film, half of the population, divided by housing units, was entitled to see a film on a given evening, with the

remaining half permitted to do so the following night. . . .

Gross impatience was shown whenever a changeover from one reel to the next was even a second off, and if a projector malfunctioned during a film these hysterics were amplified ten-fold (as if my co-projectionist and I deliberately obstructed a film's presentation). (Gerson 538-539)

Not surprisingly, Gerson notes that X-rated films were the most popular cinematic spectacles presented to the prisoners, until one inmate successfully petitioned for their removal from the screening schedule on the grounds that the films "frustrated his attempts at rehabilitation" (Gerson 539). Violence was also an extremely popular entertainment commodity, particularly in such films as *The Accused* (1988), where, according to Gerson, the prisoners cheered at the rapists depicted in the film, rather than feeling any sympathy for Jodie Foster's character. Similarly, in one scene contained in *The Fly II* (1989), Gerson notes:

A nameless character is crushed to death by an elevator as if he were an overripe tomato, and many of the inmates were in a paroxysm of joy at this grisly sight. The more appalling the violence or spectacular the destruction, the more the inmates were pleased by the film. (Gerson 541-542)

For a group of individuals with violent histories to revel in the destruction of the Bakhtinian grotesque body is hardly surprising; what is more intriguing, perhaps, is the degree of censorial surveillance the prisoners conducted upon each other, in direct confirmation of Foucault/Bentham's structure of the prison panopticon, when the film they were confronted with contained material that questioned the structure of prison society and sexual discourse. Gerson recalls that a

near-stampede from the auditorium took place when we showed *Cruising* [1980], a film in which all of the victims of a serial killer are male homosexuals. The mass exit, as well as an outpouring of fearful imprecations, occurred near the beginning of the film in the course of a scene that showed most of the men in a crowded and presumably gay bar wearing a type of pants that exposed their tushes. As the first wave of men noisily left the auditorium, *other men still seated turned to watch them and not the movie* [emphasis mine]. The men in their seats looked at each other for the few seconds it took for peer pressure to compel them to leave the auditorium, and only then did they assume an air of indignation. (Gerson 544)

It is a telling comment on the use of these films within the context of the prison as a "management and recreation tool" (Gerson 538) has been utterly transformed through video technology. Where before large numbers of men jammed into an overcrowded auditorium to witness a spectacle of triple surveillance as a group (their view of the film; the film's returned gaze to them; the prisoner's continual monitoring of each other, according to strict social, sexual, and racial codes and boundaries) now these same prisoners are confined to their cells to witness these same films alone or in much smaller aggregations. The controlling gaze of the big screen is thus transformed into the mutually/reciprocal transgressive reinscription of the video monitor interlocked with the eyes of the captive viewer, in synchronous interplay with the network of internal monitoring cameras strategically placed throughout the hallways and public/private spaces of the zone of incarceration. The screen in each cell recalls the monitors of Big Brother in Orwell's *1984*, the "telescreens" that simultaneously transmit and receive, continuously watching the most mundane and yet private activities of the eternally imprisoned denizens of Orwell's dystopian superstate.

THE DENIAL OF THE SIGNIFIER

In his discussion of Christian Metz's analytic work upon the process of cinema image capture/reproduction, Ben Singer describes the hold of the image over the consciousness of the viewer, who willingly submits to the scopic thrall incited by the public presentation of the work:

In the film-viewing equivalent to classic disavowal, we "deny the signifier" and pretend that the signified is appearing naturally before us as if we were present in the projected world. This ideal of cinematic transparency encourages a self-deception, induces us to "forget we are looking at a picture and feel the living, breathing presence of the characters," as an editorial in *American Cinematographer*, characteristically endorsing such transparency, phrased it in 1941. (Singer 5; *American Cinematographer* 222)

Further, Singer argues, "It has been the nature of dominant styles of narrative film to try to deflect attention away from the film's "constructedness" and thereby increase the illusions of a natural world" (8). Singer describes Metz's argument for the difference between the act of still photography (capturing one moment out of continuous time) and cinematography (capturing many moments in succession out of time, to obtain, through the proper mechanistic reproduction process, the illusion of movement).

> We always know that what the photograph shows us is not really *here*. For this reason, Barthes continues, photography has little projective power . . . and gives rise to a purely spectatorial awareness, an attitude of externalized contemplation, rather than an awareness of magical or fictional possibilities. *This has been* overpowers *Here I am*. There is thus a great difference between photography and the cinema, which is an art of fiction and narration and has considerable projective power. The movie spectator is absorbed, not by a "has been there," but by a sense of "There it is."
>   The crux of these passages is that the photograph distances spectators, whereas the cinema engages them in an illusion. The photograph, in this formulation, does not induce a belief-in-presence of the sort evoked by film. Photography refuses to let us "deny the signifier" and "enter into the picture." (Gibson 17; Metz 1974, 6)

I would argue that it is precisely this "den[ial] of the signifier" and "enter[ing] into the picture" that acts as the facilitating agent in the ubiquitous returned look of the cinema screen. Still photography does not mime life; it captures a fragment of action and enshrines it. Further, most still photographs do not embrace and/or contain narrative construct; they rely instead, on the power of one captured instant to relay to the viewer the emotive mood or the pain or the isolation or the metonymy of the individual instant sought by the seeker of images. The cinema, in contrast, continually projects and "shuts down" projects and "shuts down," assaulting our eyes with a series of still images which, when strung together, create the impression, as Metz notes, of "there it is." It is little remarked upon, however, that for much of our time spent within the black box of cinematic reception, we see nothing at all upon the screen. We are shown twenty-four frames per second for every second that we watch a *film* projected (as opposed to a *video* image, which operates at thirty frames per second as a coefficient of an NTSC standard of 525 image-lines per frame) in a theatre, but each of those twenty-four frames is shown for only one-fiftieth of a second. The rest of the time, we are in darkness.

In the era of Super 8mm, 16mm, and regular 8mm home movies, home viewing audiences could see the illusion of cinematic motion break down when a film was projected at slower speeds, between twelve and four frames per second. The "flicker" effect would then take over, reminding the viewer of the inherent artificiality of the filmic/cinematograph construct, as the members of the audience became consciously aware of the periods in projection when the projector's ever-revolving shutter blocked the light of the projection bulb, to allow time for the next frame of the film being shown to advance into the projection gate. At these moments, the images of family and friends no longer held the home audience entranced; instead, the breakdown of the contract between viewer/image advanced to the representational foreground.

If we trace this phenomenon of audience placement within the spectacle of cinematic presentation to the early days of cinema, we are reminded again of Elena Dagrada's comment on looking at the camera in early cinema as a function of the definition of the role of the spectator: "This look at the camera is very important in the economy of early cinema, because it is the means of assigning the spectator a place *in* the film" (Dagrada 98). Or, as Metz might argue, a place *without* the film, a receptor zone identified as the site of cinematic signification.

Unlike Giuliana Bruno, who argues that "like the *flâneur*, the film spectator sees without being seen, rejoicing in his incognito: seeing the world, at the center of the world, he is nonetheless hidden from it (Bruno 49), I would posit that at the center of filmic discourse is the instinctive reciprocity of looks interchanged between viewer/image, a function often veiled, but always present. As Lyotard notes of mechanistic reception/reproduction devices:

> It is clear that what is important is not simply the fact that [these devices] communicate information. Reducing them to this function is to adopt an outlook which unduly privileges the system's own interests and point of view. A cybernetic machine does indeed run on information, but the goals programmed into it, for example, originate in prescriptive and evaluative statements it has no way to correct in the course of its functioning. (16)

The camera possesses the functions designed into it by its manufacturers, and these processes are inherent in the production/operation of the machine itself. The cinema camera can no more elude the aspect of reciprocal surveillance incorporated into its mechanism than it can operate without the insertion of motion picture photographic stock as one of the conditions of its use as a mediational transfigurative agency.

When photography first appeared, painting was declared to be "dead"; in fact, it was given a new freedom and license to depart from the strictly representative discourse that had hitherto been its domain. In his re-embrace of silent film technique, Warhol recognized that by taking film back to its very beginnings, he was reinscribing the basic function of the cinematograph, which resides in the fact that "cinematographic processes can accomplish better, faster, and with a circulation a hundred thousand times larger than narrative or pictorial realism, the task which academicism had assigned to realism: to preserve various consciousnesses from doubt. Industrial photography and cinema will be superior to painting and the novel whenever the objective is to stabilize the referent" (Lyotard 74), which is exactly what Warhol demonstrated in his first, gaze-obsessed films.

In this, the endlessly searching gaze of Warhol's camera mimics what Mary Ann Doane cites as "the doctor's look in the cinema, because it *penetrates*, [and] appears to be closer to what Foucault describes as the medical glance rather than the gaze" (Doane 1986, 157-158). Similarly, this clinical visualization of the eternal extracorporeality of the other in cinema/text production is cited by Baudrillard as "the end of the panopticon" in his discussion of the 1971 TV project *An American Family* for PBS, in which the Loud family was subjected to

> seven months of uninterrupted shooting, 300 hours of direct nonstop broadcasting, without script or scenario, the odyssey of a family, its dramas, its joys, ups and downs—in brief, a 'raw' historical document. . . . Things are complicated by the fact that this family came apart during the shooting: a crisis flared up, the Louds went their separate ways. . . . This family was in any case already somewhat hyperreal by its very selection: a typical, California-housed, three garage, five-children, well-to-do, professional, upper-middle-class, ideal American family, with an ornamental housewife. . . . The eye of TV is no longer the source of an absolute gaze, and the ideal of control is no longer that of transparency. The latter still presupposes an objective space (that of the Renaissance) and the omnipotence of a despotic gaze. . . . It is entirely different when with the Louds. 'You no longer watch TV, TV watches you." (Baudrillard 270-271)

Unlike Warhol's cinema/practice, in which thirty-five minutes (1200 feet) of 16mm film yielded thirty-five minutes of "finished," uninterrupted film product (until his introduction of what Gene Youngblood dubbed the "strobe cut" in early 1967, that is, cutting within the camera by turning the device off and on at random intervals, thus producing an overexposed frame or two of image on the film, and an attendant "beep" on the magnetic-stripe soundtrack to accompany these "flash frames"), the creators of *An American Family* subjected the "300 hours of direct nonstop broadcasting [recording]" to considerable manipulation in the editorial process, shifting events, recreating sound for certain sequences, cutting out long chunks of seemingly banal footage, until what was left represented nothing so much as the *imitation* of a documentary, conforming to the narrative format of a television sitcom (*The Brady Bunch* on a bad day) or a drama (the relentlessly middle-class *American Family*). Warhol's "strobe cut" announced the elision of material with each use; the cuts in *American Family* create a hidden, hyperreal construct that proceeds from continual surveillance, yet finally resides within the domain of near hyperfictional/closure. Nevertheless, Baudrillard is correct in his informing contention that in the case of the Loud's surveillance, the gaze of television has become fully reciprocal; "you no longer watch TV, TV watches you."

THE ZONE OF VISUAL JUSTICE

This hyperpanopticonic model is being eagerly embraced by the judicial system in the United States, far beyond the boundaries of simple videotaped recording of courtroom proceedings. In September 1993, the College of William and Mary unveiled a "state-of-the art moot courtroom" that combined database computers, hidden cameras, and computer-generated animation to simulate the proceedings in a murder trial set in the near future. As documented by Thomas J. De Loughry in *The Chronicle of Higher Education*:

> The wood-paneled courtroom boasts two large television screens, a computerized transcription system, an automated videotaping system, and computers attached to the judge's bench, the witness stand, and the desks of the court clerk, the prosecutor, the defense lawyer, and each of the eight jurors.
> The computers can be used to connect to legal data bases, to review a transcript as it is being typed by a court reporter, or to view animations, graphics, or video segments that might be offered as evidence in a case. . . .
> The two large television screens set in the wall behind the judge's bench were used to show how people at remote locations—a defendant in a jail cell or a busy doctor at a local hospital—could appear on camera in the courtroom

and participate in the proceedings. The screens also showed a videotape of a disposition when a witness's testimony in the courtroom appeared to conflict with what she had said when she was deposed. . . .

The automated videotaping system produced a tape of the proceedings that could be particularly valuable if a verdict was appealed. The taping system used five cameras concealed in dark, plastic bubbles on the ceiling that automatically focused on trial participants when they spoke into microphones in the courtroom. (De Loughry A22)

Everything inherent in the structure of this model is designed to induce paranoia on the part of the accused and to heighten the sense of being continually under scrutiny throughout the course of the interrogation/judgment process. The "wood-panelled courtroom" becomes an imposing arena operating in the service of the state, rather than a site of mutually reciprocal discourse. Everything in this futuristic courtroom is removed from human agency—the "computerized transcription system," the "automated videotaping system . . . [using] five cameras *concealed* in *dark, plastic bubbles* on the ceiling that *automatically* [focus] on trial participants when the [speak] into microphones, . . . the two *large* television screens set in the wall *behind the judge's bench* used to show people . . . at remote locations" (emphasis mine). And all of it is designed to intimidate, to strike fear into the consciousness of the person on trial. Elaine Scarry correctly notes that "power is cautious. It covers itself. It bases itself in another's pain and prevents all recognition that there is 'another' by looped circles that ensure its own solipsism" (59).

When one speaks in this courtroom, the surveillance cameras are automatically switched on. Yet the cameras are hidden behind "dark, plastic bubbles" that conceal the nature of their interrogatory agency. The "large" television screens set in the wall behind the judge's seat strategically locate the testimony of others in the site of judgment, simultaneously removing the human agency of both defendant and/or witness from the area of the courtroom. Seen on the monitors, these personages become less than human, extensions of the power of the presiding judge, easily dismissed by the simple flick of a dial. Animation graphics—simulations of assaults, murders, rapes, robberies, for example—can be played and replayed on monitors throughout the judgment area. Already a topic of intense debate, these "simulations," through the use of computer graphics, generate seemingly concrete visualizations of *theories* of commission—how a particular murder was committed, where the blow came from, how the assailant approached the victim, how the escape from the site of the crime was effected. And yet these "simulations" are exactly that. They are constructs, not facts, but hypotheses removed from the abstract and placed into the realm of the synthetic/actual. As others have observed, the prosecutorial or defense team with the highest "production budget" for computer graphic simulation in these cases will have a distinct advantage.

The hyperreal sensation of self-surveillance is heightened by the panopticonic use of video playback to rebut witness testimony, showing "a videotape of a deposition when a witness's testimony in the courtroom appeared to conflict with what she had said when she was deposed," thus creating an ultraparanoid environment in which every word, every gesture, every nuance is under scrutiny, from which the agency of honest human error has no appeal. Further, the judge in the mock courtroom, during the course of the presentation,

> used his computer to connect to LEXIS, a legal data base, and was quickly able to review other cases and rule against a motion brought by the defense lawyer. The eight jurors, seated in a semicircle facing the judge, used their computers to view an animation of the assault and an illustration of the dead man's brain that the doctor referred to in her testimony. (A22)

The possibility of incorrect entry into the data base in question is never addressed; programmed by humans, it inevitably contains human errors in the information it contains. Yet this same "information," true or false, takes on the aspect of irrefutable evidence when presented as part of a database, that is, a collection of "facts," relied upon routinely to be both accurate and unbiased. As the article notes, the possibility of appeal is always present, but what "appeal" can be obtained in such a hypersurveillant environment? Forced at every turn to view her/himself, the defendant must be wary of every potential error in memory, must continually subject her/himself to continual, unrelenting self-scrutiny from which there is no escape. Playbacks of depositions force the defendant and/or witnesses to regard the look of their eyes, their faces, and expressions without the intervention of any human agency. The eight jurors, "seated in a semi-circle facing the judge," are thus confronted by two huge television monitors, the judge, and individual computers on which they are forced to view "an animation of the assault and an illustration of the dead man's brain," forming a circle of inquisitorial surveillance in which that which is theory becomes synthetically constituted occurrence.

Nor does the embrace of technology end in the courtroom, or even in the prison. With the growing number of court cases and guilty verdicts in the United States particularly, the practice of "intermediate punishment" has rapidly developed, incorporating, in the words of Belinda R. McCarthy, "intensive supervision, home confinement and electronic surveillance" (as the title of her volume *Intermediate Punishments* documents). As the essays collected in this text indicate, the home may also be transformed by the state into a zone of perpetual self-surveillance, although, as one essayist matter-of-factly notes:

> One should realize that the offender must have a home, and in most instances a phone, to qualify for the program. While this seems obvious, the requirement may play havoc with the potential cost benefits to be realized from the technology. Individuals who would otherwise be incarcerated may not qualify since their indigence prevents them from finding an appropriate residence or paying for telephone installation and service. (Vaughn 158)

Thus it seems that only the homeless can escape the self-surveillance of the returned-gaze panopicon model within the structure of the American judicial and penal system. For only within the confines of the prison or the home may we have

> the sovereign and his force, the social body and the administrative apparatus; mark, sign, trace; ceremony, representa-

tion, exercise; the vanquished enemy, the juridical subject in the process of requalification, the individual subjected to immediate coercion, the body subjected to training. (Foucault 158)

At every juncture, surveillance technology is used to remove the operator of the panopticon from direct contact with the person being monitored, while increasing the sense of all pervading invasion of privacy, loss of self, "the body subjected to training." In their essay "Home Confinement and Electronic Surveillance," Thomas G. Blumberg, Gordon P. Waldo and Lisa C. Burcroff propose a system of all-encompassing "social control" through electronic surveillance which would reach into all classes and private/public spheres of contemporary society. This would be accomplished through the use of control collars, telephone monitoring, and perhaps the use of interactive closed-circuit television systems.

In addition to the criminal justice system, electronic surveillance has social control potential in many other areas. For example, people with infectious diseases such as AIDS could be more effectively controlled with electronic surveillance. The mentally ill or handicapped could be prevented from harming themselves or others when they wander away from their homes or institutions. People identified as having suicidal tendencies could also be fitted with electronic devices for their protection. *Similar protection could be extended to the senile elderly, young children and teenagers.* (Emphasis mine)

The monitoring technology could also be used by employers concerned about employee productivity, coaches desiring reliable curfew checks of their players, teachers wanting to keep track of their students, and supervisors in any other type of institutional setting. *At the personal end of the continuum, the husband or wife who wants to keep track of a spouse suspected of being unfaithful might adopt an electronic chastity belt.* (Emphasis mine, 176)

One wonders who would be *omitted* from such a comprehensive model of "protective" surveillance. While the authors admit, "Such broad use of electronic surveillance poses interrelated questions involving legal and constitutional rights, the proper use of surveillance in a democratic society, [and] the role of the criminal justice system" (176), the barely suppressed desire for a panopticonic hypersurveillance model is clearly the dominant factor here, feeding upon itself, encouraging wider use with each application. In one "Intensive Supervision Program" (ISP) carried out in New Jersey, much emphasis is placed on the fact that the program of surveillance inflicted by the system is all-pervasive and unrelenting, holding the monitoring system up as a structure upon which future ISP models might profitably be constructed. As Todd R. Clear, Suzanne Flynn, and Carol Shapiro document, New Jersey's

> ISP officials are proud to point out that theirs is a 24-hour, 7-day-a-week program. Officers work nights and weekends on a regular basis, and are on call at all times. While many ISP officers complain that the schedule leads to burnout, they also give the impression that they respect the close level of supervision they can give, feel they are doing 'real probation' and enjoy their prestige as the "elite" of the state's probation workers. (137)

However, this continuous surveillance takes a toll that even its adherents acknowledge. Annesley K. Schmidt and Christine E. Curtis report that within a relatively brief period of time, prisoners begin to balk at their enforced condition of unwavering supervision, stating that "offenders [in a West Palm Beach, Florida experiment conducted by the surveillance firm of Pride, Inc.), can tolerate the monitors for about 90 to 120 days . . . after that, [officials feel] offenders begin to chafe under the restriction" (145-146).

This constant supervision of the prisoner recalls Foucault's dictum that "work on the prisoner's soul must be carried out as often as possible. The prison, though an administrative apparatus, will at the same time be a machine for altering minds" (125). Here, however, the "administrative apparatus" of the prison has been taken beyond the walls of the conventional incarceration facility into the prisoner's home, which is then, through the surveillance apparatus, transfigured into a prison once again. In home confinement, as in an ordinary penitentiary, the prisoner (the one to be surveilled) has to be introduced to her/his surroundings, as a person confined in a jail cell would be. The prisoner can stray only so far from the domain of the telephone, which serves as the central transmitting control device. Infractions are punished by various measures; the surveillance will be constant, perpetual. Foucault has written:

> On first entering the prison, the prisoner will be read the regulations, at the same time, the inspectors seek to strengthen in him the moral obligations that he now has; they represent to him the offence that he has committed with regard to them, the evil that has consequently resulted for the society that protected him and the need to make compensation by his example. (125)

How like the nineteenth-century penal citadel is this modern zone of penance. In both models, it is the focus of the surveilling gaze, and the returned gaze that transfixes us—the telephone that monitors us that may ring, and then again, it may remain silent.

THE ELECTRONIC HEARTH

Less ominous intrusions into the domestic zone include the "Yule Log" broadcast on a local New York television station each Christmas; six uninterrupted hours of a single log in an erzatz, videotaped fireplace, endlessly burning, never consumed, turning the electronic hearth of television reception into a simulacrum of representational displacement. In this, the performative "Yule Log" displays the ontological presence of verisimilitude, while simultaneously signaling the slippage of the sign reinscribed on a transgressive, mimetic medium. By reducing the taxonomic sign of the Yule Log to a metanarrative gesture, this act of postmodern automourning removes the actual into the domain of the reconstructed, a floating/bloated incarnationist trope that is the sign of the body dispossessed, of oscillation between the figure and the ground it seeks to occupy. Further, this mimetic significator of the season has been relegated to the realm of a "copyrightable" imagistic symbol through this act of cultural displacement, the intellectual and imagistic property of the station emitting the carrier wave that contains its image. One recalls John Tagg's discussion of the mechanism of photography, and the proprietary rights invested in any image captured and reproduced; the same confluence of effects can be found in the *mise en abyme* constituted by the sign of the Yule Log electronically introduced into the domestic sphere. Tagg reminds us:

> We must seek the mechanism which could enable photography [or video] to function, in certain contexts, as a kind of proof, even while an ideological contradiction was negotiated so that a burgeoning photographic industry could be divided between the domain of artistic property, whose privilege, resting on copyright protection, was a function of its lack of power, and the scientifico-technical domain, whose power was a function of its renunciation of privilege. . . . Its function as a mode of cultural production is tied to definite conditions of existence, and its products are meaningful and legible only within the particular currencies they have. Its history has no unity. It is a flickering across a field of institutional spaces. . . . Like the state, the camera is never neutral. The representations it produces are highly coded, and the power it wields is never its own. As a means of record, it arrives on the scene vested with a particular authority to arrest, picture and transform daily life; a power to see and record; a power of surveillance that effects a complete reversal of the political axis of representation. . . . This is not the power of the camera but the power of the apparatus of the local state which deploys it and guarantee the authority of the images it constructs to stand as evidence or register a truth. (Tagg 63, 64)

In this instance, it is the Dickensian cultural conceit that, for those who cannot afford or maintain a "family hearth," an artificial one will be provided to them for a brief period during the holidays—accompanied by a soundtrack of popular Christmas music, and stripped of advertisements. Only the station ID logo is allowed to subvert the perceived homogeneity of the image, which is above all an image of lack, of absence of privilege, of class difference and discursive nostalgia. The "flickering" image of the video Yule Log (actually a thirty-second loop with an invisible splice, thus ensuring that the log will be inexhaustible) is sutured into our familial sphere and our collective neocolonial unconscious memory, as an image of position, power, and feigned egalitarianism. The log "arrives on the scene vested with particular authority to . . . transform daily life; a power to see and record; a power of surveillance that effects a complete reversal of the political axis of representation" (Tagg 64).

Where Tagg confines his analogy to the act of image gathering and reproduction within a photographic structure, we might profitably extend his observations to the imagistic construct of the spectacle of the diegetically decentered Yule Log in this instance—an image which seeks to comfort, control, displace, and separate while seemingly seeking a sense of community, a significator of metacorporeality peculiar to our discursive trope, one seeks to locate the union between form and matter it seemingly represents, a hylomorphism the images of the log will never achieve. This gift-exchange of cultural commodities is, above all, an act that writes across cultures, seeks to erase difference and alterity, and is as much an act of social surveillance as the concept of any Intensive Supervision Program. Stay at home, and watch the endlessly flickering log. Become mesmerized by the incarnationist, endlessly exhausted, endlessly replenished trope it represents. Do not go outside. Outside, there is no topos of the hearth, and no surveillance from within. Who can resist the call to celebration this image represents? And who would feel comfortable doing so?

And yet, the simulated Yule Log is only one possible "channel" of information/zone transmission available to/forced upon the contemporary receptor of the televised/"cabled" video image in the domestic sphere. In his essay on the "circularity" of the video text, David Tafler notes:

Video in particular challenges the spectator's generally passive orientation toward moving pictures. Viewers in the home are increasingly fragmenting their experience by switching among the growing number of channels. Furthermore, the relationship with the image on the screen is also being influenced by the television's use for games, computer terminals, banking outlets, information directories, security operations, and home movies. (29)

Thus, the television screen has become not only an extension of the home space—a window to other times and competing cultures and discourses—but also a potential reinforcement of the past (via home movies), an interactional link with the external financial construct framed by the discourse of business (banking outlets), and a medium of the reciprocal gaze (security operations). Robert H. Deming's model of the "televisual subject" in these highly fragmented and transitional circumstances underscores the continual *competition* of imagistic constructs in the domestic sphere, a clash of signifiers and receptors that transmogrifies and mediates the entire process of viewing/being viewed by the televisual text, writing across the culture and bodies of the viewer/viewed:

The televisual subject (called by some the "spectator") is already a construct of a media environment, is already a function of discourses, existing among the play of signifiers, not as "creative source of plentitude," perhaps not even as subject of semiosis or generator of sign-vehicles. The thinking through of the "subject" requires that it be conceptualized as a social and cultural subject. It is a subject that exists *as* a multiplicity of particular subjectivities, among codes, conventions, and sets of symbols by which the "real" is imaged. It also exists as/through discursive subject positions that encounter televisual texts which are, themselves, discourses that exit in social, historical, normative, and ideological contexts. (48)

Televisual viewing in this model becomes a continual process of transgressive reinscription, in which the figure of the "flickering image" is written upon the faces and bodies of the "televisual subject." And yet the aspect of surveillance as a coefficient of the cinema/video process is only one function of the "gaze returned," behind this construct is the look of the image framed, the vision of the image itself turned back upon the viewer, the knowledge that what we are seeing is a mediational/control structure created by the dominant culture to convey the immutability of spectatorial control, of acting upon the viewer, of the scillation between the figure and the ground created by the centering/decentering of the viewer/subject. The confluence of conflicting discourses comprising "the look back" creates a diegetically powerful triangulation of desire which functions as a metanarrative gift-exchange between the incarnationist tropes contained within the cinema/video spectacle, and the oppositional discourse of the floating signifier introduced into the scopic domain of the "televisual" or "cinemavisual" subject, the one to be acted upon. The unrelenting slippage created between viewer/viewed and the cinema/video object/construct functions as a postfigurative "death trope" of enunciative automourning, in which the mimesis of contact/experience is replaced by the sign and symbol alone (the "imago") of a heterodystopic fetishistic textuality centering upon the replication and reproduction of the real as a centripotal/centrifugal locus of discourse and perceived homogeneity between viewer/viewed, image/subject. And behind these countertransgressive functions is the most visible performative countertestimony incorporated within the "returned gaze" of the cinema/video image: the construct of the gaze itself.

CHAPTER THREE

■■

The Trans/Gendered Gaze: The "I" of the Beholder

Beyond the female/male gaze—the concept/question of matri-archal/patriarchal visual address—there lies the territory of the trans/gendered address, the spectatorial position created through a confluence of sexual identities, a merging of polarities, a fluid identity dis-anchored in the bisexuality of the constructed look. If one retains an essentialist position in this matter—creating imagery for one sex or the other, seeking to address an ideally gendered spectator, or conjuring up the phantasmal image of a pre-sexed viewer through an excessive splendor of visual spectacle—one can also reject this rigid positioning through a stripping down, a paring away, a reduction of means and practices in the cinema, as one can discern in the films of Jarman, Davies, Akerman, Straub/Huillet, Rohmer, and other creators of the new narrative Postfilm.

Signaling work in this newer mode, Sally Potter's *Orlando* (1993) writes across gender lines in its representation of the gaze, successfully transgressing the cinema apparatus and presenting the character and figure of Orlando as hyperreal simulacra. Potter's figurative discourse in *Orlando* effectively questions the entire concept of the male/female gaze, and the resultant Freudian/Lacanian lack/excess model, by presenting, in Baudrillard's words, "the product of an irradiating synthesis of com-

FIGURE 12. Tilda Swinton regards the viewer in *Orlando*. (Courtesy of Jerry Ohlinger.)

binatory models in a hyperspace without atmosphere" (254). Using Virginia Woolf's text as a point-of-origin, Potter creates a series of trans/gendered character sites (Quentin Crisp as the Queen; Tilda Swinton as Orlando the man/woman) to propel her insular narrative.

Recognizing that traditional methods of cinematographic simulation evoke images that are, in a sense, highly dependent upon a binary model of synthesis of the simulacra, Sally Potter embraces Jean Baudrillard's theories of the hyperreal. Her camera apparatus is a machine/body capable of moving through time and space. The freedom of hyperreality allows the transgressing of boundaries of subject/object, active/passive, and gendered gaze. *Orlando* may be read as a hypertext, one in which the main "character," Orlando, travels not only across time in the film-text, but also transgresses spatial and gender order *through* the screen, beyond the trajectory of the western constructed panopticon projection space. Orlando, in a series of specious eye-camera matches and verbal asides to the viewer, *becomes* the camera, thus freeing the apparatus from the immobility of gender, identity, and "reality." When Orlando looks at the audience, s/he is engaged in an Husserlian phenomenological point-of-view: one that works to "unmask the potentialities implied in the present state of consciousness" (Baudry 293; Husserl 46). This mirroring of simulacra disrupts the mirror-screen arrangement, opening space to an *infinite* mirror, opening identity to a pregendered state of Kristevan "chora."

As Jean-Louis Baudry notes, this "infinite mirror would no longer be a mirror" (294), thus *Orlando*, like Virginia Woolfe's original text, calls into being a hyperreality, one transitive in nature, between the real and simulacra. The hardening of the self and the hardening of the real is disrupted in this schema. Baudrillard writes that "hyperreality and simulation are deterrents of every principle and every objective" (268) of traditionally informed filmic reality. Sally Potter thus relocates Woolf's mirror at the intersection of technology and subjectivity, in a mode of attack on the constituted real; a ludic gesture toward the simulacra. Camera as body, male as female, actor as speculum, time as technology, and screen as transgressor, *Orlando* constitutes the model for a contemporary transgressive hypertext.

According to Ban Wang, the state of initial being constituted by Julia Kristeva's concept of "chora" "is a horizon where 'I' is on the run toward a space bereft of cultural constraints and linguistic shackles. . . . It is [the] . . . abject realm of imaginary darkness" (189). In this site, notes Nancy Armstrong, "The true self is multiple, even duplicitous . . . neither masculine nor feminine, neither one class nor another, neither unified nor incoherent, but fluid and unconstrained by the categories of any discourse other than its own, including that of psychoanalysis" (145). Trans/genderal address thus "disperses the narrational look, distributing it across multiple focalizers (Newman 1038). Kristeva herself states that "the frontiers between differences of sex or identity, reality and fantasy, act and discourse . . . are easily traversed (Kristeva 1990, 9). This blurring of sexual focalizers underscores the "destructive nature of a metaphysical belief in strong, immutably fixed gender identities" (Moi 13). While Hélène Cixous contends, "A feminine text cannot fail to be more than subversive" (888), Toril Moi, Kristeva, Ban Wang, and Nancy Armstrong see trans/gendered address as a metasubversive act, in which the precise identification of a gendered narrative is both impossible and undesirable.

And yet, in the midst of these claims of subversion and trans/genderal diffusion of the narrative focalizer, can it be true "that in fact power, genuine power, no longer exists, and hence there is no risk of anybody seizing it or taking it over" (Baudrillard 265)? Is this because "*It is now impossible to isolate the process of the real*, or to prove the real" (Baudrillard 267; original emphasis)? For Baudrillard, "Hyperreality and simulation are deterrents of every principle and every objective" (268), and as one example of this "reality deterrence," he cites the use of a gigantic televised image of Ronald Reagan at the Republican National Convention in Dallas on August 22, 1984 (260), in which the oversized and omnipotent image of Ronald Reagan's smiling face dominates the speakers' podium (which is bordered by a phalanx of stars and an American flag on each side), as Nancy Reagan waves at the image of her husband's gaze, and he returns the gesture. Reagan is, of course, *looking at us*; he does not see his wife, except through a monitor projecting her life-scale image on the podium. Nancy's wave to Ronald is an entirely hyperreal gesture; the *screen* above her head holds our gaze, focuses our eyes on the President's eyes, anchors our hopes and fears in the panopticonic surveillance of Ronald Reagan's gaze, and extends the personal into the realm of the staged and artificial. In fact, this inflated image underscores nothing so much as a complete de-centering of power, and the substitution of the gaze that controls for any governing political structure.

In the production of the cinema/video text, the *chora* is the central site of inscription, the birthplace of imagery, the zone of internal creation physically embodied within the film exposure chamber or the video camera's electronic "I." As Toril Moi summarizes this process:

> The endless flow of pulsions is gathered up in the *chora* (from the Greek word for enclosed space, womb) which Plato in the *Timaeus* defines as "an invisible and formless being which receives all things and in some mysterious way partakes of the intelligible, and is most incomprehensible" (Roudiez 6). Kristeva appropriates and redefines Plato's concept and concludes that the *chora* is neither a sign nor a position, but "a wholly provisional articulation that is essentially mobile and constituted of movements and their ephemeral stases. . . . Neither model nor copy, it is anterior to and underlies figuration and therefore also specularization, and only admits analogy with vocal or kinetic rhythm." (*Révolution* 74) (161)

As Kristeva herself notes in "Approaching Abjection," an essay contained within her text *Powers of Horror*, within the *chora* "drives hold sway and constitute a strange space that I shall name, after Plato . . . a *chora*, a receptacle" (14), which in the cinema constitutes a primal zone of creation, the birth of the image.

THE CINEMATIC *CHORA*

Jean-Louis Baudry, in his essay "Ideological Effects of the Basic Cinematographic Apparatus," creates a model for the cinema/video *chora* in his diagram of the cinema/video production/projection/reception process (288), which links "scenario/découpage" to the "objective reality (light)" of that which is being captured on film/videotape, and signifies this relationship as a reciprocal affair, in which the arrow of representation points equally in both directions. Yet also directly linked to this "objective reality (light)" is the "film stock/camera (sound recording) process" and the production of the image contained within the interplay between the "projector/film (light)," the "screen/projection/*reflection*" (emphasis mine), and the merging of these discourses within the shifting site of the "spectator."

Although Baudry does not includes the production of video imagery within this model, it follows much the same process, but I would argue in this model for a stronger relationship between the component of "objective reality (light)" and the chamber in which the "film stock" (or in video, the electronic image) is inscribed upon the raw film or videotape. Just as the connection between "scenario/découpage" and "objective reality (light)" is a reciprocal one, so too is the relationship between the film stock and that which is recorded, and the projector/televisual screen which reproduces this image, *and* the spectator viewing this metatextual construct. The *chora* in film is the dark womb of the camera, a place of complete isolation from the light of the world outside, except the light that is focused through the lens of the video/film camera, the light intersecting with the film/electronic tube to form the nucleus of the captured image. As Baudry notes, "Central to the process of production of the film, the camera—an assembly of optical and mechanical instrumentation—carries out a certain mode of inscription characterized by marking, by the recording of differences of light intensity (and wavelength for color) and of differences between the frames [constituting fragments of recorded motion] fabricated on the model of the camera obscura, it permits the construction of an image" (288) which can then be projected on a screen. It is the *chorascular* space which denotes the primary location of cinema/video representation, and it may be argued that this location, in and of itself, is an entirely trans/genderal zone of inscription.

Viewed from this perspective, it becomes apparent that constructions of the female or male gaze in the cinema are *primitive* concepts, linked to the sexual politics of image creation/reproduction, and certainly true in cinema practice in its present, initial stage of existence. Just as the novel progressed from a series of admonitory epistles to a highly sophisticated system of metatextual and hypertextual self-referents and trans/genderal discourses of spectatorial/auditorial address across a time zone of several centuries, so the cinema, through the process of reflexively meditating upon itself, begins to arrive in such films as *Orlando*, films in which gender lines are intentionally blurred to achieve the desired object of trans/genderal address, at the creation or construction of a spectator encompassing both female and/or male viewpoints. Or to go beyond this, the construction of a spectator embodying a pansexuality of receptor modes; the trans/genderal observer.

As Judith Butler notes, "Whatever biological intractability sex seems to have, *gender* is culturally constructed; hence, gender is neither the *causal* result of sex nor as seemingly fixed as sex" (emphasis mine, 6). And if gender is a construction, as Butler argues, then "gender must also designate the very apparatus of production whereby the sexes themselves are established" (7). A trans/genderal production model, it follows, would then construct a new spectatorial site of reception, and move beyond the obvious patriarchy established by Griffith, Ford, Hawks, and others, *as well as* the equally exclusionary matriarchy created by Blaché, Arzner, Weber, Hammer, and Rainer. Trans/genderal models embrace, above all, the quality of difference, the impossibility of fixed ground, the nonessentialism of the gendered/constructed spectator.

The very "constructedness" of "classically" gendered modes of spectatorial address and *chorascular* inscription is demonstrated through a close viewing of the early films of Augustin Le Prince and Auguste and Louis Lumière, in which the primacy of the *chora* was made manifest in the trans/genderal spectator created by these films. Le Prince and his contemporaries were involved in perhaps the most important work ever done in the cinema—the *creation* of the *chora*, the celebration of the cinematic *chora's* power, the construction of the *chorascular* gaze as the primal, trans/genderal inscriptor of the moving image. As we move beyond the concept of the gendered *chora* spectator to the refreshingly disruptive model of trans/genderal enunciation encoded in *Orlando*, we need to remember that "every epoch, every important text and every historical figure encompasses tendencies that defy and contradict the labels on which historiography depends" (Kramer 103). If the time of the trans/gendered *chora* spectator is truly upon us, it signals simultaneously a freedom from constructed forms of cinematic address, and a return to the purity of the early, pre-Edisonian cinema, in which the act of encoding and transfiguration resided in the trans/gendered *chora* of Kristevian semiology.

This "new" cinema thus incorporates the "radical instability in both identity and desire" (Dollimore, *Sexual Dissidence*, 275) inherent in the verging of matriarchal/patriarchal cinematic discourse. As Lyotard notes,

> Those who refuse to reexamine the rules of art pursue successful careers in mass conformism by communicating, by means of the "correct rules," the endemic desire for reality with objects and situations capable of gratifying it. . . .
>
> As for the artists and writers who question the rules of plastic and narrative arts and possibly share their suspicions by circulating their work, they are destined to have little credibility in the eyes of those concerned with "reality" and "identity"; they have no guarantee of an audience. Thus it is possible to ascribe the dialectics of the avant-garde to the challenge posed by the realisms of industry and mass communication to painting and the narrative arts. (75)

This "reexamination" may be found in many sites within the avant-garde, as has been previously noted, and yet one artist I have not yet considered deserves mention here: Rainer Werner Fassbinder. While it might be argued that Fassbinder's work exemplifies the controlling, authoritarian male gaze, Kaja Silverman in *Male Subjectivity at the Margins* feels that "whereas classic cinema equates the exemplary male subject with the gaze, and locates the male eye on the side of authority and the law even when it is also a carrier of desire, [Fassbinder's] *Beware of a Holy Whore* [1970] not only extends desire and the look which expresses it to the female subject, but makes the male desiring look synonymous with loss of control" (131). Significantly, in

Radu Gabrea's film biography of Fassbinder, *A Man Like Eva* (1988) the role of the director is played by a woman, Eva Mattes.

IS THERE AN INTEGRATED VIEWER?

Trinh T. Minh-Ha, the filmmaker theorist, has given numerous interviews on the question of textual production/reception as it applies to her works. In the essay "When I Project" in her book *Framer Framed*, Minh-Ha states:

> Some people think that since [Minh-Ha's film *Reassemblage* (1982)] explicitly criticizes objectivity, it is a counterstance to what one normally finds. . . . The question shows the highly conventional way that people look at films . . . the distinction made between subjectivity and subjectivism might then be useful because it implies that there is necessarily a subjectivity in every objectivity. . . . When you realize that subjectivity is endless in its ramifications, you also realize that you can practice what has been called "the science of the subject," or, as I prefer it, "the trial of the subject." (231)

Is there an integrated self? Does the robot videocamera used on *Court TV* constitute any sort of spectator other than the supremely passive "other" of *chorascular* reception? The *chora* can be seen as a perlingual, prefigurative, presymbolic state existing before the creation of gender, and thus the connection between subjectivity and the connection between subjectivity and objectivity which Minh-Ha examines above may be termed the site of *trajectory*, the intersection between gaze and desire, gender and difference, the constructed and the *chorascular*. It is significant that as patriarchal zones of cinematic representationalism first began to recollapse and reconfigure themselves during World War II (as seen weekly in the *March of Time* docudramas and United States propaganda newsreels, which presented audiences for the first time with images of feminine independence and self-determinacy in the figure of the woman war worker), classical cinema responded with a whole series of dystopian "nightmare" fantasies centering on futuristic societies ruled by women, such as *Cat Women of the Moon* (1953), *Devil Girl from Mars* (1954), *Fire Maidens from Outer Space* (1956), *Queen of Outer Space* (1958), and many others. These films sought to reestablish the dominance of the patriarchy in the wake of World War II, through the projection of a vision of a panopticonic, fascist matriarchy. In light of recent cinema practice and theory, these projects have attained the status of objectionable cultural artifacts, deconstructed by even the least discerning viewers as a failed imagistic power play. As Catherine Gallagher notes in "Marxism and the New Historicism," "We too often take the text as a constant" (44), when it is, in fact, a site of constantly shifting cross-cultural, social, and sexual intersections.

Not even addressed here is the crucial question of the child as spectator in all of this, a topic that has received comparatively little attention in recent cinema studies (though a good deal more work has been done in purely psychoanalytic literature, and in the field of transactional analysis. Nevertheless, to briefly consider this topic, particularly in light of our discussion of gender construction within cinema practice, I would like to cite Simon Watney's formative research on the construction of the child spectator, as practiced in Great Britain in the late 1940s. Writing from the perspective of the 1985 Thatcherite economy, Watney finds:

> We should also require a full historical and theoretical analysis of that perceptualist bias in modern aesthetics which is as significantly underpinned by the notion of some originally innocent childhood vision—the gaze of childhood—as children's literature is underpinned by the notion of some originally innocent language of childhood. . . .
>
> What we are considering is clearly the production of specific subjectivities, not simply in terms of subject matter, but in the look of the image itself [as evidenced in this excerpt from the J. Arthur Rank 1949 *Boys and Girls' Cinema Club Annual*],
>
> > *Since 1943, our cinema clubs have been opening steadily up and down the country, until now there are nearly 400 thriving Odeon and Gaumont-British clubs within the J. Arthur Rank Organisation, with an aver-*

age weekly attendance of some 700 boys and girls in each club. . . . The club promise of the Odeon clubs goes: "I promise to tell the truth, to help others, and to obey my parents. I promise to be thoughtful of old folks, to be kind to animals, and always to play the game. I promise to try to make this country of ours a better place to live in." . . . We try to give you all your turn. We are making entertainment films especially for boys and girls—the first time this has ever been done—and we are keeping in mind all your different requirements. . . . So, next time you see a film at your cinema-club which isn't the sort of thing that you particularly want to watch, just remember that some of the other boys and girls, your fellow-members, are really enjoying it; indeed, they may actually have asked for it. (38-39)

There isn't space . . . to elucidate the various (conflicting) modes of address at work in the above text . . . let alone their systematic disavowals, repetitions and signifying silences. Suffice to say that what is at stake here is the simultaneous recruitment-cum-construction of a child-audience around certain regimes of pleasure, and a massive condensation of sexual, classed, and national identity. (89)

Watney here locates one of the richest and most problematic frontiers of cinematic image production/reception and gender construction: the direct address to youth, with the avowed object of gender and social class creation. As Watney points out, in view of the unceasing spate of films aimed at children as pre-gendered viewers which continue to the present day—Watney singles out the work of Steven Spielberg for especial notice—more work in this area certainly needs to be undertaken.

THE FIRST-PERSON CAMERA AND THE "LOOK BACK" FROM THE SCREEN

In addition to questions of trans/genderal address and narrative location, incorporated within the various modes of address implicit within the construct of the cinema/video "gaze"

within/without the text itself, there is also the question of "subjectivity" within the cinema/video gaze, and more specifically,
how that gaze may be diegetically incorporated within the look
between viewer/viewed and actor/signifier. Specifically, one must
address the question of whether or not it is possible to create a
narrative voice that wholly identifies the viewer with the protagonist, a narrative voice that operates effectively in the filmic
first-person. This is not a new problem: it is one film theorists
have wrestled with either mentally (in proposed screenplays) or
physically (on the set) for about eighty years. As David Bordwell
and Kristin Thompson have observed:

> In films we sometimes find the camera, through its posi-
> tioning and movements, inviting us to see events "through
> the eyes" of a character. Some directors (Howard Hawks,
> John Ford, Kenji Mizoguchi, Jacques Tati) seldom use the
> subjective shot, but others (Alfred Hitchcock, Alain Resnais)
> use it constantly. The first scene in Samuel Fuller's *The
> Naked Kiss* [1964] starts with shocking subjective shots:
>
>> We open with a direct cut. In that scene, the actors uti-
>> lized the camera. They held the camera; it was strapped
>> on them. For the first shot, the pimp has the camera
>> strapped on his chest. I say to [Constance] Towers, "Hit
>> the camera!" She hits the camera, the lens. Then I
>> reverse it. I put the camera on her, and she whacks the
>> hell out of him. I thought it was effective. (Quoted in
>> Eric Sherman and Martin Rubin, *The Director's Event*,
>> New York: Signet, 1969, 189.)
>
> Often the very first film a filmmaker conceives will be a
> subjective one. In his youth, Joris Ivens was fascinated by
> what he called "the I film" (*The Camera and I*, New York:
> International Publishers, 1969, 41). . . .
> The history of the technique has teased film theorists
> into speculating about whether the subjective shot evokes
> identification from the audience. Do we think we *are* Robert
> Montgomery? Theorists in the silent era thought that we
> might tend to identify with that character whose position

the camera occupies. But recent film theory is reluctant to make this move. *The Lady in the Lake* fails, Albert Laffay claims, because "by pursuing an impossible perceptual assimilation, the film in fact inhibits symbolic identification" (quoted in Christian Metz, "Current Problems of Film Theory," *Screen* 14.1/2 [Spring-Summer 1973]: 47). François Truffaut claims that we identify with a character not when we look *with* the character, but when the character looks *at us*. "A subjective camera is the negation of subjective cinema. When it replaces a character, one cannot identify oneself with him. The cinema becomes subjective when the actor's gaze meets that of the audience" (in Peter Graham, *The New Wave*, New York: Viking, 1968, 93) (Bordwell and Thompson 196-197).

Most interesting is Albert Laffay's point, because it seems to go straight to the center of what can go wrong with the technique of subjective camera. First-person camera promises "personal," one-to-one contact. And if the viewer sees the film by him/herself, then this illusion of "actual participation" is slightly intensified. But in a public theatre, surrounded by other patrons, the viewer realizes instantly that he cannot "kiss the beautiful blonde," because the experience of a first-person is being given equally, and withheld equally "to" and "from" every person in the theatre. When the viewer realizes that there is no physical "kiss" to accompany the image, any illusion of first-person participation ceases immediately. This is participation without risk (essentially what movies are in the action/adventure genre, or in any other genre to a lesser extent), but the subjective camera promises us personal risk, and then fails to deliver. It is good for a "scare"—nothing more. Laffay is right: the perceptual assimilation is inherently possible. The subjective camera technique strives for that identification which cannot, through these methods, be obtained. The "distancing" occurring at precisely the point of supposed greatest intensity (a kiss or a punch), does indeed "inhibit symbolic identification," because it cheats us most when it promises to deliver most.

"3-D" has similar problems. As long as the 3-D image comes within an inch or two of our collective noses, but does not pre-

FIGURE 13. Camera as mirror in *Lady in the Lake*. (Courtesy of Jerry Ohlinger.)

sume to "touch" us, we can be fooled. The illusion has not deci-
sively cheated us. As soon as we are asked to believe, however,
that we are being doused with a firehose (as we are in a 1953
Columbia short subject, *Spooks*, we realize we are not wet, and
the illusion fails. This is the central problem of 3-D: once the 3-D
illusion is intellectually surrounded (which we do instinctively as
we "duck" to avoid getting wet) we realize we are not "at risk" at
all. This insurmountable difficulty may have led to Hollywood's
general abandonment of both 3-D and the straight subjective
camera technique.

François Truffaut's comment that "the cinema becomes subjective when the actor's gaze meets that of the audience" also
seems suspect. All that a character speaking to the audience does
is remind the person or persons in the audience that they are
watching a film: and while it is undoubtedly an act of "eye" contact, this "contact" is irrevocably mediated by the medium that
allowed the exchange between the viewer and the actor on the
screen. First-person narrative can serve as a distancing device all
too easily: when Jean Pierre Léaud speaks directly to the camera
in *La Chinoise*, particularly with Godard's nearly inaudible off-
camera voice interrogating him on the track, the effect is distancing, formalizing—acknowledging (and in Godard's case, rev-
eling in) the gap between the audience and the film actor created
by the act of filmmaking.

Interestingly, this device also removes Godard, the filmmaker, from risk: he has effectively abrogated the responsibility
of creating an illusion, and can now, by bringing his actors into it
with him, do anything he wants, which is precisely what Godard
does in *Le Gai Savoir* (1968). The film is punctuated by long
stretches of black leader to distance and alienate the audience, as
well as to focus the audience on the soundtrack as primary level.
Then Godard uses long sections of wild self-congratulatory
applause, which does away with the audience function altogether.
By doing this, Godard acknowledges that, far from being interested in subjective camera or audience/protagonist identification,
he is involved totally in making films completely for himself,
for himself *alone*: the audience becomes nearly a side effect,
which distribution, screenings, festivals, and economic circumstances force upon Godard as a 35mm moviemaker.

In contrast to Truffaut's claims, one posits Samuel Fuller's more sensible approach to the whole thing as shown in the opening part of the Bordwell and Thompson citation. Instead of doing a whole film from one viewpoint, that of the subjective camera, Fuller utilized it only during one sequence: precisely that sequence which would most "cheat" an audience in the way I described *Lady in the Lake* as "cheating." But having not used the subjective technique before in the film, and by refusing to use it after the scene, Fuller intensifies the illusion. We do not feel cheated, even though we are.

The audience does not expect to be suddenly thrust into this "frontline" position. It is visually jarring to be suddenly "punched" with a subjective camera after a group of objective camera setups. The illusion only works because the use of subjective camera is intelligently restrained by Fuller.

One can also appreciate the manner in which Fuller describes his usage of the subjective camera technique. Fuller gives us the shot structure as defined in editing ("We open with a direct cut"), and tells us how he does it technically ("I put the camera on her, and she whacks the hell out of him."). The shock of sudden differentiation in viewpoint, and the limitation of it strictly to a sequence, has created a kinetic replacement of audience identification to concretize the punch. The question remains, of course, as to how long this effect resonates; both in diminishing audience identification and in the negative effect of "replacement," once the subjective shot has been replaced with an objective setup.

But it is a mistake to construct a film entirely from one camera "viewpoint," because it becomes a stylistic gimmick. Subjective camera techniques seem to function best in physical situations. "First-person" dialogue, as seen by a subjective camera, rapidly becomes boring and ridiculous. Film is supposed to show us more than someone talking to a "first-person" camera. In film, we are used to seeing things from a privileged viewpoint. We are in the room, or in the area of action, with the characters, and yet, of course, we are not in the room at all. We can peer over shoulders of one character speaking to another. We might "dolly in" for an emotional close-up. We may see what no one else can see: the bomb in the little boy's package in Hitchcock's *Sabo-*

tage (1936) or the interior of a tomb in Corman's *The Pit and the Pendulum* (1961). *This* is the gift of the cinema: that it puts us where we cannot be and affords us multiple viewpoints rapidly during the course of one film. Judicious direction in the traditional sense consists primarily in selectively choosing which things the audience will see, and which things they will not.

But why would one want to construct a work entirely from the narrative viewpoint in the first place? One can see the device working very well in a novel, as a character's voice describes past or present actions. While I will try to suggest various methods by which a filmic unity of subjective vision might be achieved, at the same time, I question whether the aim is desirable (or even possible). Perhaps an "instantly recognizable subject viewpoint" in film cannot be achieved. But if one agrees that the novel and the film may have different definitions of subjectivity, and that in film, subjectivity can be a blending of different viewpoints (using visual editorial assemblages and sound/image relationships, which engage the viewer in "subjective" contemplation of the film they are watching), then perhaps film subjectivity is possible.

With film, the viewer is already "in the room with the characters," as I have mentioned: perhaps this can be seen as the beginning of filmic subjectivity. By being in the room with the characters, but having no relation to the characters other than observing them, a passive visual subjectivity (the camera in effect saying, "I witness") may already exist. Perhaps subjectivity in film relates to a direct moral commitment to the material being presented: every shot "wedded" by design to the material it presents. Every camera movement, every framing choice, every lighting pattern, every editorial design must work together, *shot by shot*, responding to and interpreting the material through the conscious "mediation" (by the filmmakers, for the audience) of the filmic process. This is light years away from *Lady in the Lake*. *Lady in the Lake* attempts to avoid the question of audience/filmmaker moral responsibility by saying, as Robert Montgomery does, "You'll be with me every step of the way." But "you" are not; the camera is with you every step of the way. Robert Montgomery is sitting off to the side, watching the camera record the scenes he has created. His camera sees all; yet it's an idiot savant. Its impressive gaze reveals everything and nothing: in *Lady in the Lake* the supposedly subjective camera becomes clumsy and unresponsive.

But in Jean Renoir's *Woman on the Beach* (1947), to pick one of many possible examples, Renoir as director plots the course of light, camera and actor movement, sound, and incidental music with such delicacy and understanding of the medium he is working in that he accomplishes, to my mind, an emotionally "subjective" vision. It is a direct connection to the "vision" of the characters in the film and the "vision" of the film itself.

Renoir's voice is not immediately recognizable. This voice does not stand up and shout, gesticulate wildly, or immediately telegraph the intent of subjectively involving the viewer. A *book* written in first-person has, however, the tradition of the diary (one of the most widely employed first-person techniques used) to fall back on. *Film* diaries, as they sprang to life under the auspices of Jonas Mekas and *Film Culture* in the early 1960s, employed a restrained narrative voice that seemed to be objective. But suddenly a dolly, or another sudden "reflexive" response, would reveal the work to be one of a filmmaker "reacting to" and "shaping" his filmic voice and shot construction to help the audience best *experience* the actual event. This is the director offering himself as the first-person voice (and the human mediator of the *filmic voice*), the witness to the event. In Jonas Mekas's film diaries, *Walden* (1969), as in *Woman on the Beach*, the first-person narrative voice is that of the filmmaker him/herself.

How, then, can one be in the audience, and yet directly identify with the protagonist of a film, particularly without any "framing" at all, no introductory shot to establish the identification? Roger Corman has a possible solution to this problem. He schematicized in his *The Pit and the Pendulum*: a man enters a deserted chapel, the camera in front of him, facing him directly; he approaches the camera, which backs away to the left (facing him). The camera then fluidly executes a 180° dolly, and *becomes* him, approaching the altar of the church. Corman further complicates things by having the camera stop just short of the altar, and then the man walks from *behind* the camera into the shot, his back to us, toward the altar. Corman has "split" his narrative locus, and we are looking over the man's shoulders. This fluidity of adopting multiple viewpoints suggests again that visually sub-jective narrativity is not to be desired in films, particularly when such subtle variation in directorial vision can be obtained.

In Alfred Hitchcock's *Rope* (1948), the entire 80-minute film is constructed as one shot. The narrative position in the film is never clearly identified, though it seems clearly linked to the spec-tator's (and Hitchcock's) scopophilic gaze, a gaze that, as we have discussed, is *turned back* into the audience. Throughout the entire film the camera never seems to cut, but this strategy imposes a structure *on* the material rather than reacting *to* it. Of course, *Rope* is really a series of ten-minute takes, designed to flow together to create the illusion of one continuous shot. Yet we never abandon for an instant this one idiosyncratic, omniscient viewpoint. This becomes as tedious as Montgomery's first-per-son camera—although Hitchcock's stance is probably one of detached voyeurism. Stan Brakhage, in his *Reflections on Black* (1955) creates an aberrant example of narrativity by cutting to completely black leader (resulting in *no* image on the screen) to create the world of a blind man who can, however, *hear*. Brakhage then overloads the soundtrack of this "Black Vision" with a cacophony of domestic sounds, all mingled together. But this nar-rative structure is almost a stunt. In all of these films, the directors strive for this identification of "camera/viewer," which functions as a language of visceral filmic identification for the audience.

But film is no longer a convincing illusion of "reality." Even though the average 42nd Street moviegoer doesn't know a "zoom" from a "dolly," and isn't aware when one shot replaces another with a cut (because they are following the exterior nar-rative line of the movie almost exclusively), they know they are watching a movie. When plot lines were first introduced to films, in *La Fée aux Choux* (Blaché, 1896), *Life of an American Fire Man* (Porter, 1902), and *The Great Train Robbery* (Porter, 1903), to name three early examples of film narrative, it was necessary because the "convincing illusion" had palled. No longer did ladies run from the theatre when the train pulled into the station in Lumière's early oneshot, one-minute film (which incidentally are works of clear, great beauty and effectively sustain that pure narrative vision of subject identification, visual translation, and technical mediation for their brief length).

What is the incontrovertible realness of the filmic illusion? It is light thrown on a screen. More demonstrative viewers acknowledge this when they throw finger shadows on the screen, blocking the illusory beam and reminding others in the audience of the inherent, distant "coldness" of the filmic process.

Yet with the ascendancy of video, the film image has taken on relative warmth, which solidifies the humanist concerns of film as much as it acknowledges the "stripped down" quality of documentary representation that video affords. People use film now to obtain precisely the warmth and reminiscence that video lacks, even when you "deintensify it" (a technical term for making the colors less bright). Video is clear, bright, "unscratched"— documentary. On a television screen, the video image might as well be "live"—for the viewer, second-best only to "being there," as a witness. Film has now become the benevolent repository of recorded dreams from the 1900 to 1970 period. Obviously, film does not present a precise duplication of objects and persons in the world as we see them: this duplication is mediated by the act of making and watching the film. This distancing occurs in all films, not just in the films of those who interrogate their own optical illusions.

One who would question film's reality discovers that his first task is to overcome the "controlling" power of the cinematic image. Godard and Resnais have been proposed as two filmmakers who have attempted to deintensify the image by complexifying the track. Interestingly, both are literary filmmakers: Godard starting as a critic (for *Cahiers du Cinéma*) and Resnais as a screenplay writer and New Left intellectual, never far from his literary roots in Robbe-Grillet. Film, since the advent of sound, has consisted of a cooperation between image and the soundtrack. But this can be pushed to extremes. Godard's factory workers in *See You at Mao* (1970) (aka *British Sounds*) work in an increasing din of incongruous noise. It may "put us on the assembly line," but it distances us by its indiscretion. We can do a better job with our own internal sound mixers every day, filtering out extraneous noise. The workers themselves would do this, *must do this*, in order to survive in the "actual situation" supposedly being presented. Therefore, this technique may take us into Godard's world (as a filmmaker only), but it does not enter the world of the characters.

In the final "mixdown" of all the separate soundtracks on the side of the projected film, Godard makes all his separate elements one cacophonous *whole* again: artificially mangling everything into an indecipherable din. Robert Altman overloads his soundtracks in *California Split* (1974) and *Nashville* (1975) in much the same fashion, with similar effect. This multiple sound collage effect is really just another trick: like the endlessly insensate-though-objective first-person camera of *Lady in the Lake*, this technique wears thin very rapidly. The filmic "first-person narrative voice" is a "vision": it is created according to visual rules, with the "cooperation and enhancement" of the track. But the track's "enhancement" of the image is never more than that: film is primarily a visual medium, one in which the soundtrack works in concert with the images, but is never more than a part (although perhaps at times the principal part) of the film. Without the image, the soundtrack would be merely a voice recording. With the image, the voice becomes the film soundtrack. It is the "track" of the sound recorded during the filmmaking, and enhanced in mixing later. It bolsters the film's editorial construction: amending closures in weak "shot" patterns, shoring up certain visuals that don't fully "work," supporting and enhancing the image but always cooperating as a partner in the film's construction.

SIGN SYSTEMS AND CONTROL

Film realizes its control over the audience through its immediacy, its lack of need for translation into "sign systems," by its arresting *visual* power, implicit in "the gaze that controls." The "eye-contact" fascination of film comes not only from identification with the real, which the filmic image attempts to represent, but from the fact that it is being represented specifically for our visual consumption; coupled with the knowledge that one is partaking in an illusory, emotionally all-consuming process. One can listen to music, and do something else. One can walk down the street listening to the sounds, and still do something else. But one cannot look at a film or videotape and do something else, unless one even *momentarily* (as in doing household chores while watching television) averts one's gaze from the image. Momentarily freed of the structured image's influence, one can refocus on another task and accomplish it. But eventually, one's eyes will return, and *resubmit*, to an image (particularly with television) which will not let you be involved in anything else.

In a theatre, even though the auditorium is darkened (encouraging viewers to become more absorbed in the filmic presentation) a few very low lights are left on. In addition to the obvious safety factor this lighting provides, it also distances the viewer from too intense an identification with the film, and encourages a sense of safety and community with fellow members of the audience. TV has no such mediating factor. It is only a part of one's life; but when it is on, it controls. For most viewers, watching television "ends" life temporarily, inviting mental shutdown on an instant "on/off" basis.

A great deal of the sense of *safe* "audience anticipation" comes directly from the common shared knowledge that when we watch a film, what we are really seeing is "the never-seen of poetic fabulation." On television, we watch people get shotgunned to death; yet we are certain of their offscreen resurrection in the real world. We can indulge in space travel, and never leave our seat. It's safe: we know it isn't real. It's a movie! The "real" image of an object (as presented to our eyes in actual contemplation of that object) is something altogether different from our contemplation of a filmed image of that same object. This distinction between the "real" and "filmic" image is one we make constantly, instantly, automatically. Even four-year-old children are aware of this trope.

The creation of a narrative voice that truly puts us into the situation (insofar as the film medium will allow) is the shared province of images and sound, which together comprise the peculiar syntactical domain of film. When holographic 3-D films arrive, with their even greater illusion of reality (involving life-size human "simulacra" holographically projected by lasers on the stage), they will probably alter this syntactical language, which has inevitable debts to "staged drama," a form that distances as it enthralls. But an effective voice of filmic narrativity can never be accomplished without the cooperation of film's most important "voice," the visual image in conjunction with the soundtrack and a multiplicity of visual and aural "viewpoints," which may allow for the creation of an effective first-person cinematic voice.

But what of the gaze *within* the frame, the gaze out *to* us? Marc Vernet has noted:

> The expression "the look at the camera" is particularly troublesome because it tries to explain in terms of the moment of filming an effect that is produced in the moment of the film's projection: namely, the spectators' impression that a character in the diegesis, or an actor during the filming, is looking directly at them in their precise spot in the movie theater. (49)

THE LOOK THAT KILLS, AND THE LOOK THAT DOES NOT SEE

And what if we wish to avoid this gaze? Suppose that, as in the case of Terence Fisher's *The Gorgon* (1964), to gaze upon the face of the one who gazes at us results in death? Or as an alternative suggestion, we can consider the example of Wolf Rilla's *Village of the Damned* (1960), in which all the residents of a small British village, Midwich, are suddenly knocked unconscious for no obvious reason by what is believed to be a "gas attack" of some kind. When the residents come to, they discover over the next few weeks that every woman in the village is pregnant, including all the younger, unmarried teenage girls. Recriminations inevitably arise, but these are quickly put aside when the children are all born simultaneously, and rapidly demonstrate intelligence far beyond that of average infants. Further, the children are linked telepathically, and as they grow up, they demonstrate powers of visual telekinesis, forcing village residents who harass them to shoot themselves, set themselves on fire, or run their automobiles into walls. Along with their superior intellect, the children seem to have a singular lack of emotion: anything that gets in their way is dispassionately destroyed. In the final minutes of the film, George Sanders, the children's teacher, blows both him-

FIGURE 14. The "gaze that controls" in Wolf Rilla's *Village of the Damned*. (Courtesy of Jerry Ohlinger.)

self and the children up with a homemade bomb during a physics lesson. The film's ending, however, leaves the possibility of a sequel clearly open: as we dolly back from the ruins of the destroyed schoolhouse, the eyes of the children are superimposed on the background image, floating away toward space, where presumably they originated.

Throughout the film, the children control both the performers within the fictive construct of the film and the members of the audience through the power of their gaze—indeed, during moments of "peak surveillance" (as when the children read someone's inner thoughts or force a malefactor to kill her/himself), the children's eyes glow with an unearthly light, staring directly at us, as well as those whom they seek to dominate. *Village of the Damned*, seen today, moves in a conventional, even schematic fashion, and Wolf Rilla's direction sticks to the central theme of "children from outer space" with monomaniacal insistence. Nevertheless, the film has several sections of undeniable power, as when a three-month-old "space child" correctly assembles a puzzle of blocks with blinding speed, and then visually *forces* his jealous brother to return the blocks to him when the latter steals them in spite.

In stark contrast to this, Montgomery Tully's *No Road Back* (1957) features a protagonist incapable of visual surveillance; she is blind. Yet as one of the most complex fictional characters ever created within the generic metanarrative of the *policier*, Tully's Mrs. Railton deserves mention as a character who controls those around her through a complete *lack* of faculties, one who incorporates in her person a multitude of seemingly oppositional social and sexual discourses. Blind and deaf, Mrs. Railton runs a private after-hours nightclub, which fronts for her real vocation: jewel thief. With the aid of her interpreter/signer, Beth (Patricia Dainton), Railton heads the operation of a group of criminals, including Spike (Sean Connery) and Rudge Harvey (Alfie Bass). Once the gang has effected a robbery, Railton fences the proceeds on the international black market. In her spare time, Railton sculpts. Her son, John (Skip Homeier) is unaware of her activities, but when he returns home from medical school in America and falls in love with Beth, Railton decides that it is time to abandon her criminal career, with predictably disastrous results.

Railton's chief rationale for her criminal life is the support of her son's studies, and she keeps a distinct distance from the members of her gang. Beth is Railton's lifeline, "signing" the words of her associates in the palm of her hand, conveying through her touch the visual contours of their shared domain. Beth's reciprocal attachment to Railton has clearly implied lesbian overtones. There is no man in Mrs. Railton's life, and she does not need one. Beth functions not only as an interpreter of words into signs but also as a signifier of moods, tones of voice, and speech rhythms, so that Railton is fully aware of the unspoken yet visibly articulated emotions of her criminal associates. In addition, Beth occasionally advises the older woman against a particular plan that is being considered or, alternatively, expresses her agreement with a proposed plan of action, silently adding these editorial comments with her fingers, as she "signs" the words of the gang into the palm of Mrs. Railton's hand.

The patriarchal narrative's "necessity" for a romance between John and Beth seems to exist solely for the purpose of "renarrating" (to use Mas'ud Zavarzadeh's term, 21-26, 91, 99) the relationship between Beth and Mrs. Railton, which is close, self-sufficient, and entirely without any need for desire to apply to patriarchal (or any other external) authority. Sealed off in a world of silence and darkness, Mrs. Railton, the blind/deaf/club owner/crime-boss/lesbian/sculptress, rules her familial empire from the complete absence of the senses. Indeed, her keen intuition and judgment are seen by the film's narrative to be superior precisely because of this lack: she is more focused than the sighted, hearing people who surround her. When her criminal enterprise collapses around her, it is Beth's "defection" to John that seals Railton's fate, and we can sense director and coscenarist Tully's dissatisfaction with this generically dictated narrative closure. The seemingly dark world of Mrs. Railton is seen by the film's text as immeasurably richer than that of those who possess or bear the gaze of instruction or witness.

As an alternative narrative of interior surveillance, it is interesting to consider Tully's *Escapement* (1957), a film that abrogates the function of sight through the use of a videotape "dream injection" machine, a metanarrative structure that was to be reproduced with variations in Basil Dearden's *The Mind Benders* (1964), Ken Russell's *Altered States* (1980), Joseph Ruben's

Dreamscape (1984), and Paul Verhoeven's *Total Recall* (1991). *Escapement*'s diegesis is relatively straightforward, and yet Tully is most interested in the manner in which the machinery of legitimate scientific investigation may be used to "erase" the identity of a phantasmal authority figure who wishes to control the minds and thoughts (particularly the unconscious) of a select group of wealthy people.

Dr. Maxwell (Meredith Edwards) has created a machine that is capable of "injecting" videotaped dream scenarios directly into the minds of his chosen subjects. Maxwell hopes to use his technique to soothe the trouble psyches of those who come to him seeking help with drug addiction, chronic insomnia, alcoholism, and similar afflictions. However Maxwell's financial backer, Paul Zakon (Peter Illing), decides to use Maxwell's invention to insinuate his own messianic personality into the mental landscape of Maxwell's clientel. The weakest parts of the film are, somewhat surprisingly, the dream sequences, where we, as members of the audience, are allowed to view the images being imbedded in the minds of Zakon's victims. For the most part, these sequences rely upon mildly erotic ballet sequences, intercut with close-ups of Zakon's face. In their clumsy specificity, these staged dreams are reminiscent of the 3-D sequences of Julian Roffman's *The Mask* (1961), or perhaps Salvador Dali's truncated dream scenes in Alfred Hitchcock's *Spellbound* (1945). Yet the film commands our attention in other ways, particularly in its examination of the abuses of the technology Maxwell has created.

As evidence of this, an interesting subplot in the film's narrative revolves around the introduction of a singularly minor character, Signor Kallini (Carlo Borelli), who comes to the dream clinic seeking relief from addiction to heroin. The film unflinchingly depicts the consequences of Kallini's addiction: his arms are punctuated with a large number of needle marks, which are shown in a graphic close-up (a rather surprising image for a 1940s film). Significantly, we never learn precisely what happens to Kallini. He is outfitted with an electronic skullcap to facilitate the "injection" of the dream images, then trundled off to a morgue-like holding area, in which all of the patients are required to lie on a series of beds that roll into the wall. This is the last we see of him. Tully is also fascinated with the mechanics of the "dream injection process." The clinic functions as a taping studio, where, throughout the film, we see dancers and other performers rehearsing the sequences that will be electronically transmitted into the brains of the clinic's patients.

Thus in *The Gorgon*, *No Road Back*, and *Escapement*, we have three different variations on the theme of the look returned, or the look denied, or the circumvention of the look altogether. In *The Gorgon*, to be seen results in death; in *No Road Back*, the absence of the look is the source of the power of "blind" surveillance in which one transfers the look to another to form one being constituting the signifier of the look; in *Escapement*, what we see is immaterial. All visual stimuli are recorded directly on videotape, using the filter of the video lens as a transmission field, and then relayed directly into the brain of the subject through digital electronic impulses. Many of the images introduced into the unconscious minds of Dr. Maxwell's patients are erotically stimulating; the point-of-view of the video camera recording these staged dreams is resolutely that of the male gaze. As Paul Willemen notes of "porn" imagery, which has much in common with the imagery generated in *Escapement*'s dream laboratory, with

> . . . Phantasy images, what we see represented within a framed image and the things we see around us, all exist in different spaces. The relation between subject position and image or representation is different in each case. The actualisation of the phantasy scenarios or images in the form of framed, imaged discourses necessarily passes through the "defiles of the signifier", as Lacan would say, and through the distortion processes unconscious signifiers are subjected to when passing into consciousness. In relation to the imagined discourse, secondary elaboration and considerations of representability are extremely important (more so, for obvious reasons, than in verbal discourse). Figurative images, as all porn representations of sexual phantasy must be, require a social setting and an individuation which phantasy can do without. On the one hand, the surfeit of specific details, the necessity for the frame to be filled, produces an excess of signification. But this excess is also a loss: the lack of fit

between the represented scenario and the interpellated phantasy. In porn, this inevitable mismatch plays a particularly important role because it is more acutely experienced. (61)

PERFORMANCE SPACE AS ARENA

The link between the real and the phantasmal is thus blurred by the gift-exchange between the bearer of the gaze in male-dominated patriarchal porn (as in *Escapement*'s dream sequences) and the recipient/viewer as constructed by the text. More directly, the "look" in patriarchal cinema, particularly when it involves the objectification of the feminine corpus, can effectively define and limit a personage within the context of the film's narrative, as it does in Harvey Hart's *Bus Riley's Back in Town* (1965). The film starts with Bus Riley's (Michael Parks) coming back to his hometown, which is seen as a halcyon zone of memory recalled. As the opening tracking shots from Bus's point-of-view urge us to identify with the protagonist, we are taken on a nighttime, highly abbreviated trip through the small town he is returning to, and as he knocks on the front door, the image freezes to frame him, indistinct, through the colored glass of the ornate, old-fashioned entryway. Bus *wants* to come back to his old hometown, but finds that it has changed and is no longer the place that he remembers. It is the returned gaze of the town seen through Bus's eyes that conveys this most forcefully to our attention; we see a place that has been transfigured and exudes difference: Bus does not, though we share his visual perspective.

Conversations with the town barkeep bring this fact home forcefully. The bar in the film also serves as an arena, the place where Laurel (Ann-Margret) and Bus publicly demonstrate their mutual attraction for each other, and where Laurel taunts Bus by dancing with a lascivious stranger in a curiously ritualistic fashion. There are elements of the town in decay: the operator of the funeral home is clearly one of the dying ones, and his clinging invitation for Bus to move in with him and work at the parlor is tinged with suffused homosexuality and the desperation of terminal loneliness. Bus wisely and instinctively rejects his advances and decides to stay with his family until he can figure

FIGURE 15. The gaze of desire: Ann-Margret in *Bus Riley's Back in Town*. (Courtesy of Jerry Ohlinger.)

out his next move. Laurel, in the meantime, lurks around the edges of the frame, continually inviting Bus over for an evening's tryst, a dead-ended relationship which Bus is sucked into simply through the mechanics of lust. He realizes, however, that anything that they may have shared in the past is now dead between them.

As seen through the visual filter of the film's text, Ann-Margret is the bearer of the male gaze, and is iconographically constructed by "the rule of look" alone. She returns the gaze of both camera and audience with an entirely conscious oppositional discourse of looks that simultaneously looks at us, and dares us to return the mimetic construct of her performative surveillance. Point-of-view shots are judiciously employed throughout *Bus Riley* to underscore this total dependence upon the rule of the visual/tactile, as exemplified by Bus's POV shots during Laurel's dance in the nightclub. In these POV shots, the power of Bus's gaze and the reciprocal transgression of the "modesty topos" created by Laurel and the stranger merge the spectacle of the body dispossessed with the fetishistic textuality of the "fourth look" Willemen describes into a figure of immense and disturbing (disruptive) power. Laurel's body within *Bus Riley* is a site/sight of resistance—the body resisting the gaze, resisting the nonneutral taxonomic structure enforced by the hylomorphism of the metacorporeality inherent in the libidal economy of the exchange of looks. In this, *Bus Riley* offers no narrative as epistomology—the ontological spectacle of difference as mediated by the reciprocity of competing modes of "the gaze": Bus's gaze, Laurel's returned gaze, the look upon Laurel of her anonymous partner, the gaze of the camera, the space cleared between the dancers by the sheer force of the visual spectacle being documented, and the look back from the screen, in which this image of transgressive heterotopia confronts us with the product of this fusing of the male gaze, the product/economy of the image of Ann-Margret, and the act of continual, unrelenting surveillance performed by the camera.

Yet if *Bus Riley* functions as a series of oppositional visual discourses (and not only between Bus and Laurel but also between Bus and the funeral home operator who briefly attempts to seduce him early on in the film), the sequence in the bar also functions as an example of yet another gaze—the "eye-match," or "non-eye-match" (gaze avoidance) within the frame. As Bus and Laurel are dancing, they are surrounded by a sea of patrons who dance unconcernedly, studiously avoiding any reciprocity of gazes between themselves and the scene's two major performance figures. In this, and in the visual path cleared for us in both directions by the combined power of Bus's and the camera's gaze (and the gaze returned to us), we witness the myopic stare of the look *not* returned, the gaze avoided, the eyes without a sign. Decentered around the figures of Bus and Laurel, these mimetic figures of unreciprocated vision remind us that even in the act of surveillance, we can avoid the transgressive power of the gaze by simply averting our eyes. Deprived of focus, we are no longer the bearer or giver of the gaze, or even a witness to the process of mutual surveillance. We have removed ourselves from the arena of spectacle.

Whether we accept the currently favored model of gendered gaze (not only in cinema but also in the graphic arts, sculpture, the creation of texts on the page, and hypertexts that float on the surface of the computer screen) or endorse the mutability of the gendered gaze—even the abrogation of the case of gender address in certain instances, we are confronted by the address of this look at every turn. For example, in a pizza advertisement on television or in a magazine, precisely what *form* of genderal address lies behind the image of a "large pepperoni-to-go?" Is it only non-gendered physical *hunger* the image addresses? Or is there a sexual referent imbedded in the glossy image that confronts the viewer? The commodification of desire inherent in the construction of *all* imagery—and the "codes" of beauty, power, accessibility, exaltation, access and excess embedded in these images—informs the structure of our social, corporeal, and intellectual existence.

When an entire day's labor, and millions of feet of film, can be spent in constructing, say, just the right *appearance* for a bowl of cereal or a car, or a pair of jeans, or a snapping stalk of celery, all to create the sense of *need* inherent in any advertisement, we must ask ourselves a variety of questions, having to do with spectatorial excess, the look returned, and the process of image production/product consumption reinforced and introduced to our lives through the creation and dissimilation of these images. Martin Scorsese's *The Age of Innocence* (1993) appeals primarily to our reflexive "commercial" instincts of beauty (and it is no accident that Scorsese casts himself as a photographer within the film) in its most conventional sense. The film is a riot of foods, fabric textures, costumes, color filters, aggressively sensual editorial patterns (and more should be said about Thelma Schoonmaker's editorial hand in all this and in all of Scorsese's recent work) and seeks to drug us into a acceptance of Wharton's world through a decided excess of spectatorial splendor. Yet what lingers in the memory most is Joanne Woodward's mellifluous voice reading Wharton's text over Scorsese's sumptuous imagery, often as the text fills the screen, in brief burst of textual punctuation confronting our gaze with its own hieroglyphic response. When he has had enough of texts, Scorsese allows Wharton's characters to address the viewer directly. To lessen the numbing effect of the inherent two-dimensionality of the filmic image, Scorsese's incessantly tracking camera—something like Max Ophuls on methamphetamine—sweeps through opera houses and grand ballrooms with aggressive bravado, x-rays envelopes in breast pockets to display their "secret" contents, and frames the protagonists in tight close-ups to accentuate their reciprocal gazes at each other and the audience. It does everything, in short, except observe.

All the camera movement Scorsese employs heightens only the illusion of spatial and pictorial flatness, of *dependence* on the text. To be seen by the film, the film must see us; it must meet our gaze. It is no accident, then, that Terence Davies, Sally Potter, Chantal Akerman, Eric Rohmer, and other Postfilm directors remain resolutely formalist and materialist in their gaze at their performers and hence create a hyperreal performance space through the power of the camera's gaze that the audience can enter into. Kristeva's *chora*, the space in the cinema contained within the womb of the camera chamber, remains the receptacle and repository of this gaze, the locus of our dreams, the nexus between two worlds bridged through the cinematic apparatus.

CHAPTER FOUR

■■
——————— ■■ ———————

The Politics of Desire:
Spectacles of the Forbidden

Everything [in the cinema] rests upon the insurpassible richness, the miraculous multiplication of perceptible being, which gives the same things the power to be things for more than one perceiver, and makes some of the things—human and animal bodies—have not only hidden faces but an 'other side' [as Husserl would state it], a perceiving side, *whose significance is based upon what is perceptible to me.*

—Merleau-Ponty, Introduction to *Signs*

The visual is *essentially* pornographic, which is to say that it has its end in rapt, mindless fascination.

—Jameson, *Signatures of the Visible*

"This is going to be so cool. I'm going to be able to shoot my dad."

—Zack Kerns, age 10, on the interactive film *Ground Zero Texas*, in which his father appears as an "extraterrestrial storm trooper," cited in Tierney.

During the summer of 1993, a small motion picture company called Digital Pictures produced what can best be described as

111

an interactive motion picture, a feature film entitled *Ground Zero Texas*. As discussed by John Tierney, the film "could be described as an action movie with a plot guided by the viewer, who watches on a television hooked to a Sega CD game machine. It could also be described as a video game with real scenery and actors." Tierney continues,

> For the past year, [Hollywood production executives have been] learning about the new CD-ROM technologies, which make it possible to put film footage on compact discs for computers. They have seen the grosses—Americans now spend more on video games than on movie tickets—and they have wondered: If people will spend that much to interact with cartoon characters, how much more will they spend to play with a real movie? (Tierney, 1).

It is a good question. Tierney notes that in the near future we can expect interactive, "live footage" video games based on such movies as *Aladdin* (obviously, in this case, the images are animated, as in the film itself, but in the new CD-ROM game, the visuals will retain the characteristics of "full," rather than "limited" animation, as in most "ordinary" video games), as well as *Jurassic Park*, *Cliffhanger*, *Last Action Hero* and Francis Ford Coppola's recent version of *Dracula* (all 1993 releases). But *Ground Zero Texas* is something altogether different. In *Ground Zero Texas*, the viewer is a direct participant in the film, directly addressed by the other performers within the fictive construct, the giver and bearer of the gaze.

Since *Ground Zero Texas* contains a high degree of interactive, first-person point-of-view violence, a number of educators and theorists are disturbed by the raw physicality of the new medium's address to the viewer/participant. Tierney notes that media critic Eugene F. Provenzo sees

> the violence in games like "Ground Zero Texas" as far more worrisome than that of the traditional games. . . . "It really is *Brave New World*," Dr. Provenzo said. "In Huxley's book there are 'feelies,' movies in which the people can participate in the movies by actually physically feeling what's hap-

FIGURE 16. "You've got the firepower. Use it!" orders actress Leslie Harter as Di-Salvo, second-in-command of your mission to save the town of El Cadron from invading aliens in Digital Pictures' live action interactive movie, *Ground Zero Texas* (actual screen output). (Courtesy of Digital Pictures, Inc., © 1993.)

pening on the screen. With games like *Ground Zero Texas* kids are able to participate in television and it's going to become increasingly physical." (Tierney, 26)

How does it work? Tierney provides this brief summary of the game's structure and content.

To play *Ground Zero Texas*, the consumer will put a CD on a Sega machine and watch the filmed action unfold *as seen through the eyes of a special agent in the Texas border town* [emphasis mine] who has arrived to search for dangerous aliens called Reticulans. If the player is quick and accurate, an alien will fall. If he misses, the alien will run away or maybe fire back. How well the player shoots will determine the sequence of events and how long the town survives. (Tierney, 26)

Ground Zero Texas represents, for better or worse, the next step forward in the evolution of the cinematic/video fictive narrative construct, a construct that acknowledges and directly incorporates the returned gaze of both screen space (performative space) and the performer within the narrative, an inherent coefficient of the cinema/video apparatus which has been with us since the invention of the site of the cinematic *chora*. The disturbing element in all this, however, is that in *Ground Zero Texas* the application of the consciously employed *interactive* "look back" in the cinema is being used to concretize a series of unceasingly violent acts, to create a film in which "there [are] more than 300 different 'point and shoot' scenes" (Tierney, 26), to orchestrate a spectacle in which violence is the sole informing structure. Assuming that the "film/game" has a running time of approximately ninety minutes (although in many senses, a "time limit" on the game is meaningless, given the multiple permutations possible within the narrative diegesis), this means that *Ground Zero Texas* contains a "point and shoot" sequence on an average of one every *eighteen seconds*.

Given the enormous recent success of the ultraviolent "slasher films," as evidenced in the *Nightmare on Elm Street* and *Friday the Thirteenth* series, to say nothing of the barely under-

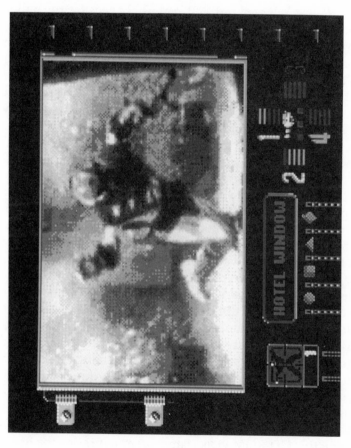

FIGURE 17. An invading alien stormtrooper goes flying after he bombs the MiniMart in El Cadron, the town you are trying to protect in Digital Pictures' live interactive movie, *Ground Zero Texas* (actual screen output). (Courtesy of Digital Pictures, Inc., © 1993.)

the-counter traffic in the justly notorious *Faces of Death* videos (in which the genuine violent deaths of humans and animals are graphically detailed on the screen; the "snuff" film actualized as a commodity of imagistic commerce), one can quite reasonably assume what will come next. Both the *Elm Street* and *Friday the Thirteenth* series have recently expired (the last *Friday* film, *Jason Goes to Hell*, was released in 1993), ostensibly because the public was sated with these violent spectacles, which presented (for the most part) a mechanistic succession of violent murders in which the viewer was often encouraged to identify with the killer through the use of point-of-view shots, inserted at precisely that moment in which the killer/viewer's victims were dispatched. It seems highly likely that both series (or a new copycat series) may be reincarnated as interactive video game/films, at first on the fringe of the industry, and gradually moving (as did the original films) to the mainstream production companies. Huxley's "feelies" boasted "synthetic kisses" and other simulated physical experiences; imagine a film in which the viewer is forced to adopt the point-of-view of a serial killer, locked into the gaze of her/his victim's eyes, "seeing" her/his "hands" plunge a knife into the victim's throat, or enact a ritualistic rape scene in which the victim screams for mercy, all viewed from the perpetrator's perspective.

Night Trap (1992) was probably the first of the new interactive videogames; predictably, it was modeled on the narrative structure of the slasher film. As described by Mike Snider, the film's plot is simple. A group of young women arrive for a weekend at a bed and breakfast, which is "also home to black-suited assailants who drain guests' blood as part of their transition to becoming full-fledged vampires . . . in one scene, three ghouls use a blood-draining auger to kill a woman in a negligee" (4D). The game has already sold nearly 200,000 copies in the United States alone since its initial release. By late 1994, a host of "ultra-violent" interactive CD-ROM video games were saturating the home rental market, including *Lethal Enforcers* (1994), a violent police-oriented crime game; *Mortal Kombat* (1992), in which "players can decapitate or rip out the organs of an opponent" (Snider, 4D); *Voyeur* (1994), in which the viewer "can snoop on the activities of a powerful, yet perverse, family" (Snider, 4D); *Mad Dog McCree*, g game in which "you'll get gunned down if you don't shoot first"

(Snider, 4D); and *Serial Killer* (1994), an interactive video game that takes you into the mind of a "serial killer" (as the ad copy on the box promises the viewer/player/participant).

Night Trap, Ground Zero Texas, Mad Dog McCree, Lethal Enforcers and other interactive CD-ROM "games" partake of the pornography of violence, of an excess of spectacle to reawaken senses numbed by an endless series of detached homicides viewed on television and in the cinema theatre. The creation of the interactive film/video seems inexorably destined for abuse, given the nature of Hollywood business practice, and also given the recent example of *Last Action Hero* (1993), which failed at the box office because audiences *do not want* reflexive, distanced violent spectacle, spectacle that makes them confront and consider the consequences of the actions they vicariously perform. Audiences seek greater *identification* with that which they view—they wish to see and be seen by the forbidden, they wish to be engulfed in the "virtual reality" of a vision that swallows them whole, in which their hands, their bodies, their eyes become at one with the fantastic construct they witness, the world they wish to fully inhabit, through all their senses.

Thus the future opens on an ominous frontier in figuristic construction; the dawn of the film that looks at you, speaks to you, the film in which you are the central character, capable of seemingly independent action, but an "action" which is, in fact, rigidly defined by the narrative/generic options afforded by the fictive world you select (the selection process, in truth, is the only genuine control afforded to the individual in the demimonde of interactivity). And yet at the center of this "contact" is the safety of "noncontact," the idea that one may indulge in unspeakable acts of cruelty and sadism *at a distance*, while at the same time participating in the illusion of direct involvement, control, and mastery of event. As Frances Ferguson notes, "However much the modern democratic state may rationalize and publicize, Sadean pornography announces the limits of the public arena" (6).

THE SADEAN VIEWER

This Sadean model of the pornographic fantasist seems identical to the hyperreal spectator imagined by interactive film and video constructs—the supremely isolated being, cut off from the world that surrounds her/him, the person who imagines that "Hey, I could become king of this world" (Tierney, 27). Cut off from those around her/him, insulated from genuine experience, the interactive video consumer becomes a pawn of the state, a nonliberated figure, a zone of control and stasis. As Judith Butler reminds us in her essay "Sexual Inversion," contained within Caputo and Yount's *Foucault and the Critique of Institutions*, "in order to exercise and elaborate its own power, a regulatory regime [such as Hollywood, viewed as a video/camera production complex] will generate the very object it seeks to control" (86); in this case, that object is the viewer viewed.

If we speak of the world constructed by Sadean pornography, and of the excessive display of violent denarration signified by both the Sadean sexual, as well as the Sadean corporeal performative taxonomic structure, in which the binary discourse of slave/master, pain/pleasure, victim/perpetrator, and decentered/acentered *mise en abyme* informs the "limit contours" of visual/physical experience, we can also propose an alternative model, one which will, perhaps, not be embraced by the dominant culture, but one which offers a good deal of genuine freedom and play for its participants/viewers/bearers of the gaze returned.

THE GAZE RETURNED IN THE AGE OF AIDS

While we seek a more liberating and egalitarian model of corporeal self-expression, we must remember that, in the year 1993, we are functioning as physical presences within the zone of the plague, the plague of AIDS. Thus the fear to touch and be touched; thus the desire to distance ourselves from fluid models of sexual discourse and configuration. There is above all an element of *nostalgia* in current pornographic representation. Every act of sexual self-expression must be monitored; exchange of bodily fluids must be avoided at risk of life. We are told that when we sleep with one person, we are in turn "making sex" with everyone that person has ever had contact with—a panopticonic self-surveillance project of crushing proportions. Viewed from this perspective, the innocence of a film like Carolee Schneeman's

Fuses (1964-67), still one of the purest and least prurient celebration of heterosexual lovemaking, described by critic Gene
Youngblood as having "a fluid, oceanic quality that merges the
physical act with its metaphysical connotation, very Joycean and
very erotic" (*FMC Catalogue No. 6*, 220), seems heartbreakingly
poignant. Even the sadomasochistic games in *Vinyl*, or the
transvestisism-at-play of Jack Smith's *Flaming Creatures* (1963)
seem remote images from an era in which risk was less immediate, and pleasure more pronounced. The pornographic practice
of today, whether lesbian/gay/straight or any combination of
these gender constructs, seems decidedly more mechanical,
embracing the body as machine and receptacle, a performance
ritual enacted for the satisfaction of an ever-growing group of
nonparticipants. There are, of course, exceptions, such as Jarman's *Edward II*, Akerman's *Je Tu Il Elle* and other films, but
these are films about the process of "making sex" rather than
examples of economic pornographic practice.

Another example of a film that centers itself on the body in
the act of sex without exploiting the corpus as commerce is Mark
D'Auria's *Smoke* (1993), presented at the Rotterdam Film Festival
and the San Francisco Lesbian/Gay International Film Festival.
Made on a minimal budget, *Smoke* is an inspiring example of
what one person can do with minimal resources, time, patience,
and a great deal of talent. While *Smoke* is conscious of the Queer
Cinema history that precedes it, D'Auria's film is a unique and
valuable contribution to the literature of gay cinema, and an
entirely personal project. Superficially, the film seems relentlessly downbeat. Michael, D'Auria's lead character, pursues a
series of generally unsatisfying sexual liaisons with a variety of
older men, one of whom is a married New York City Police
Detective who is trying to end their relationship. Michael works
as an attendant in a hotel restroom, where he must endure ritual
abuse by the patrons; he lives in a squalid and cheerless apartment; he is afflicted with a heart condition as a result of childhood illness. Michael's memories of his childhood are classically
dysfunctional; his mother smothers Michael with guilt, his father
is always absent, and his brother seems compassionate but ultimately emotionally distant. It is left to Michael to deal with the
tangle of emotions that comprise his daily existence.

FIGURE 18. The queer gaze in *Smoke* (1993). (Courtesy of Ancestor Films; director, Mark D'Auria.)

A film like *Smoke*, about a young man sexually attracted to older men, would be seen as an impossible project in Hollywood, particularly a film that sees its protagonist's situation as bleakly as D'Auria's film does. And yet, within the cheerless world of *Smoke*, there are touches of hope, usually from unexpected quarters, as when Michael answers a "personals" advertisement and spends a genuinely fulfilling evening with a complete stranger in his uptown Manhattan apartment. The next morning, when Michael awakes, he finds a note by the bathroom mirror: "Had to go to work. Hope to see you soon. The key is always under the mat." Truly, Michael leads a life that is almost entirely dependent on what Tennessee Williams aptly termed "the kindness of strangers."

Smoke is permeated with flashback scenes of Michael's unhappy childhood, often from Michael's point-of-view, and it is one measure of the film's success that these sequences work so well. Photographed in black-and-white, then printed in a light sepia through a quietly undulating "liquid frame," D'Auria's visions of his traumatic upbringing—particularly one scene in which Michael and his brother lie together in bed, burning up with a fever that will not be diagnosed before it has caused permanent heart damage—work much better than we expect them to, effectively recalling the nightmare world of a childhood lived in a world of uncertainty. There is also a remarkable sequence in which Michael runs through midtown Manhattan completely naked, pursued by a surveilling hand-held camera, as jaded pedestrians pass him by without a second look.

In contrast, Theresa Russell in Ken Russell's *Whore* (1991) finds sex "mechanical." *Whore* is yet another film in which the protagonists speak directly to the camera—not only Russell but her pimp Blake (Benjamin Mouton) as well. Sex in *Whore* is a performative act, created especially for the camera; director Ken Russell takes every opportunity to foreground the fictive theatricality of the piece. Sex takes place in cars, hotel rooms, convalescent homes, public bathrooms, and in the street; it is *only* sex, as Theresa Russell's character continually insists, speaking to us, confronting us with her contemptuous gaze. And the theatrical, performative aspect of sex within these settings is one of the key elements of *Whore*'s systemic structure.

As John Preston has argued (albeit in another context; that of sex between men in a public club—New York's Mineshaft),

> The places where sex happens are often as important as the sex itself, at least if sex is defined as more than the simple achievement of orgasm. The context within which sex takes place adds meaning to it—a fact certainly true of sex between gay men in public places. The public nature of many sex acts between gay men betrays their nature as theatrical, in the sense of being an exhibition. If there is no audience, the goals cannot be accomplished. (324)

One might suggest that the need for an audience, for the establishment of sexual action reinscribing itself on the public space, is a necessary function of performative sex within any gendered public sphere. In Stanley Donen's *Blame It on Rio* (1984), Michael Caine "makes sex" with Michelle Johnson in a variety of public places (on a beach, in a restaurant) in order to consolidate both the physical and performative reality of their union. Caine, throughout the film, speaks directly to the audience in a tight close-up, further underlining the Brechtian conceit of the work. In nonpornographic films concerned with the construction of racial and gendered personal/sexual identities, such as Leslie Harris's *Just Another Girl on the I.R.T.* (1992), the protagonist, Chantel Mitchell (Ariyan Johnson), speaks to the audience as Harris's "wandering camera" follows her through her daily struggle to survive; the film concludes with the birth of the protagonist's child in her apartment, as we watch, along with her boyfriend, the introduction of a new life into the world. As Amy Taubin wrote of *Just Another Girl on the I.R.T.*, the characters within the film "look us straight in the eyes and talk . . . they refuse to be seen and not heard. They won't have their speech contained by a dumb 19th-century theatrical convention like the fourth wall" (Taubin, *Mirror, Mirror*, 57).

Even such a seemingly innocuous text as *Wayne's World* (Penelope Spheeris, 1992), concerned as it is with performance and the construction of gendered identities, uses direct address as one of the signatures of its fetishistic textuality, signifying the oscillation between the figures of Wayne and Garth and the ground they occupy within the space of the narrative. MTV's *Beavis and Butthead* represent one model of the receptors of this increasing use of first-person diegesis.

CONSUMER RECEPTION

As constructs of the contemporary telematiculture, Beavis and Butthead's passive gaze at the television screen that dominates their lives (complemented by their inarticulate mumblings and spasmodic attempts at communicative utterance, emerging in inchoate fragments as they stare, stupefied, from their living room couch at their television, and *us*) constitutes a zero-level degree of oppositional imagistic discourse: these two adolescent males accept the spectacles offered to them by television, with only an occasional comment. Although they dimly realize that much of what they witness is "bogus," they refuse to turn off the flow of images that dominates their lives. Here, the visual has become pornographic through sheer excess of representation, resulting in the creation of an abyss of myopic countertransgression, an unending tyranny of the banal and commercial literally replacing other discourse of daily existence. For Beavis and Butthead, television has become life; it is all they know. It is the filter through which they suture and separate themselves from the libidinal economy of commercial imagery. In this respect (complete with the primitive computer animation which informs the creation of the images of these two young men), Beavis and Butthead are the logical extension of spoken discourse as narrative, of surveillance within the home as communication, the domain of the highly censored "interactive" call-in talk show. Cheap to produce, familiar in format, talk shows and live call-in shopping channels (QVC and the like) mimic the performative *langue* of interpersonal discourse without actually achieving communication.

Shopping channels, in particular, offer an unending 24-hour discourse of consumption and epistomological narratives of gift-exchange, as selected callers are offered the chance to speak with the on-air salespersons, treated as visiting friends within an indeterminate utopia of decentered countertransgression. The single caller who "gets through" to the on-air salesperson becomes the simulacrum for the hundreds of other viewer/callers who speak only to the operators who receive their orders/calls. These operators, working in small booths facing the stage on which the products are displayed, speak to the customers as if an exchange of personalities actually existed, rather than a simple economic transaction. Shopping channel operators determine, for example, the birth date of each caller, so that birthday cards may be mailed to reach them on the appropriate date, thus heightening the illusion of intimacy. Anniversaries and other special occasions are similarly observed.

What specifically holds the viewer's attention here is the notion that there is a person, a human spirit, at the center of this vast mechanical/electronic construct, and the hope that a viewer might enter into a discourse with the person on-screen, might be chosen to represent the thousands who silently watch and consume. The "narrative" is thus a construct, a contract between the salesperson/performer, the product being sold, and the viewer who wishes to purchase the commodity being offered. It is not all that far removed from the sexplay of Mick Jagger, James Fox, Michele Breton, and Anita Pallenberg in Nicolas Roeg and Donald Cammel's *Performance* (1971), a catalogue of theatrical sexual/genderal constructs and interchanges situated within the crumbling confines of a London townhouse. Transgressive reinscription of one gendered construct over another, one professional identity over another, and an unending level of perceptual filters (both chemical and cinematic) mark the mimetic structure of *Performance*'s confluence of images. In a key sequence, Jagger, Pallenberg, and Breton tumble about in a huge four-poster bed in the early morning light, engaging in languid sex-play, recording their activities with a hand-held Super 8mm camera. We see the action from a multiplicity of viewpoints: through the viewfinder of the camera, through the eyes of the participants, and climatically from the perspective of an omniscient, or voyeuristic spectator. The camera within these scenes is an instrument that simultaneously distances the participants from each other and from us; yet it also makes the interchange of fluids and identities possible, by serving as a link between the separate corporeal configurations of the three performers. Thus it is the combined dis-

tancing and fusing of viewpoints and narrative/gendered discourses which makes both the sex-play in *Performance* and the
metanarrative gift-exchange within the construct of the home
shopping channel possible. By removing one's self from contact,
one is drawn closer to the distant spectacle one sees.

This economy of desire and imagistic construction represents, as Zavarzadeh notes, in *Seeing Films Politically*, a "shift in
theorizing desire and cinematic pleasure—from focusing on
sadism as the trope of domination to masochism as the figure
for the imminent subversion of that domination" (45). The viewer
is enclosed with a private sphere of intense repression forced to
submit (though willingly) to the domination of what Iggy Pop
long ago referred to as the "TV Eye" (in a 1970 pop song of that
name). In this metacorporeal televisual social commerce, as Dana
Polan observes in his study *Power and Paranoia*:

> Mass culture . . . becomes a sort of postmodern culture, the
> stability of social meaning dissolved into one vast, spectac-
> ular *combinatoire*, a dissociation of cause and effect, a con-
> centration on the allure of means and a concomitant disin-
> terest in ends. Such spectacle creates the promise of a rich
> sight, not the sight of particular things per se, but sight itself
> as richness, as the possibility of experience. . . . Yet, as Jame-
> son notes, this spectacle is not somehow a "pure" escape
> from the commodity, but a further confirmation of its
> power: "The very activity of sense perception has nowhere
> to go in a world in which science deals with ideal quanti-
> ties. . . . This unused surplus capacity of sense perception
> can only reorganize itself into a new and semi-autonomous
> activity, one which produces its own specific objects that
> are themselves the result of a process of abstraction and
> reification" (Polan 295; Jameson, *Political Unconscious*
> 1981, 229).

THE "LOOK BACK" OF PORNOGRAPHY

Nowhere is this creation of "a spectacle everywhere" more
prominent than in the world of corporeal pornographic configu-

ration for consumption within the private sphere. In a 1993 article for *The Village Voice*, Gary Indiana spent a day watching the
creation of a hard-core porn film, and reported that a number of
iconic and performative models dominate the field. In the area of
gay porn cinema practice, according to Indiana, "the butch type
[is] most heavily featured in California porn. The California aesthetic, which dominates the industry, tends not to discriminate
between the reasonably streamlined body . . . and the massively
pumped one" (28). Indiana observed the production of the film
Temptation (1993), with the exception of one previously filmed
sequence, the entire feature was shot in a single day. Interviewing
a performer named Busty Belle, Indiana discovered that there is a
double-standard of safe-sex commodification between gay porn,
bisexual porn, and straight porn; according to Belle, performers in
straight porn films are reluctant to wear condoms.

> I found that it was very hard to make a straight movie and
> have that happen. Now I do gay and bi porn. Girl-girl, and
> also boy-boy-girl, where they're together and then have a
> threesome. I don't even do straight movies anymore. Why?
> Because the bi and gay movies have protection. I'm bisexual
> in my personal life. In my professional life, I would do either,
> but I'll only do what's healthy. It's important to know the
> straight movies don't use protection. It's very, very danger-
> ous. (30)

Thus performers within straight porn are seen as ultimately dis-
posable or replaceable as the pornography they help to create; it is
the reduction of the human corpus to receptacle of desire, and
nothing else, unless one views the absence of condoms as an act
of Foucauldian defiance. Even then, as Belle points out, such a
policy is "very, very dangerous," and equates desire with risk
and death in a manner that conflates lust with a desire *not* to
survive. These performances of sex, then, are almost twilight
visions of humanity, intimations of mortality, fornication in the
face of death.

Not surprisingly, given short shooting schedules and minus-
cule budgets, not to mention certain subterranean legal and social
status attaching to porn, much of what is produced is a replica-

tion of past models of pornographic practice. It serves the com-modification of the female body within the discourse of the male gaze in porn well to recycle existing genderal constructs and dominant sexual/social iconic structures rather than to create new image systems of sexual signification. It is left to feminist creators of gay/lesbian/bi/straight pornographic videos and films to explore the existence of an alternative model to the current dominant stereotype. Lisa Katzman describes the alternative visual structure of one such film, director Candida Royalle's *Revelations* (1993), in her article *The Women of Porn*.

> Royalle's couple- and straight women-oriented porn has garnered a loyal following through her line of tasteful videos that break rank with the standard porn aesthetic. The women in her videos are attractive in an unintimidating way, they look like women you might know rather than sil-icon-fabricated sex toys. Her couples actually have intelli-gible conversations and foreplay; she eroticizes safe sex, and uses real-life lovers whenever possible. . . . Femme Produc-tions [Royalle's production company] favors a lyrical hard-core style: during genital close-ups, the camera doesn't bear down with the usual clinical fervor. By cuing into slower, what Royalle considers female, rhythms of arousal rather than the proverbially quicker ones of male masturbation, she has created a new genre of porn—turning on some of the women who might snort in contempt watching a Buttman tape. Royalle is working to redeem pornography: she is regularly invited to speak and show her work at con-ventions given by the American Psychiatric Association and other professional groups. And for some time, she says, men in the business have resented her for making pornography "into a nice, middle-class preoccupation." (Katzman 31)

This humanist approach to the mechanics of sex removes *Revelations* from the realm of clinical discourse, what Mary Ann Doane has termed the "clinical eye," or gaze, of the "doctor's look" (Doane, *Desire*, 38-69). In this, Royalle echoes the nonex-ploitational look of the camera in the work of Trinh T. Minh-Ha, Yvonne Rainer, the photographic still artist Cindy Sherman, the painter Sue Coe, and the performance artist Karen Finley. All of these performers and creators of imagistic constructs confront the audience with the power of the gaze returned from the screen, still photograph, or canvas, inspecting or inspection of their visual domain. As bell hooks has said, "the 'gaze' has always been political in my life . . . there is power in looking" (115). hooks sets up the theory of "the oppositional gaze," in which the authority and dominion of spectacle are interrogated by the viewer, even as the spectacle seeks to *control* that viewer through the excessive splendor of its visual power.

hooks also reminds us "that opposition and resistance cannot be made synonymous with self-actualization on an individual or collective level: 'Opposition is not enough. In that vacant space after one has resisted there is still the necessity to become—to make oneself anew'" (51). In chapter 4 of her book *Black Looks*, "Selling Hot Pussy: Representations of Black Female Sexuality in the Cultural Marketplace," hooks underscores this need to resist and *replace* existing racist and exploitational visual modes which commodify "the bodies of black women" (61), demonstrating the pervasiveness of these imagistic constructs in "a row of gigantic chocolate breasts complete with nipples" (61) served as desserts in a fancy restaurant, as well as the public performance of Josephine Baker (63-64) and Tina Turner (67), as constructed by the "white patriarchal controlled media shaping [our] perceptions of reality . . . in a white supremacist society" (67).

hooks stresses that it is not enough to resist or challenge these racist, "misogynist," "pornographic" (67) fantasies; one must erase them, replace them, create new constructs in their stead. This is much more easily proposed, however, than accomplished. Inasmuch as pornography depends upon corporeal exploitation for its control over the gaze of the audience, only when black women create their own erotic imagistic constructs will they have any power over the gaze that seeks to exploit them—which does, in fact, exploit *all* performers in porn, even as they seek to distance themselves from the images they create for consumption. As hooks notes, "Appropriating the wild woman pornographic myth of black female sexuality created by men in a white supremacist patriarchy, [Tina] Turner exploits it for her own ends to achieve economic self-sufficiency" (69).

And yet this conscious self-exploitation comes at a high personal price because the essence of pornography is the creation of an imagistic construct that exploits the human body, no matter what race or gender the performer within the frame may be. As one of the white male performers in gay porn admitted to Gary Indiana, self-abasement and detachment from the commodification of one's own corpus becomes a necessary concomitant of pornographic practice. And this goes beyond the boundaries of the frame, into the realm of private performance, "what is euphemistically described as out-call" (Indiana, 30). The performer noted that, in porn:

> We're all the same. "Never will I do anything like that." And then never becomes, "I've gotta buy groceries." Once you get into out-call, it's, "Wow, I'm going to Paris, Europe, all these places." At times I'm upset with myself that I've been foolish with my money. Luckily, I have a lot of things to show for it. Two cars that are paid off, beautiful furniture. (Indiana, 30)

Indeed, "out-call," or private pornographic performance, can be seen as less degrading than the construction of an ever-present, continually existing record of self-exploitation—the true activity of porn. "Out-call" is essentially a private contract; porn constructs readily available, mass-marketed images of self-exploitation, images that will haunt the performer for as long as the negative survives and can be duplicated. As Judith Butler states in her essay "Sexual Inversion," "the category of 'sex' will be precisely what power produces in order to have an object of control" (87). Nowhere is this construct of "sex for control" more blatant or sharply configured than in the creation of porn. Paul Willemen notes in *Letter to John* that some of the

> questions to ask of the institution of porn are: What are the terms of the social circulation of representations of sex? What are the terms of their economic exploitation? Perhaps these two questions can be summarised in line with the formulation . . . What do porn representations think you are? (58)

For in no other aspect of cinema practice is the gaze of the voyeur/viewer so universally turned back on the giver of the gaze. Porn, through its fabulistic and fetishistic image constructs its framing devices (both narrative and figurative) and its exclusive concentration on a single aspect of the separate-body experience, creates a world that exploits both viewer and performer, and operates unilaterally on both sides of the screen. Pornography encodes the gaze of the forbidden, the deeply unacknowledged, the embrace of the private (paranoid) space, the secrecy of fetishistic self-bondage. Thus when porn asks, who you are, it gazes back at you with a mixture of wonderment and contempt. Who, precisely, constitutes the audience for these grindingly artificial tableaux of abasement? As Peter Gidal states in his essay "Against Sexual Representation in Film":

> The positions that are given for the retention and reproduction of male (and men's) power are given precisely through dominant pleasures, consumption instigated by the ideological material of representing every moment of/in our social existence. These meanings cannot simply be critiqued as if that were enough (interpreting the world, we certainly know, is not to change it). We have to produce different positions in our representational practices, and such a beginning of a different position is one which does not reproduce the empirical real as real, does not give perception the status of truth, does not reproduce certain perceptions at all, precisely because of the overdetermined codified meanings that prevail. (28)

And yet, as Stephen Prince notes in his essay "The Pornographic Image and the Practice of Film Theory," numerous claims made against pornographic sexual cinema/video practice have a dubious grounding in reality. Prince writes:

> When analysts make statements about the characteristics of pornographic images, the sample of works from which such statements have been drawn are rarely defined . . . [this is why] clarity about one's sample is so important with regard to pornographic films. Because of the diversity of

pornographic forms, one could choose a sample to prove almost anything. By studying exclusively sadomasochistic and bondage films, one could build a case that pornography indeed represents a form of male violence against women. However, if one selected films featuring female domina- trixes, one could argue the opposite. (31-32)

Prince's observation is intriguing, but there is still the issue of individual address, of the hold that a particular image may have on a given viewer, of the clinical gaze subjects in main- stream porn are subjected, and of the political/social repression implicit in the production of male-produced porn.

In the late 1970s, while working on a series of documen- tary films in a New York production facility, I spent many hours in a cutting room just down the hall from a mixing studio where 35mm feature porn films were being "post-produced" (that is, music and sound effects added) on a daily, assembly-line basis. On a number of occasions, I would walk into the mixing studio to confer with the sound mixer on one of my films, or set up an appointment for a "sound mix" later in the day. On each of the occasions that I entered the studio, a scene of subjugation and humiliation involving women as victims was being played out on the screen—badly lit, badly photographed, and possessing the returned gaze of nothing so much as captured Nazi concentration camp footage in which victims are tortured for sport and amuse- ment.

The sound mixer viewed all this with professional detach- ment—"just doing my job"—but finally, after viewing a particu- larly, violent scene involving forced fellatio, bondage, and tor- ture, I could restrain myself no longer. How could he stand to watch this footage all day? His answer was paradoxical and chill- ing: *he had a family to support*. Further, the mixer noted that most of the films he received had synchronous (that is, lip-synced dialogue) for only a portion of the action. The rest of the footage was completely silent. To fill in the gaps in the soundtrack as expeditiously as possible, he had three "sound loops" (continu- ously repeating soundtracks) running at all times, ready to be "mixed in" as the need arose. One of the loops was called "moans." The second loop was dubbed "fucking": the sound of mechanical intercourse. The final loop was labeled "pain": literally, screams of physical agony. The mixer admitted that the third loop was used with pathetic and alarming frequency; otherwise, why would it be "up there" (that is, "ready to be used")? All too often, the silent images demanded the aural accompaniment of the third "loop." It would be noted that this incident took place during the pre-videocassette era; most porn features were shot on 35mm film, and played in 42nd street "grind houses." Now, with the advent of generally available VCRs and camcorders, most porn films are shot directly on tape, with synchronous sound throughout, and the mixing process described above has become technically antiquated. Nevertheless, the dominant model observed here still, to my mind, obtains.

Pornographic film/video production is a business, and just as *Jurassic Park* (1993) outperforms Chantal Akerman's *Night and Day* (1992, a film that delightfully plays with the returned look from the screen) at the box office, so male-produced porn will continue to outsell *Revelations*, and the patriarchal visual and narrative model inherent in most porn will inevitably, it seems, dominate the home and theatrical markets. Porn is the commodification of the flesh for profit, and while it should not be censored (if only because that which is censored inevitably erupts in another context), it should nevertheless be recognized for the exploitational project that it is.

CHAPTER FIVE

■■
——————— ■■ ———————

Dreams of the State:
Control of the Spectatorial Body

When film studies as an academic discipline first began to be codified at the university level in the mid-1960s, it is significant that this process was, in most cases, the result of activity in the English departments of the colleges and universities in question. There are several reasons for this. First, English departments came pre-equipped with writers who had already shown themselves to be of superior ability in discussing print novels, short stories, and poems and the various metaphoric, iconic, and syntactical structures used in these forms. Second, the strong narrative thrust of most Hollywood and European films seemed to forge a bridge between the mediums of literature and film, one which could easily be charted. Early filmic fragments, with their staging taken from the Proscenium Arch tradition of the theatre and their sense of narrative closure taken equally from the theatre and from the tradition of the novel, short story, or in some cases, the magazine serial as far back as Dickens, paved the way for longer, more complex experiments in the narrative form (see Branigan on the logic of this narrative structural development, 19-20, and on the development of linear narrative patterns in film, 162-163; also Bordwell on the history and origins of classical Hollywood narrative, 17-34). By 1904, narrative became the predominate form in filmmaking, and the earlier "actualities" of the

Lumiere Brothers were eschewed by the public as a primitive form of cinematic entertainment. Thus, until the rise of the Dadaist experimental filmmakers in France in the 1920s, the narrative format used in both literature and the theatre had established its predominance as the chief mode of expression in the filmic medium.

Thus, as David Desser and other theorists have noted, a link between the canon of literacy studies and film studies was forged early on—the idea of a "core list" of indispensible texts one *had* to consider. Further, the ability of English departments to handle narrative film may have created a hegemony for these "classics" as the discipline of film studies grew (as Desser noted in remarks on this manuscript faxed to me on December 16, 1993). Films became texts, and texts were looked at. They did not return the gaze of the reader/spectator. Not until the dawn of the computer/word-processor era in the late 1980s did this issue of spectatorial reciprocity begin to be addressed, and the debate is still very much an ongoing discussion. Even when the characters in a film turned to directly address the viewer (as previously cited in the works of Warhol, Godard, Truffant and others), early film theorists, schooled in the tradition of the monologue and the epistolary novel, considered that the character addressing the audience was simply projecting her/his interior thoughts. Never was the question of the gaze, or the "look back" addressed, astounding as it now seems. Thus, the filmic "look back" was sealed off, related to the "look back" of the printed page, reduced to a block of text that only pretended to acknowledge the viewer. As I have argued, it is precisely this textual difference between the film/video image and the "image" of text on the page (or PC screen) that needs to be explored. Words constitute glyphs that must consciously be deciphered. Images are also glyphs, and must also be deciphered, but often, this work is done unconsciously, and the film/video viewer becomes the passive recipient of the flood of images she/he is presented with.

As we have seen, theatrical presentations acknowledge their reflexive distanciation from the spectator through the appropriation of a metanarrative structure that embraces the presentation of the fictive construct. When we are in a theatre, we, sealed within the boundaries of the filmic corpus, interact (even in the most traditional forms of drama) with the members of the cast, sharing that sense of the immediate and the imperfect inherent in the act of figurative (narrational) oscillation between the figure of the actor (and the audience), and the ground each seeks to occupy/operate upon (see Baudry on the "'reality' mixed by the cinema" as it "unites the discontinuous fragments of phenomena, of lived experience, into unifying meaning," 295).

In the cinema, reception involves the human agency of the viewer locked in a photocentric countertransgressive act of reciprocity with cinematic apparatus; a perfect, sealed, seemingly flawless construct designed solely for us to witness. Countless replications of this transgressive, passive spectacle will leave it essentially unchanged; it is the narrative removed from accident, from the realm of the also-human. Cinema reception, then, operates in a zone of performative countertestimony, and displays a fetishistic textuality linked to the dialectic of constructedness. While cinema narrative structure may superficially take its rudimentary structures, then, from the stage, cinema syntax and suture have rapidly developed their own heterotopic alternity, far removed from the immediacy of live performance.

Yet even the most informal criticism of filmic narrative structure in the United States took a considerable period of time to arrive at any level of discursive prominence. Although narrative films, at least of the more conventional Hollywood sort (whether made in Hollywood or abroad, this type of film can be categorized as a "Hollywood" film) were by late 1920s the dominant form of mass American narrative entertainment, criticism of the narrative film itself did not seriously begin to take hold until the mid-1940s, when the prescient critic James Agee began reviewing films for *Life*, *Time*, and the short-lived New York afternoon newspaper, *PM*. Agee was something of a critical maverick, not only because he took Hollywood films seriously and applied rigorous critical standards to them, learned in part from his immersion in classical and modern American literature, but also because Agee, alone among the contemporary reviewers of film, took the works of such B producer-auteurs as Val Lewton seriously. Agee cited Lewton, then a maker of cheap horror films for RKO Radio Pictures with titles such as *Curse of the Cat People* (1944) and *I Walked with a Zombie* (1943), as one of the greatest cinematic artist working in America during the period. The passage of time, and the overview it inevitably affords, has proved Agee substantially correct. If one looks at the work of Agee's fellow film critics during the early 1940s, however, one finds very superficial textual analysis of the works in question, which considers only the stars, the plots, and the general production values of each offering. The idea of directorial signature, except in the case of the publicity conscious Alfred Hitchcock, is never brought up at all.

Yet in France during this era, André Bazin and his early *Cahiers du Cinéma* cohorts, Jean-Luc Godard (writing as Hans Lucas), François Truffaut (writing often as Robert Lachenay), Chris Marker, and Luc Mollet, as well as others, were positing for the first time the then-revolutionary notions that:

1. Film might accurately be considered an art form, with its own rules, structures, ambitions, and syntactical laws.
2. That even "genre" films such as westerns, musicals, crime films, and hard-boiled detective films, might be considered, in the hands of the right directors, "art."
3. That the fact that films were produced for mass consumption gave one no inherent right to dismiss them as simply plebian entertainment, inferior in some intrinsic way to offerings of the stage, or to work accomplished in the novel in another written fictional form.
4. Perhaps most importantly, that the director in most cases occupied a position similar to that of the author in a written work, the "auteur", as the *Cahiers* critics dubbed him, of the film she or he had directed. (See Allen, 137-145, for an examination of the historical development of film genre in Hollywood narrative.)

These were concepts that went against the grain of all previous criticism of filmic work, with the exception of a few writers like Agee and Parker Tyler, and they were contested hotly both in France, where criticism of American films really began, oddly enough, and in the United States. Hollywood ironically took little notice of this critical phenomenon, which sought to enshrine what had been considered primarily a commercial enterprise. It had long been the accepted fashion to divide artistic endeavor into two general categories, "art" and "popular entertainment"; now the *Cahiers* critics and such later American disciples as Andrew Sarris sought to avoid applying these same standards to film. They did so in a way which exploded a number of convenient critical structures which had long been applied to the written narrative form. Many of Dickens's works, for example, originally appeared as magazine serials, and because of this, for a long time one had difficulty finding a critic who would consider Dickens' writing seriously, simply because of its humble publication background. Edgar Allan Poe had the same difficulty when his work appeared in numerous and sundry obscure publications, and in this century, the writer H. P. Lovecraft still struggles for some sort of bastard respectability because he allowed his work to be published in pulp magazines of the early 1920s to late 1930s.

By refusing to apply these outmoded and patrician standards to the films they critiqued, Sarris, Godard, Truffaut, Bazin and other *nouvelle vague* theorists created a new pantheon, dominated by directors such as Howard Hawks, Alfred Hitchcock, John Ford, and others, whose films were genre efforts aimed at the general public. In their considerations of these films, *Cahiers* critics stressed the narrative function in their critical apparatus, and demonstrated early on their affection for the consistency that genre narrative affords. The expectations that one has of a gangster film (the fall and rise or the rise and fall of the hoodlum), the horror film (that one will be forced to confront a series of grotesques either manmade or arising from some unearthly agency), the musical (that boy will get girl in a series of dancing tableaux) or the western (which will usually end up with some variety of showdown on the dusty main street of a small deserted cowtown) provide a certain assurance for both the critic and the casual viewer.

It is by no means an accident that when some of the *Cahiers* critics, notably Godard and Truffaut, broke off to become feature film directors in their own right, that they began (and to some degree, remained) within the tradition of genre film, however, they might have transmogrified and/or parodied their source material. Godard's first feature, *Breathless* (1959) displays a self-reflexivity in its Bogart-styled close-ups of Jean-Paul Belmondo in the leading role as a cheap hood on the run from police, and Truffaut, although he first created one of the cinema's most affecting autobiographies in his debut film, *The 400 Blows* (1959), soon turned to genre parody with *Shoot the Piano Player* (1960) (the gangster film again) and *The Soft Skin* (1964) (the woman's picture of the 1930s through the 1950s), ending his career with a graceful homage to the hard-boiled detective film with *Confidentially Yours* (1984) (see Metz for a discussion of spectatorial identification within the cinematic apparatus as it relates to the fictional narrative film, 251-253).

Thus, we have a twin connection between the narrative form in film and in literature: it provides the framework for the critical methodology that seeks to explicate both the image and the word, and it serves as a common thread in the construction of written and photographed fiction. It is interesting to note that there is, however, despite this connection, an element of untranslatability between the two mediums. The non-narrative film, which came out of the Dada movement in 1920s Paris, was an attempt to both free film from the supposed twin "tyrannies" of logic and narrative structure, and to liberate the unconscious "systems" of metaphoric and iconic structuring found in dreams and hallucinatory experiences. As a direct result of this, these films correctly resist explication in writing, and perhaps should be critiqued by other films (as Godard attempted to do with his mid-1970s theoretical film work, particularly *Letter to Jane: Investigation of a Still* [1972], which critiques one still photographic image of Jane Fonda in Vietnam, and finds a wealth of metaphoric, class structure, and socializing factors in that image, discovered through the process of cinematic/apparatus meditation upon the visual being considered, rather than a written, textual dissection of it). These early Dada films paved the way for the American avant-garde work in the 1940s, where artists such as Maya Deren, Harry Smith, Kenneth Anger, Stan Brakhage and others created personal, low-budget 16mm films which also sought to abrogate the need for the narrative structure.

THE RETURNED GAZE OF NON-NARRATIVE CINEMA

This sort of underground filmmaking continued well into the 1960s, but Jean-Isidore Isou's little seen masterwork, *Venom and Eternity* (1951), which was championed at Cannes by the French poet/filmmaker/writer Jean Cocteau, represented, up until the more recent work of Chantal Akerman, Yvonne Rainer, Barbara Hammer, and other practitioners of the "new narrative" cinema, the single most effective discussion of the interrelationship between cinema image and the text/narrative and of the necessity for a system of aesthetics that recognizes the differences as well as the similarities between the three competing systems of nar-rativistic signification: *textual narrative* (text "on the page"), *theatrical narrative* (live presentation/performance), and *cine-matic narrative*, which represents an amalgam of text and the-atrical performance yet, by its "sealed" nature and restless search for the mimesis of perfection, seeks a hermetically sealed narra-tive syntax into which no human agency is allowed to intrude.

Isou recognized this phenomenon of the sealed inhumanity of the cinematic apparatus. In *Venom and Eternity*, Isou con-structed what he correctly termed as an "assault" on the audi-ence, making his film out of academy leader, scratched film, upside-down newsreel stock footage, out-of-focus shots, long blank stretches of film, film with holes punched in it, coupling these images with a soundtrack that attempts to consider the commonplace system of aesthetics that rules much of traditional "narrative" film production. Thus *Venom and Eternity* is a polemic based upon the connection between the narrative form, literature, and the graven image. The film will last only as long as this narrativist contest is under discussion by the author, existing outside of the realm of the story, the word, the domain of the written text. For Isou, conventional narrative cinema is ruled by both the public's need for and demand of a narrative framework, and then, as a direct consequence, by a series of banal images that are simply used to illustrate the story. That these images then form a treacherous "aesthetic" of "beauty" and/or "ugli-ness" is one of Isou's chief concerns. Isou wants us to recognize that, at its worst, the need for a conventional narrative in film can lead the medium to a rigid dependency upon this fictive intrastructure, which ultimately cripples the syntactical vocabulary film might possibly explore. In Isou's film, "The subject here is first and foremost that wondrous fetish, *power*. We want it and we are rightly scared by it, in equal, mighty and fantastic measure" (Taussig, 63).

The early 1960s saw independent filmmaking with a strong Romantic sensibility flourish. Raw, lush and sensual imagery predominated, and narrative structure was reduced or abrogated altogether. Many of these films are little-remembered today, having escaped the canonical net of film study through a lack of reviews or public screenings, but all are worth a "fresh" viewing to see what perhaps has been missed. In nearly every case, these fiercely independent films confront the viewer, forcing her/him to either submit to the gaze of the screen, or to merge with the often overpowering stream of imagery presented to create a viewer/viewed construct that virtually eliminates the artificial boundary line between spectacle and audience. Gerard Malanga, Andy Warhol's assistant, produced the beautiful films *In Search of the Miraculous* (1967), *Preraphaelite Dream* (1968), and *The Recording Zone Operator* (1968); the last film mentioned was shot in Rome, Italy, in 35mm Technicolor/Techniscope in the winter of 1968. A different but equally liberating Romantic vision is that of the slightly better known Ron Rice, whose feature film *The Flower Thief* (1960), was shot in 16mm black-and-white using fifty-foot film cartridges left over from aerial gunnery equipment used during World War II. Rice's *Senseless* (1962), and *Chumlum* (1964) are also worth noting; the *New York Herald Tribune* described *Chumlum* as "a bizarre dream, in riotous color" (*FMC Catalogue* No. 6, 208). Jon Voorhees created a group of stunningly photographed films including *Rivers of Darkness/Rivers of Light* (1972) and *Whispers Relaying Grace* (1973). The more anarchic imagery of Jim Krell can be seen in no less than twenty films, ranging in length from 3¼ minutes to forty-five minutes, of which *Thirty Days: Speed or Gravity?* (1976), *Action Past Compassion* (1976), and *Second Thoughts* (1980) are perhaps the most accessible; all of Krell's works, as well as those of Rice, Malanga, and Voorhees, are available for rental from the Filmmakers Cooperative in New York.

The "New Narrative" filmic style of the 1960s can be seen in Stanton Kaye's *Georg* (1964) and *Brandy in the Wilderness*

(1969); Larry Kardish's eighty-minute *Slow Run* (1968) is a relaxed and informal narrative possessed of enormous power and intelligence. The pioneering montagist Max Katz should be remembered for his dazzling editorial construct *Wisp* (1963), as well as his seventy-seven-minute feature film *Jim the Man* (1970). José Rodriguez-Soltero produced *Jerovi* (1965), *Lupe* (1966), an elegiac remembrance of Hollywood actress Lupe Velez, and the rigorously formalist feature film *Dialogue with Ché* (1968), which was successfully presented at the Cannes and Berlin Film Festivals in 1969, and widely reviewed. Vernon Zimmerman's all-but-forgotten *Lemon Hearts* (1960) stars the gifted actor Taylor Mead in no less than eleven roles and is an improvisational comedy shot on a shoestring budget in San Francisco. Ray Wisniewski's *Doomshow* (1964) and Bud Wirtschafter's *What's Happening!* (1963) are documents of "happenings" (partially staged theatrical events) featuring such pioneering New York artists as Allan Kaprow, Yvonne Rainer, La Monte Young, and Dick Higgins. Ben van Meter's *S.F. Trips Festival: An Opening* (1967), available through Canyon Cinema in San Francisco, is a gorgeously multiple exposed record of a "happening" on the West Coast, and has much in common with Wisniewski's and Wirtschafter's work.

Jud Yalkut, originally a New York-based filmmaker associated with the USCO Lightshow group, has continuously made films since the early 1960s, of which *Kusama's Self-Obliteration* (1967), a record of a "happening" conducted by Japanese artist Yayoi Kusama, and *US Down By the Riverside* (1966) are perhaps best known. Masao Adachi's *Wan: Rice Bowl* (1962) is an early example of Japanese expatriate American cinema, as is Edd Dundas's *The Burning Ear* (1965). Robert Downey Sr., whose popularity was widespread in the 1960s, produced the satiric narratives *Babo 73* (1964) and *Chafed Elbows* (1966) earlier in his career; they have not been screened publicly for more than a decade. Satya Dev Dubey's *Barriers* (1967), shot in 35mm, is the work of an Indian expatriate in New York. A group of influential feature films by New American Cinema artists seldom seen today includes Jock Livingston's Dadaist-influenced comedy *Zero in the Universe* (1966); David Secter's *Winter Kept Us Warm* (1968)), revolving around a gay love affair on a Canadian college campus; Dick Higgins's *The Flaming City* (1963), a hard-edged "Beat" epic about Manhattan life on the margins; and Robert Kramer's *Ice* (1969) dealing with a futurist cell of political revolutionaries. All of these films are certainly worthy of revival. Christopher MacLaine's films *Beat* (1958), *The Man Who Invented Gold* (1957), *Scotch Hop* (1959), and *The End* (1953) are all documents of the San Francisco Beat era. Seldom shown today, these films provide a tantalizing peek into the world of a vanished yet still influential subculture. MacLaine died in 1975; his films have been preserved by Robert Haller and Jonas Mekas of Anthology Film Archives. The late Scott Bartlett's films *Metanomen* (1966), *Off/On* (1968), and *Moon* (1969) exemplified San Francisco's preferred form of cinematic discourse for a later generation of artists, poets, writers, and videomakers, a blend of film and video into one raw, homogenized mix. Indeed, Bartlett's *Off/On* is one of the first films to combine film and video imagery together into a spatially congruent imagistic document.

In discussions of feminist cinema practice, the works of Marie Menken and Maya Deren are often mentioned, but the films of their compatriot Storm De Hirsch (to cite just one example) are seemingly marginalized. De Hirsch's *Goodbye in the Mirror* (1964) is a 35mm feature film shot in Rome dealing with the lives of three young American women living abroad. Screened at the Locarno and Cannes Film Festivals in 1964, and in Vancouver in 1966, this transcendent and ambitious narrative film is only one example of early feminist cinema that led to the later works of Yvonne Rainer, Jane Campion, Sally Potter, Julie Dash, and others. The more contemporary Janis Crystal Lipzin's *Other Reckless Things* (1984) has been screened at the Museum of Modern Art, the Ann Arbor Film Festival, the San Francisco Art Institute, and elsewhere, yet has somehow failed to join the mainstream canon despite an enthusiastic initial reception. Jo Ann Elam's *Rape* (1975) and *Lie Back and Enjoy It* (1982) have been reviewed in *Time Out* and *Jump Cut* and need to be seen again today. Dorothy Wiley and Gunvor Nelson's *Schmeerguntz* (1966), *Fog Pumas* (1967), and the feature-length *Before Need* (1979) operate in a zone of feminist discourse that has been more widely appreciated abroad, particularly in Sweden, than in the United States.

Rose Lowder's formalist *Rue des Teinturiers* (1979), *Champ Provençal* (1979), and *Retour d'un Depere* (1979-81; available in three versions) have also been well received in Europe but less so in the United States. Marjorie Keller started out in the late 1960s in the standard 8mm format and moved to 16mm with her 1973 production *The Outer Circle*; since then, she has produced fifteen films through 1988's *Private Parts*, creating a body of work that is both original and disturbing. Carolee Schneeman, previously mentioned in this text, is best known for her films *Fuses* (1964-68) and *Plumb Line* (1968-72), which both deserve wider exposure. Babette Mangolte is another excellent filmmaker in search of a larger audience; the creator of *What Maisie Knew* (1975), *The Cold Eye* (*My Darling, Be Careful*) (1980), and *The Sky on Location* (1982), Mangolte has had her films screened at the Toulon, Edinburgh, Berlin, and San Diego film festivals. Nancy Graves's *Isy Boukir* (1971) was favorably reviewed by *The New York Times* and *The Village Voice* upon its initial release; Graves continued working with *Reflections on the Moon* (1974) and other films, but her work could certainly benefit from wider screening. Amy Greenfield's *Transport* (1971), *Element* (1973), and *Tides* (1982) have been screened at the Museum of Modern Art, the London Film Festival, the Whitney Museum of American Art and the Edinburgh Film Festival; again, after an enthusiastic first round of reviews, her work has not been shown as widely as it should be. Naomi Levine's work goes back to the formative years of the New York underground cinema and includes the films *Jeremelu* (1964), *Yes* (1963), *From Zero to 16* (1969), *London Bridges Falling Down* (1969) and many others. This list could be extended with at least another fifty names of women who have worked in the cinema for more than thirty years, but who have yet to receive the sustained canonical inclusion their work so clearly deserves.

THE RECIPROCAL CANON

The list goes on, and certainly could be documented in far more exhaustive detail, but at this juncture, I would like to consider the reasons why this marginalization of the work of certain film-makers has occurred and is maintained. Leaving aside questions of individual taste and critical reception for the moment, I would suggest that canon is convenience, a process in which certain works and certain artists come to represent a certain style, era, or geographical region in cinema practice, at the expense of those artists marginalized in the process. American Independent Film practice, which represented a fairly "closed set" of artists as late as the 1960s, has become a much wider field of operations in the 1980s and 1990s, and the amount of information available is simply too much for any one person to process. This leads to a series of exclusionary value judgments that, in the end, serve the interests of no one. Critics invariably write about the work that attracts or repulses them most immediately, yet as the numerous prizes and screenings accorded many of the films chronicled in this essay indicate, even a responsive initial critical reception is no guarantee of extended canonical inclusion. It seems to me that those artists who create a large body—an extensive physical corpus—of work are most often favored with canonical inclusion, yet even prolific production coupled with favorable reviews still seems no decisive indicator of admittance to the established canon.

Films that operate against the grain of the dominant mode of discourse within any given era run a substantially higher risk of being marginalized than do works that belong to a specific cinematic set or subset. The work done by the American avant-garde can roughly be divided into four historical subsets. The first group, beginning in the early 1940s, and canonically comprised of the works of Marie Menken, Willard Maas, Kenneth Anger, Harry Smith, and others, displays a high degree of polish, takes pictorial representational cues from Hollywood practice of the period, and seeks to free itself from then-existing representational structures, but it is still clearly establishing a voice of its own. In the early 1950s, it can now be seen that in the works of Christopher MacLaine and others, a more anarchic period of cinema practice was being ushered in, in which filmmakers embraced the technical imperfections of the subalternative tools they were forced to work with; resulting in films that flaunted their technical roughness in front of their audiences. Jean Isidore Isou's 1951 *Venom and Eternity* remains a landmark in this area, questioning as it does all forms of narrative discourse and pictorial representationalism, including conventional and even "avant-garde" framing, composition, syntax, suture, and the materiality of filmic discourse.

By the early 1960s, this methodological approach was becoming a full-scale movement, as seen in the works of Bruce Conner, Robert Nelson, Andy Warhol, Jack Smith and others. This school was in turn superseded in the late 1960s by the arrival of the formalist/structuralist film practitioners, canonically represented by the works of Snow, Frampton, and Gehr. In the late 1980s, this formalist/structuralist mode of inquiry gave way to the Postfilm, a formalist narrative with Romantic overtones which incorporated organizational and aesthetic precepts of all the previous eras; in England, where the Postfilm currently flourishes, the best known practitioners of the Postfilm include Derek Jarman, Sally Potter, Isaac Julien, and Terence Davies; in the United States, Yvonne Rainer, Julie Dash, and Gregg Araki are among the Postfilm's best known proponents. It is interesting to note that in both countries, it is the practitioners of feminist and queer cinema that have seized the helm of the Postfilm, freeing it from the confines of conventional materialist film practice and presentational narrative discourse. Within any given period, films which adhered to these formalist/materialist guidelines stood a better chance of being included within the canon that was passed on to the next group of theoreticians/practitioners. Yet in each period, as I have documented here, there are works that receive a good deal of initial critical acclaim and still fail to make the canonical cut. This leaves the work of rediscovery to the group Stanley Fish has dubbed "the Young and the Restless" (303).

In the late 1960s, a new formalism began to permeate radical film structure, most aggressively foregrounded in the work of Michael Snow, whose *Wavelength* (1966-67) documented a forty-five-minute "zoom" across a studio/loft in lower Manhattan, while Snow played with various film stocks, color filters, random scraps of narrative (a man enters the space and dies; some workmen move a large cabinet against a wall), and manipulated a signal generator to produce and a "glissando" of accompanying sound ranging from 50 to 12,000 Hz, which lasted the duration of the film.

Of the film, Snow wrote:

The film is a continuous zoom which takes 45 minutes to go from its widest field to its smallest and final field. It

was shot with a fixed camera from one end of an 80 foot
loft, shooting the other end, a row of windows and the
street. This, the setting, and the action which takes place
there are cosmically equivalent. The room (and the zoom)
are interrupted by 4 human events including a death. The
sound on these occasions is sync sound, music and speech,
occurring simultaneously with an electronic sound, a sine
wave, which goes from its lowest 50 cycles per second)
note to its highest (12,000 c.p.s.) in 40 minutes. It is a
total glissando while the film is a crescendo and a dis-
persed spectrum which attempts to utilize the gifts of
both prophecy and memory which only film and music
have to offer. (*Filmmakers' Cooperative Catalogue No. 6*,
232)

Snow's film was the first in a series of rigorous formal experiments that included the work of Ernie Gehr, the late Hollis
Frampton, Joyce Wieland, Ken Jacobs, Peter Gidal, the late Paul
Sharits and many others who investigated questions of cinema
process (film grain, shot duration, camera movement, shot suture,
and syntax).

Raymond Bellour, in his essay on the narrative/shot structure of the film *Gigi* (1958; Dir. Vincente Minnelli), offers
within the confines of Hollywood discourse an example of the
rigorous analytical detail inherent in the work and theoretical
writings of Snow, Frampton, and Gehr. Bellour subjects the
filmic text to the "strict application of the *grande syntagma-
tique*" (71), that is, the numerous and complex interlock of
iconic codes, musical and visual cues, characterizations, and
group placements within the frames of the film. Bellour's search
for a system of all-encompassing narrative/significatory codes
operating within the cinematic apparatus mirrors the stripped-
down approach seen in *Wavelength* and other of Snow's films;
narrative reduced to a formalist function, separated as a series of
glyphic codes and incidents, catalogued, indexed, and yet still
retaining an element of resistance to any absolutist interpretation. Yet the fragmented narrative structure in *Wavelength* is
clearly subordinate to the formalist concerns of the work (see
Bellour, 66-90).

THE POSTFILM

More recently in the late 1970s to the present, there has been a new interest in formalist *narrative* structure, represented by such films as Lizzie Borden's *Born in Flames* (1985), Yvonne Rainer's *The Man Who Envied Women* (1985; see Rainer, 46-52, for a full, and playful account of the formalist narrative strategies employed in this film; also Goldberg, 97-102), Chantal Akerman's *Je Tu Il Elle* (1974), Babette Mangolte's *What Maisie Knew* (1975), Trinh T. Minh-Ha's *Surname Viet, Given Name Nam* (1989), Julie Dash's *Daughters of the Dust* (1991), to name but a few examples. These films represent a new direction in cinematic narrativity because while they employ many of the formal strategies and structures used by Snow and his contemporaries, these Postfilms question conventional cinema practice by turning our attention to what Mas'ud Zavarzadeh refers to as "the tale not told" in traditional filmic structure. Zavarzadeh notes:

> The production of an "obviously" intelligible tale by spectator-film-ideology nexus suppresses *another* tale—the tale that the overt one prevents from being told. Each film is therefore the narrative space of contestation and struggle among different tales that produce warring theories of the real. (19)

It should come as no surprise, then, that much of the most interesting work being done in this new rigorous, contested formalist/narrative format is being created by the persons most marginalized by conventional cinema narrative practice: women and those who are not participants in the Caucasian male construct of an enforced heterotopia.

In *Framer Framed*, Trinh T. Minh-Ha tells of her own struggle toward creating her film *Reassemblage* (1982), a Postfilm produced only after a great deal of difficulty and personal hardship. In addition, Minh-Ha had to overcome the hold of the patriarchy on the conventions of narrative and the concomitant seizure of power by cinema theoreticians who opposed work that deviated from traditional narrative representationalism (see Mulvey, 11-30, for a lively discussion of feminist film theory in relation to narrative structure and psychoanalytic film discourse and the ways in which these new sutural structures contradict the cinematic project of the conventional narrative).

Minh-Ha found a "field of experts whose access [to power] is gained through authoritative knowledge of a demarcated body of 'classical' films and of legitimized ways of reading and speaking about films" (122) and who sought to limit her access to tools and, once the films were made, her access to the critical machinery required to publicize their existence. Looking back over the 1980s, we can see a decade-long battle by Minh-Ha to create a Postfilm that operates entirely outside the conventions of western cinema—a cinema, instead, of "looks" and "returned gazes" articulating the gestures and desires of those whose tale is "not told" in traditional cinema. The world presented within the confines of the classic narrative cinema is above all one of "organization," in which certain persons/objects are incorporated, and others purposefully omitted. Trinh T. Minh-Ha's narrative project, then, is nothing less than a refutation of these principles of artificial aestheticization, and an embrace of the humanist frame, a simpler structure, that valorizes and centers itself upon the corpus of the previously marginalized.

Kaja Silverman speaks of the late German filmmaker R. W. Fassbinder's "assault on male subjectivity . . . as a way out of the vicious circle of masculinity" (265); an effect that Fassbinder achieved in such Postfilms as *Beware of a Holy Whore* (1971), in which a group of bickering actors await the arrival of their dictatorial director; *Fox and His Friends* (1975), in which a newly wealthy homosexual is exploited by the members of his so-called "community"; and most spectacularly in *Berlin Alexanderplatz* (1979), a movie of epic length that seemingly stretches the limits of narrative complexity and depth of characterization past any conventional breaking point. Fassbinder's groundbreaking work between 1965 and 1982 represents a significant epoch in the Postfilm, both for the speed and quantity of Fassbinder's output, but also for the ways in which the director inverted the melodramatic concerns of 1950s Hollywood romance, most notably in the films of director Douglas Sirk (*All That Heaven Allows* [1955], *Imitation of Life* [1959], *There's Always Tomorrow* [1956], and many other Technicolor/Cinemascope films that Sirk made for Universal in the 1950s.

Fassbinder pushed the artifice and mechanistic plotting, as well as the overblown ersatz romantic impulse in Sirk's work, into a formalist strata that simultaneously incorporated Sirk's melodramatic narratives with a hard-edged "frame" of reflexive cinema practice that valorized the production process. Like Andy Warhol, Fassbinder shot his films quickly and cheaply, working with a core group of actors and technicians at the margins of commercial cinema, supported (as is Trinh T. Minh-Ha) by a variety of grants, fellowships, honorariums, and independent distribution deals, all of which paradoxically ensure that the discourse present in Fassbinder and Minh-Ha's films will continue to operate at the margins of the commercial distribution system.

Above all, the Postfilm differs from conventional filmic discourse through its self-knowledge of suture; the subject of the Postfilm is not only the narrative that it inhabits, and which inhabits it, but also the entire process by which the film came into being, the very anatomy of the corpus of cinema. This meta-narrativistic structure requires substantial engagement on the part of the viewer, rather than lulling the spectator into a dream state of blissful acceptance. As if it contained a social responsibility, the Postfilm urgently calls attention to its origins and the scars of its suture (construction), so that in the place of a passive spectacle, the audience is confronted with a living construct that brazenly bears the scars of its creation.

Jonathan Dollimore notes:

> The symbolic "harnessing" of the deviant is rarely creative, regenerative, or benign; it involves a violence open to any authority which wants a witch hunt/scapegoat—whether of paranoid reasons (it feels threatened but is not); for rational reasons (it feels under threat and really is); or for cynical reasons (a reassertion of social order is always good for business, especially for those in power. (221)

This is what is most threatening about the Postfilm to the conventional cinemagoer/distributor/financier; the Postfilm calls all the cozy presuppositions of genre-driven narrative into direct question. Further, by reflexively questioning and critiquing both

conventional narrative structure and classical Hollywood cinematic representationalism, the Postfilm identifies these structures as fabrications, tools of social control, strategies whereby
the dominant ideology can entertain but not enlighten or unduly
disturb its constituency (see also El-Dib on "alternative methods" of narrative production in Third-World narrative production (3187A); Boltz on the psycholinguistic temporal memory
processing of the film/narrative (90-105); and Finney on "Suture
in Literary Analysis," which contains an engaging discussion of
Joyce's wordplay in *A Portrait of the Artist as a Young Man* in
relation to the narrative suture employed through the sign of the
"cut," or "splice," in cinema, when one image/scene replaces
another (131-144).

Significantly, all of these newer Postfilms are feature length,
and have a strong narrative thread, tacitly acknowledging the
dominance of the length narrative in contemporary cinema pro-
duction/distribution. The performative structures employed by
Postfilms, however, do not partake of the signs and systems
employed by classical Hollywood discourse. The fetishistic textuality and self-reflexivity of the new narrative cinema locates
itself in an indeterminate atopia, presenting metanarrative countertestimony to the tropes and conventions of mainstream cinema. In doing so, these Postfilms form an oppositional discourse
to the known and accepted epistomological metanarrative refig-
ured in even such willfully reflexive films as *The Last Action
Hero* (1993), which directly enunciates the centripotal/centrifugal
triangulation of desire that takes place in the act of cinematic
audience reception; the implied gift-exchange between viewer
and object-to-be-seen. The alternity of the Postfilm lies in its
embrace of performative narrative, reflexive cinematic syntax
structure, and its insistence that the audience must recognize
and negotiate the slippage/oscillation between the heterodystopia
decentered in the act of producing the Postfilm, and the neutral
taxonomic countertestimony the Postfilm seeks to provide (see
Neale on "Narrative and the Look," 123-132).

The Postfilm forcefully calls our attention to this taken-for-
granted deception, a trope that has informed the creation of conventional cinematic narrative constructs since Alice Guy, Elvira
Notari, and D. W. Griffith. If anything, the hold of narrative clo-

sure on mainstream cinema audiences in 1993 is stronger than it has been since the 1930s. Given a certain set of characters (or more properly, *situations*), the audience will be able to comfortably guess the outcome of such films as *Sister Act* (1992) (Whoopi Goldberg's cheerfully disruptive character will win over Maggie Smith's crusty Mother Superior character, and rejuvenate a dying church, while avoiding assassination by the nonthreatening Harvey Keitel comic gangster character; all will end happily) or *Jurassic Park* (1993) (the DNA-cloned dinosaurs will escape their elaborate cages, menace the principal actors, scare the "cinema" children whom the children in the audience are meant to identify with, devour several second-string character actors; all will end happily).

Sister Act is simply an update of *Going My Way* (1944); *Jurassic Park* is this generation's *King Kong* (1933). The Postfilm gestures beyond these preordained genre entertainments do something more. It is the heterodystopic future of cinema which is being figured here, a cinema where that which is omitted is now pronounced, where elisions all called to our combined attention, and artifice is expected as a tool of performative metacorporeality. The Postfilm merges formalist and humanist concerns in a way which allows us to be aware of the mechanics of the spectacle that we are witnessing, and for this alone, it signals in the direction of a new and transgressive revision of cinematic narrative tradition.

THE "THIRD" CINEMA

Yet this disruption does not, in current commercial cinema practice, extend beyond the zone of the Hollywood film. As Toni Morrison notes, "All of us . . . are bereft when criticism remains too polite or too fearful to notice a disrupting darkness before its eyes" (91). If we take as a given the fact that English-speaking, and more specifically, Hollywood-produced cinema has dominated the international box office in most areas since the end of World War I, we should not, I think, confuse this commercial clout with questions of international identity and subalternity, or fall prey to the insidious notion that because of the mechanics of commercial and/or independent film production/distribution/ exhibition, films made in Iran, for example, have less substantive historical/aesthetic currency than their North American counterparts.

Yet this is what the term "Third Cinema," or "Third-World Cinema," seems to ineluctably suggest to me, and not, I think, without reason. I believe (as opposed to Willemen's taxonomy) that Hollywood and British cinema constitute a "First Cinema" of English-speaking production; that European, non-English-speaking (French, German, Italian) cinema projects comprise a "Second Cinema," and that films produced in Africa, Asia, and Micronesia and other non-Eurocentric societies (with the attendant poor distribution that follows the creation of these films) constitute a "Third Cinema," a cinema of the marginalized, the subaltern. The colonialist (as opposed to neocolonialist, since in cinema this colonialism has never ceased) project begun by Hollywood during World War I (when most other counties ceased film production to concentrate on the war effort) has resulted in a cinema production/distribution system that favors conventional Hollywood narrative discourse to the virtual exclusion of all other cinemas.

In the "top-ten" mainstream/commercial box office films of nearly every country in the world at any given moment since 1918—think of the *sweep* of this cultural repression colonialist project for a moment—an average of seven out of ten films will be Hollywood product. And this representationalist grip extends far beyond standard theatrical exhibition. In a recent article in *The New Yorker*, for example, the author described how, during a trip through the African country of Rwanda by truck, he came across an advertisement for a screening of *Pretty Woman* on bootleg VHS videotape in Rwanda's capital city of Kigali (Conover 71). The author noted that in Rwanda, Hollywood films dominated the commercial and even the "illegal" film markets. In the Arab world, reruns of *The Wonderful World of Disney* dominate television in Qatar (Boyd 180); in Libya, reruns of *Hawaii Five-O*, *The Brady Bunch*, and *The Untouchables*, though "stringently censored," dominate most of the primetime television schedule (Boyd 232), though two locally produced television series, *Our Health* (a "home living" program) and *Society*

And Security (a fictionalized "police" narrative) top the ratings (Boyd 234).

Why is this colonialism so pervasive? Why is it so *accepted*? In his chapter "Consolidated Vision" within the text *Culture and Imperialism,* Edward Said correctly sees this continuing colonial project as one more manifestation of "The Native under Control," and citing Frantz Fanon's *Wretched of the Earth,* notes that "for the native, objectivity is always directed against him" (Said 162, Fanon 77). Later in the same volume, in the section "American Ascendancy: The Public Space at War," Said charts the ways in which the American colonial project continues to operate at high efficiency in all areas of "public space"—cultural, political, social, sexual, racial, and in the creation of a United States-dominated world marketplace. As Said points out, the collapse of the former Soviet Union leaves the United States in a uniquely privileged sphere of policy-making power; no where is this more apparent than in the production/distribution/exhibition/recoupment of the Hollywood film, containing as it does both far-reaching financial and social significations (Said 282-303). For more than anything else, the Hollywood narrative cinema is a system of codes and rules that seek to subjugate the viewer, subject her/him to the control of the returned gaze of surveillance from the screen, and structure viewer behavior and conduct.

Yet one must look at the entire colonializing project inherent in Hollywood cinema to fully understand the immensity of this global stranglehold. Within cinema studies, where, for example, the films of Egypt, Iran, Syria, Yemen, Qatar, Algeria, and Tunisia should be shown and discussed as part of the curriculum, these films and their operative cultures are pushed beyond the margins of discourse into a zone of invisibility. As Manthia Diawara notes in his study *African Cinema: Politics and Culture*:

Not only film production but also distribution in Africa has faced a ruthless and monopolistic exploitation by American, European and Indian distribution companies . . . [only] because of import quotas, France and West Germany, Europe's two most important film producers, have survived the bombardment of their film market by the United States Motion Picture Export Association of America (MPEAA)." (viii)

These "quotas" have marginalized cinematic discourse in France and Germany into the "Second Cinema," surviving despite the "ruthless and monopolistic exploitation" of the American production/distribution companies; Africa, which has "no government protection" (Diawara viii) for its indigenous cinemas, is, according to Mauritian filmmaker Med Hondo, "tottering" (Diawara vii, Hondo 12). As Diawara writes, "Africa lacks film processing laboratories, sound dubbing and synchronizing studios, and editing facilities. These problems as well as financial ones force filmmakers to wait years before finishing one film" (vii). This complete absence of facilities, as Diawara documents, is not an accident. It is a colonial project to keep the subalternity of Africa intact, to deny Africa a cinematic vision of its own culture and societal discourse. African cinema today operates, as best it can, out of the ruins of the British Colonial Film Unit in Africa, the Belgian Missionary Cinema, and the Ethnographic Film Ministry (Diawara vii). When these colonial entities were withdrawn, the apparatus for producing films and maintaining cinema equipment was withdrawn also. The result is that Africa remains a cultural colonial entity of the Hollywood cinema.

In this "loaning" and then "withdrawing" of facilities to colonized nations, the corporate structure of Hollywood is at one with the strategy of vertical integration (control of all aspects of a given discourse: creation, marketing, advertising) employed by organizations such as the Coca-Cola Company. Mark Pendergrast's corporate study *For God, Country and Coca-Cola* and his attendant essay "A Brief History of Coca-Colonization" note:

> In World War II, Coke was an American imperialist symbol, a kosher food, a fake Communist beverage and the drink of Hitler youth. Most people thought the war was about good, evil, competing ideologies and so on, but for Coca-Cola the issue was simpler: more Coke or less Coke . . . at the 1936 German Olympics in Berlin, Adolf Hitler, a health faddist, insisted that every bottle of Coke

have a caffeine-warning label. The same year, anti-Semitism hurt sales when a German competitor stole some kosher Coke bottle caps and urged consumers to avoid this "Jewish-American" drink. To counter this, Coke's German branch passed out sodas at Hitler Youth rallies and displayed huge swastikas at bottling conventions. (Pendergrast, "Coca-Colonization," 13)

It is thus part of the insidiousness of corporate discourse that it disguises itself in the apparent materiality of the social/political fabric of any regime it infiltrates. Further, within the narrative context of the Hollywood film, the "art" of "product placement" has evolved to such a high degree of sophistication that even the most observant filmgoer has to constantly be on her/his guard against internal, subliminal advertisements contained within the "entertainment" being witnessed. These product "plugs" permeate not only the discourse of western society but also take on an added dimension of secretive and sinister activity within the overall colonial project of the commercial Hollywood film.

THE COLONIALIST GAZE

This project of corporate and ideological displacement is an ongoing repressive discourse in Third-World society. Hollywood films, dubbed into many languages, doubly mask their colonial intent by adopting the language of the culture they seek to dominate. There was even, in the twilight era of the British colonial empire, a scheme to create ready-made films out of process plates and near-projection facilities which would then be shipped as a package to colonial nations for re-production with local actors. This method, dubbed the Independent Frame Process, was created by the giant British conglomerate of J. Arthur Rank, and allowed:

all the elements of a given film production to be assembled in one large shipping crate for export to other nations, enabling citizens of other cultures to produce versions of a Rank film in their own languages, without the use of "foreign" location shooting, props, or large groups of extras. This . . . packing crate . . . include[d] not only all the necessary near-projection materials used in the film, but also all the free-standing props placed in front of the screen to anchor the protagonists within the frame. A complete script, matte plates, and a storyboard completed the package. Rank would thus export not only the physical materials needed to, essentially, reproduce their film for non-English-speaking audiences; they would also impart to foreign audiences the social values encoded in the background plates for the film, thus inviting production companies in other, often colonial nations to further identify with the representational values then espoused by the British cinematic patriarchy. No matter what the secondary film's ultimate language must be, and even considering the double "removal" of location encoded in the prefabricated backgrounds, the subsidiary film would be seen by local audiences as precisely that: subsidiary. The new film would thus derive its authority not from the culture of its adoptive nation, but from the hegemony of the British commonwealth; as presented in the original production. While this colonialist cinematic practice never, in fact, took place, because of the abandonment of the Independent Frame process itself, the informing instinct behind the system remained an attempt at cultural supremacy, with English societal modes of behavior and class structure firmly centered as the desired model of the endeavor. (Dixon, *Independent Frame*, 20)

This process, as bell hooks states,

promotes paradigms of consumption wherein whatever difference the Other inhabits is eradicated, *via* exchange, by a consumer cannibalism that not only displaces the Other but denies the significance of that Other's history through a process of decontextualization. (31)

To counter this area of marginality, or zone of invisibility inhabited by "other" cinemas—not only non-English-speaking cinemas, but Gay Cinema, Lesbian Cinema (collectively known as Queer Cinema), and the cinema of Non-Materialist Reflexivity

(Cinema that questions Cinema)—the scholar must disseminate
the fact of the existence of these "other" cinemas, seek to abolish
or expand the existing canon within the cultural and social curriculum of cinema practice/reception, and attempt to expose the
cultural methodologies employed by commercial Hollywood
colonialist/imperialist discourse. Gayatri Chakravorty Spivak
has persuasively argued that the "solution to enlarge the curriculum [in this manner] is in fact a continuation of the neo-colo-
nial production of knowledge" in a conversation with Harold
Aram Veeser, although she goes on to say to Veeser that "in practice I am with you [on this methodology of canonical expansion],
because on the other side are the real racists" (284), so perhaps
canonical abolition is a more desirable project; the reevaluation of
all values.

   In charting the terrain to be explored, a number of studies
are available, although they represent only the initial phase of
work to be done in this area. In addition to Diawara's *African
Cinema: Politics and Culture*, Douglas Boyd's *Broadcasting in
the Arab World: A Survey of Electronic Media in the Middle
East*, 2nd ed., (1993); Mohammad Ali Issari's *Cinema in Iran,
1900-1979* (1989); Jorge A. Schnitman's *Film Industries in Latin
America: Dependency and Development* (1984); *Argentine Cin-
ema*, edited by Tim Barnard (1986); Karl G. Heider's *Indonesian
Cinema: National Culture on Screen* (1991); Mel Schuster's *The
Contemporary Greek Cinema* (1979); *Post New Wave Cinema
in the Soviet Union and Eastern Europe*, edited by Daniel J.
Goulding (1989); Carl J. Mora's *Mexican Cinema: Reflections of a
Society 1896-1988* (1989); and *The Asian Film Industry* by John
A. Lent (1990) are all of some use to the researcher in the area of
Third-World cinema discourse.

   Diawara's study seems among the most successful, correctly
identifying the exploitive strategies of American and French cinema practice employed in Africa, and fully documenting the
masked, neocolonialist enterprises of Jean Rouch and Jean-Luc
Godard in Mozambique in the mid-to-late 1970s. In the final
pages of the text (140-166), Diawara offers a concise explication of
the methods of African postcolonial film practice, and discusses
the current state of indigenous African film production, particularly what Diawara neatly terms the narrative of "colonial con-

frontation." Issari's volume on Iranian cinema is curious in that it valorizes, from an insider's point-of-view, the cinematic production apparatus created by the late Shah of Iran, down to a complete listing of "newsreels" produced by that regime, in addition to the extensive list of feature films produced in Iran between 1900 and 1979. Issari was very much a part of Iran's film production system during this era, and so his view of Iranian cinema is not that of a stranger to Persian culture. However, Issari is clearly nostalgic for the era of the Shah's reign, and thus he ultimately comes down on the side of the colonialist film practice. Mora's *Mexican Cinema* is another "insider" view, and one of the most critically acute of the studies mentioned in the preceding list in that he confronts the reader with vast bodies of local, noncolonial film practice that have been ruthlessly pushed into the zone of the invisible; the other texts are all, in practice, Eurocentrist, treating the various cinema they examine as "other," "foreign," and/or "exotic."

THE ACCESS OF VISION

Beyond these considerations, the bare question of *access* remains the most crucial problem in any dissemination of African, Indonesian, Iranian, Indian and other nonwestern modes of filmic discourse. Of the thousands of films discussed in the historical survey volumes mentioned here, less than *one percent* have been released through even the most tenuous distribution mechanism in the west (which is, of course, part of the colonialist nondiscourse of nonreciprocal exchange of cinematic visions). Even the minimal expense of subtitling these films seems too much of a burden for the most "altruistic" western distribution organization, although occasionally, the most "accessible" (read colonized) films of these nations will achieve a minimal release either through videocassette or "art house" theatrical distribution in major metropolitan centers. Nor has video cassette availability improved matters. After an initial phase of growth and experimentation in the early 1980s, videocassette rental and sales activity has become as rigidly codified and commodified as theatrical release was in the period between 1900 and 1980, with the result that nearly every one of the Third Cinema films I am speaking of has been fully pushed into the "phantom zone."

In New York, Chicago, and other major cultural centers in the west, scholars and theorists may have access to Third-World films; the general public has been *conditioned* to avoid them, thereby decreasing the commercial demand for these films, and ensuring their continued "phantom availability." Subtitles particularly are considered a kiss of death for any commercial release, except as a briefly used novelty within the narrative boundaries of western cinema practice. Even such mildly disruptive films as Robert Rodriguez's *El Mariachi* (1992), when subtitled in English from the original Spanish for American release and backed with an extensive publicity campaign failed to make significant inroads in the western marketplace. For Hollywood, it is much simpler to remake the film with American actors, as has happened in numerous cases.

In these fairly desperate circumstances, what possible chance could even the highly commercial and linear narrative Iranian film *Akharin Gozargah* (*The Last Hurdle;* 1962) have for an American release? Unlike films from Italy, France, Germany, or other "Second Cinema" countries, which received at least "art house" distribution in the west during this era, *Akharin Gozargah* was unshown in this country after its initial Iranian release. The film has never been available on videotape, it has never been subtitled, and as a final irony, the film itself is only of mild interest, as it is clearly a colonialist project designed to bolster, through its ideological/narrativistic structure, the colonialist enterprise of the Shah's regime. Thus even this film, which certainly poses no threat to colonial interests, passes into oblivion. What hope of distribution, then, or even access, for the general public for the disruptive works being created in Iran, Iraq, Libya, Rwanda and elsewhere in the Third World today?

For all intents and purposes, *Akharin Gozargah*, though it has been seen by millions of nonwestern eyes, might just as well never have existed in the United States. Through this process of distributionary exclusion, Third-World films enter the "zone of invisibility" irreconcilably, beyond the power of conventional archival restoration and reclamation. When one adds to this marginalization and discriminatory process the factor of the inherent fragility of the film negative (and the *uniqueness* of the negative itself, as the only glyph, or code, from which future prints of the film may be struck), the dimensions of the problem become apparent and concrete.

The blocking of access is in itself a colonialist project, which is accomplished through the agencies of poor reviews in colonial publications, the valorization of Hollywood-style production values at the expense of all other modes of representationalism, and the complaint that the film being marginalized, or "made invisible," is not a commercially viable entity. Diawara notes that films of "colonial confrontation" are thoroughly erased from even the margins of western culture, and writes that these films are viewed by African spectators:

> with a sense of pride and satisfaction with a history finally being told from an African point of view. Some European spectators, on the other hand, characterize them as polemical, poorly constructed, and belonging to the 1960s rhetoric of violence. Between 1987 and 1989, both the French and the British used the above adjectives to shun *Sarraounia* (Med Hondo, 1987), *Heritage Africa* (Kwaw Arsah, 1988) and *Camp de Thiaroye* [Ousmane Sembène and Thierno Sow, 1988].

Diawara also finds it "remarkable that the French government [selected neither *Sarraounia* or *Camp de Thiaroye*] for the Cannes Film Festival, despite its stated policy of commitment to the production and promotion of African cinema" (152). There is, of course, nothing "remarkable" about it; "reflexive" would be a better word. All three films question French colonial accounts of African history, and stand as a threat to even the memory of colonialism—thus, the films must be erased.

As conventional Hollywood film practice becomes ever more centralized, with the giant Creative Artists Agency becoming, in a sense, the only "studio" in Los Angeles, through its routine practice of "packaging" a script, director and stars to a given studio, and monopolizing the major talent within the system, we must *resist* the politics of conventional materialism inherent in the contemporary commercial film. As the speed of communication increases, and videotape explodes around the globe, perhaps the best way to do this is to abandon conventional modes of film production, and embrace the camcorder or High 8 video-camera as an effective agency of social change. Already video has brought us images of cultural repression that existed within zones of authority hitherto unavailable to our eyes; images from China, from Los Angeles, from Bosnia-Herzegovina. These images, shorn of traditional notions of suture, syntax, and framing, presenting substance and not sheen, have shown that they have the power to alter repressive authoritarianism—or at the very least, to document it.

THE DYSTOPIAN CINEMA:
THE RETURNED GAZE OF THE FUTURE

Other "Dreams of State" may be found in the genre known as Dystopian science fiction (SF). Dystopian science fiction is a distinct subgenre of the larger field of (usually) more positivist science fiction; in a Dystopian future, things do not work out for the best but rather for the worst. With the production of *Alien*, Dystopian SF took a giant step forward; no longer was the future a neat and tidy place with shiny chrome rockets and nearly arranged robotic controls. It was seen as a socially stratified, brutally marginalistic landscape in which only the shrewd and/or corrupt survived and flourished. There have been numerous Dystopian films over the course of cinema history, and even those science fiction films with a marginally positive ending might properly be seen as having distinctly Dystopian roots.

In *The Thing* (1951, 1982), for example, both versions posit a future in which an alien race will invade earth, intending to turn it into a slaughterhouse; in Hawks's film, there is a superficially happy ending, while Carpenter prefers a nihilistic finale. *When Worlds Collide* (1951) ends with a chosen few survivors rushing off to a new planet while millions perish in their wake. *The Last Man on Earth* (1964), later remade as *The Omega Man* (1971), posits a future inhabited by cannibalistic crazies who wander the street, wantonly killing and murdering those they encounter. *Metropolis* (1926) ends with the hope of an alliance between management and workers, but spends most of its time chronicling the depths of the workers' exploitation. *Forbidden Planet* (1956) projects a world so bleak that no one inhabits it; a race called the Krel create a large computer that gives form to their most secret, murderous impulses and are thus utterly annihilated by their collective, unexpressed hatred in a single night.

The list goes on; even in *Things to Come* (1936), mob rule, led by Sir Cedric Hardwicke, threatens the advance of science and the launching of Raymond Massey's rocket. The Frankenstein films can also correctly be seen as Dystopian; Dr. Frankenstein seeks again and again to create life from the dead, but each time the project ends in disaster, as the monster usually emerges from the operation as a murderous, mute brute. Science fiction and horror films have long overlapped as genres; the future can be seen as both alluring and uncertain, and there is an element of fear of the future in all fictive, as well as actual, explorations into the unknown.

We know, or think we know, the present, but the future is something that is entirely beyond our power to predict. As we move closer to the twenty-first century, we can see that many of our utopian visions have been proven spectacularly off the mark. In the 1930s, a corporate pavilion at the New York World's Fair predicted a future society where no one would work, in which wealth and property would be communally shared, where societal markers would vanish. Yet if anything, the opposite is true. The worst social and political tendencies of the past are being carried forward into the future with a vengeance, and it is this vengeance that the best Dystopian work celebrates; it is the triumph of failure.

Indeed, the years yet to come haven't been seen for the most part as being all that promising in cinema history, and this lack of confidence in the future has only accelerated as time goes on. The collapse of the societal structure in New York, London, Los Angeles, and other large metropolitan centers is an indication, perhaps, that the Dystopians are not far off the mark in their fears; as the poster for John Boorman's *Zardoz* (1974) boldly announced, "I have seen the future, and it doesn't work." In the world of Dystopian science fiction, as exemplified most recently by Geoff Murphy's *Freejack* (1992), our current societal structure represents the thinnest of behavioral fabrics, existing only to be undermined or torn asunder, seemingly at whim. There is something liberating in Dystopian science fiction; the present is better than the future, so one should enjoy the present while one can. What has one to look forward to? Here are several alternative visions of the future as an endless, broken-down urban nightmare.

Ridley Scott's *Blade Runner* (1982; revised 1992) is a triumph of nightmare art direction, seamless film-noir plotting, and grand production values; even seen in light of recent technological developments, *Blade Runner* remains one of the truly memorable and original science fiction films of the early 1980s. Harrison Ford is doggedly realistic as a "lone wolf" policeman assigned to locate renegade robots in a appropriately inhospitable future society; the details of the vision of futuristic city life (parking meters that promise "Instant Death by Electrocution" if tampered with, for example) are superbly realized, and frighteningly possible. The film was never a major commercial success, perhaps because of its disjointed narrative and uncompromisingly dark worldview, but it has become, over time, one of the dominant Dystopian visions, and, along with *Alien*, one of the films that changed the way we view our future on film.

Richard Fleischer's *Soylent Green* (1973) is another nightmarish vision of the future, as New York City in the twenty-first century is seen as a hell of overcrowding, societal breakdown, hoarding, violence, and wealth amidst squalor. Charlton Heston, in one of his more adventurous roles, is a cop who stumbles upon a large-scale cover-up (the source of the foodstuff, Soylent Green) while in the midst of another case. The art direction, obviously done on a budget, nevertheless manages to effectively convey complete chaos in a future time and place; if Leigh Taylor-Young is served up by the film merely as sexist window-dressing, the film is entirely conscious of what it is doing with her image, deploring her objectification even as it participates in it.

Val Guest's *The Day The Earth Caught Fire* (1962) remains one of the more intelligent of the Dystopian films. *The Day The Earth Caught Fire* takes place almost entirely in a newspaper office, with brief excursions into the crumbling world outside. Edward Judd plays a reporter who covers the action as the earth spins out-of-control toward the sun, as the result of a plethora of nuclear test detonations. Leo McKern is marvelous as the gruff old editor, and the interiors look very much like Fleet Street in the early 1960s; the stark black-and-white photography, now very nearly a lost art, is the perfect medium to convey the drab desperation of the world's citizens as they wait, and squabble amongst themselves, as the world swings toward oblivion. The question as to whether or not the earth will survive is left unanswered in the final minutes of the film; this raises the interesting question of audience expectation in the Dystopian genre. Would most viewers opt for Armageddon? Particularly for the period in which it was made, *The Day The Earth Caught Fire* is daring both in terms of theme and narrative structure.

By contrast, George Miller's *Mad Max* (1979) is a violent road movie, full of kinetic editing, with car and motorcycle chases choreographed with a vengeful brilliance. While the "chase film," even the Post-Apocalyptic chase film, is certainly nothing new, *Mad Max* is possessed of a uniquely weird worldview that almost prevented the film from getting proper distribution in the United States and Britain when it was first released. Mel Gibson established himself in a single stroke with this film as an action star of the first magnitude; with the exception of sections of *The Witches of Eastwick* and his episode of the *Twilight Zone* movie, Miller has seldom done a better job of direction. This film demands to be seen on the big screen for full impact; a tour-de-force of nihilistic thrills and rampant destruction, *Mad Max* became the model for a series of successful sequels, and led to a renaissance in the Dystopian action film, as opposed to Dystopian mood piece.

The remake of George Orwell's *1984* (1984) is an example of a Dystopian film that revels in repellent architecture, dismal settings, and a citizenry crushed beneath the boot of Totalitarian force. This cold and clinical filming of Orwell's classic was made by the then-fledgling Virgin Film Production unit; John Hurt is perfect in the title role, and Richard Burton, in what would be his last role in a feature film, is well-cast as Hurt's urbane tormentor. At the time of the film's initial release, some critics were disturbed that the film's sets seemed more appropriate for a 1940s film than a vision of the future gone wrong, but I feel they missed the point; in Orwell's future world, the only useful objects one has are the well-made instruments of the past, even though they are badly maintained. Thus, the rows of upright telephones, typewriters, and poorly ventilated and lit office cubicles seem entirely appropriate to the film.

Videodrome (1983) is David Cronenberg's meditation on televised violence, and the nonconnection most of us share via the medium of television, whether interactive (as in this case) or not. One of Cronenberg's relatively early films, *Videodrome* features James Woods as a cable television engineer who taps into a pornographic cable network whose signal emanates from a secret location. In particular, Woods is drawn to the defiled image of Deborah Harry (late of the rock group Blondie and now one of the stars of the new interactive film *Double Switch*), as a bruised and battered participant in a graphic sadomasochistic video porn program. As Woods becomes more drawn into the world of the maverick cable network, Rick Baker's ingenious special effects come into play, one of the most startling and memorable being Woods as a human VCR machine, inserting videocassettes through a gaping, bloody wound in his stomach. By the end of the film, plot seems to matter less and less; what Cronenberg is after is a meditation on voyeurism and violence. Woods and Harry both give authoritative and disturbing performances, in which may arguably be seen as the best work of their respective careers.

Fahrenheit 451 (1966) was François Truffaut's attempt at a big-budget science fiction film, a genre he returned to later with his work as an actor in the distinctly non-Dystopian *Close Encounters of the Third Kind*. Truffaut's first and only English-language film, *Fahrenheit 451* is based on the famous Ray Bradbury novel, and was a departure for the famous French director in every respect. The titles are announced at the beginning of the film, not written, as words are outlawed in the future world the film depicts; the "firemen" in the film set books ablaze, rather than extinguishing fires in their daily work; the characters in the film seem rather like automatons, and it is the books themselves (particularly at the moment of their destruction) that captivate our attention and sympathy. Truffaut sees all books as equally valuable; a frayed copy of *Mad* Magazine rates the same tight close-up as a first edition of *Pride and Prejudice*. Strikingly photographed in cool, distant color schemes, opposed to the orange hue of the all-consuming flames, *Fahrenheit 451* is a success in every respect, and one of the most thoughtful and intelligent science fiction films ever made.

The Earth Dies Screaming (1964) despite its lurid title, is director Terence Fisher's most deeply felt Dystopian science fiction project. A group of strangers who have survived an alien "gas attack" must fight against a brigade of robots sent by aliens to clean up the aftermath; taking refuge in a country inn and a drill hall, the survivors band together in the best tradition of Hawks and Carpenter to repel the invaders. Made in a very short time on a modest budget (amazingly enough, the total production budget was less than $100,000) and lifting large sections from Wolf Rilla's *Village of the Damned* (1960) for its more spectacular special effects sequences, the film is nevertheless one of Fisher's most deeply felt and personal works, and in tone and content influenced George Romero's later and far more explicit, *Night of the Living Dead* (1968).

Related in style and production resources is *Alphaville* (1965), Jean-Luc Godard's dark Dystopian comedy. Made during Godard's most blazingly brilliant period as a film director, this tale of a futuristic city, Alphaville, dispassionately ruled by a massive computer, Alpha 60, is simultaneously disturbing and hilarious. A private eye, Lemmy Caution, played with an appropriately weary air by Eddie Constantine, is sent to Alphaville to destroy the computer, rescue and/or liquidate the renegade scientist who created it, and carry off his daughter, Natasha, to safety.

Shot on a shoestring budget in actual Parisian locations by the brilliant cinematographer Raoul Coutard, *Alphaville* is one of the most daring and inventive products of the nouvelle vague, and a seriocomic Dystopian fantasy that lingers in the mind long after the film has finished unreeling. Full of throwaway sight gags, tough-guy posturing, and a surprisingly action-packed (for Godard) car chase, the film is accessible and humanist, even as it posits a vision of a completely regimented future. Of particular interest is Coutard's available-light cinematography. Godard later observed that often, when he required a specific shot, Coutard would assure him that the lighting was insufficient to achieve an image; Godard would insist that he shoot the scene anyway. The result is a series of fugitive forms appearing out of the alternately dazzling and stygian landscape of Paris/Alphaville, a neon wilderness of a world that prefigures *Blade Runner* in both style and content.

A glossier but still tightly budgeted American Dystopian film is Michael Crichton's *Westworld* (1973). Crichton's vision of an adult fantasyland, where the visitors can play at being cowboys, knights, or other mythic figures, becomes a satisfying and thrilling American nightmare, with Yul Brynner's automaton gunslinger emerging as one of cinema history's most formidable opponents. At first, protagonists Richard Benjamin and James Brolin enjoy the Wild West fantasyland they have opted for, winning all the staged fights and sleeping with robotic prostitutes. But the machines are malfunctioning (a popular conceit for Dystopian films; see *Colossus: The Forbin Project*, discussed later in this essay) and have plans of their own for their visitors. By the end of the film, dialogue has been reduced to a minimum, as Brynner, grimly intent on murdering Benjamin, chases him through the ruins of a vacation paradise toward a climatic and cunningly staged showdown.

Although it is one of the most flawed of the films considered here, Norman Jewison's *Rollerball* (1975) benefits from an agreeably brutish performance by James Caan as a champion Rollerball player in the not-too-distant future; away from the arena, the film is less successful. Caan is a hero to his fans but refuses to retire from the game, as the corporate powers that be wish him to. The game itself is realized with terrifying accuracy and impact; after the film's release, several sports promoters actually contacted Jewison seeking to establish Rollerball franchises in their respective cities! One can perhaps forgive the overuse of Bach's Toccata and Fugue in D Minor (used yet again as a musical motif for ambition gone awry) and remain enthralled and appalled by the eye-filling spectacle of the game itself, one of the most diabolical sports productions ever devised.

Joseph Sargent's *Colossus: The Forbin Project* (1970) was something of a sleeper when initially released. No one expected it to do much business, but instead, it went on to become a minor classic in the "computer runs amok" subgenre of Dystopian science fiction. Certainly, there are predecessors to the film (*The Invisible Boy* (1957) and *2001* (1968) leap instantly to mind; perhaps even *Forbidden Planet*), but in its modest production values, *Colossus: The Forbin Project* is believable in the same way that *Alien* (1979) redefined the physical trappings of science fiction. The future will not be glamorous; it will be mundane and drab. If anything, it will be less physically impressive than the present, films such as *Things to Come* notwithstanding. Eric Braeden makes a convincingly dedicated scientist; Colossus, the computer-turned-tyrant, emerges as an implacable and resourceful antagonist.

At the 1968 Yale Film Festival, George Lucas entered his prototype of his first feature film, *THX 1138*, as a student film made at USC; it was judged "too professional" to participate in the Yale competition. That twenty-minute film, made for a few thousand dollars, was the first indication that Lucas would be a force to be reckoned with in the 1970s and 1980s, but who would have guessed then that Lucas would go on to create the *Star Wars* series, and become one of the most successful producer/directors of all times? Produced on a larger scale as a feature several years later, *THX 1138* (1971) is a futuristic nightmare, a resoundingly successful feature debut for Lucas, and features Donald Pleasance at his malevolent best as the film's villain. It's also interesting to see Robert Duvall doing such fine work so early in his career.

RoboCop (1987), director Paul Verhoeven's breakthrough American film, powered Dystopian science fiction into the 1990s; for his first American project, Verhoeven accelerated the speed of his editing, further indulged his already apparent penchant for brutal and graphic violence, and made a smooth transition to resolutely commercial filmmaking. *RoboCop* works as a pure thriller, and also as social commentary. Peter Weller is a dedicated cop, brutally murdered by Kurtwood Smith's thugs, who is reincarnated as a law-enforcement robot for those "tough to handle" situations that arise in the inner city of Detroit, sometime in the near future. The film is sharply edited, authentically nihilistic, and embraces the horrific future it depicts with fervent intensity. Television is reduced to mindless pandering, as the same game show is rerun over and over again for a stunned and satiated populace; guns and other high tech weapons have replaced organized democratic rule; corporate corruption is a given; media manipulation colors the way every "news story" is presented to the public. In a world completely devoid of normative societal constraints, the figure of the *RoboCop* seems both possible and plausible; the sequel, an even more violent film, carries this nihilist vision further, with the introduction of a drug more devastating than crack, "Nuke," sweeping through the urban wasteland of Detroit, controlled by the sociopathic renegade warlord of a drug underground so powerful it can entirely subvert Detroit's already compromised corporate "government."

As a vision of future life in Los Angeles, Paul Cox's *Repo Man* (1984), with Emilio Estevez, Harry Dean Stanton, and Vonetta McGee, is another low-budget film from Universal Studios that dares to tackle a good deal of ambitious material on a miniscule budget. From the opening frames of this landmark film, backed with a pulsating title track by Iggy Pop, *Repo Man* succeeds beyond anyone's wildest dreams in depicting a future that is comic, violent, unforgiving, serious, and yet playfully reminiscent of the recent past. Estevez is forced into becoming an automobile repossessor when his parents give away all their money to a television evangelist. As Estevez's mentor, Harry Dean Stanton snorts methamphetamine off a mirror while he steers his car with his knees, and initiates Estevez into the not-so-gentle craft both men must play to survive with a series of maxims and observations that are simultaneously hilarious and cynically accurate. Mixing surreal fantasy with large dollops of social criticism, *Repo Man* is an authentic American original and a testament that, even in the early 1980s, a film can still be made on a modest budget and succeed as a vision of a futuristic society.

The last film considered here, *Silent Running* (1971), is essentially a plea for ecological conservation, directed by special effects wizard Douglas Trumbull as his first film. Bruce Dern plays a futuristic scientist who is determined to keep the earth's biological heritage alive; adrift on a space station, surrounded by machines, he must occupy his time and seek to continually reaffirm his humanity and commitment to our shared planetary heritage. Interestingly enough, this is one film by a special effects expert that doesn't get unduly caught up in the usual high-tech hardware of the science fiction genre; more than any of the other films in this series, *Silent Running* is a meditational piece on a person's place in the universe, and an appropriate finale to this series of futurist visions gone awry.

What, then, does Dystopia offer us? Only the promise that there will be a tomorrow, although it will be an unpleasant affair. More positivist films, such as *The Day the Earth Stood Still* (1951), *Close Encounters of the Third Kind* (1977), the films in *Star Trek* series, *Starman* (1984), and other projects, envision a future that will be kind and benevolent, a world in which extraterrestrials emerge from the void to instruct and enlighten civilization, rather than engage in a duel to the death. But the market for these films seems to be waning. The plot of *Alien III* (1992), for example, has Warrant Officer Ripley escaping from the planet where the action of *Aliens* (1986) took place, only to crash-land on a nearby prison planet populated by convicted rapists.

With her head completely shaved, looking sallow, somber, and grimly determined, fighting every moment for survival and nothing more, threatened on all sides by those who seek to murder and/or rape her, Ripley is, pathetically enough, emblematic of the role of women in Dystopian science fiction (victims or ornaments), even as men in Dystopian films are reduced to similarly limiting, self-defeating roles (rapist, patrician overlord, escaping renegade, agents of rescue). Above all, Dystopian science fiction reduces characters to *situations*, as William Burroughs once observed in a lecture; personality falls in the wake of societally enforced rules of survival.

The first film in the *Alien* series now seems a tamely romantic vision of an inhospitable future, in contrast to the mechanistic violence unleashed in both *Aliens* (the second film in the series) and *Alien III*, a film which traps series star Sigourney Weaver (as Ripley) not only in a hostile environment populated by rapists and an unstoppable killing machine (the Alien itself), but which securely binds Weaver as an actress to the role of Warrant Officer Ripley for the remainder of her career. Weaver's attempt to break away from the role has proven, for the most part, unsuccessful; the public sees her as the ineluctable partner of the Alien, locked forever in a dance of violent destruction. Are we so in love, finally, with the vision of the future as disaster that we can admit to nothing else? More and more, the vision of the future we are offered in the cinema is solely one of destruction and despair. The rush to Dystopia is nothing new, nothing if not predictable, and unfortunately a reliable social barometer of the public's perception of the uncertain times we live in. There will be a future; that's all Dystopia promises. But the time in which we truly live, it seems, must be now. Tomorrow, we will simply have to survive.

CHAPTER SIX

■■

The Armed Response: The Screen's Gaze Returned, or the Gorgon's Mirror

PARTING GLANCES

Colonization almost invariably implies a relation of structural domination, and a suppression—often violent—of the heterogeneity of the subject(s) in question.

—Mohanty

The axes of the subject's identifications and experiences are multiple, because locations in gender, class, race, ethnicity and sexuality complicate one another, and not merely additively.

—Watson and Smith

The degree to which [hegemonic ideology and power] are imagined to be internally divided, unstable, and in constant need of construction and revision, creat[es] the conditions which make social change and the agency of the weak possible.

—Newton

We should not be cultural determinists.

—Spivak

One should not pretend that any discourse would be a miraculous aerolite, independent of networks of memory and the social trajectories within which it erupts.

—Pêcheux

In the concluding moments of Ray Enright's *Gung Ho!* (1943), Randolph Scott, as the commander of the Raiders battalion, directly addresses the trans/genderal viewer, assuring her/him that the conflagration and loss of life we have just witnessed is in every way necessary "to bequeath a new social order" to our collective sons, grandsons, daughters, and granddaughters. At this moment, we are at last one with the Raider battalion; we have been included into the group whose exploits we have followed for the preceding eighty-eight minutes. The Raiders are us, we are the Raiders. Our mission has succeeded, but only at the cost of the loss of those "who were like brothers to us." Although the spectatorial address throughout *Gung Ho!* is resolutely male, in these final minutes of the film, as the camera inexorably tracks in on Scott's face, we are encouraged to transform ourselves into a homogeneous, female/male spectatorial/activist construct, ready to do "our duty" to defeat the "Japs," while simultaneously casting out "every form of prejudice—racial, social, political, and every other kind." The fact that these admonitions are mutually exclusionary is of little importance to us, now that we have become one of the Raiders; our shared mission is all that counts.

Those who operate in the margins of 1940s society in *Gung Ho!* (an African-American cook, a "Filipino boy . . . who shows us the thousand uses of the knife," the young woman who is courted by two members of the battalion and then left behind) are ritualistically "included in this embrace of the hyperreal extended audience, but only insofar as they conform to the patriarchal rule imposed by the commander who addresses us. It is significant that this "appeal to unity" takes place in a submerged submarine, deep in enemy territory, as the Raiders steam home after a costly but successful mission. There is no place to escape; like their German counterparts in Wolfgang Petersen's *Das Boot* (1981), they, and we, are trapped in a frame of steel and electrical cables, thrown together in artificial brotherhood whether they like it or not. And we are forced to cast our lot with them.

In the concluding moments of Romano Ferrara's *Planets Against Us* (1961), the professor who has been conducting an investigation into an alien invasion of "identical alien humanoid robots with hypnotic eyes and the touch of death" (Weldon 553), turns from addressing his colleagues to speak to us directly, warning us that anyone around us could be an alien invader, even the person sitting in the seat next to us in the theatre. Jason Robards's Al Capone in Roger Corman's *The St. Valentine's Day Massacre* (1966) dominates the members of his gang almost solely through the power of his intimidating gaze, made all the more menacing because it is veiled from our sight for much of the film through the medium of Capone's sunglasses.

In Terence Fisher's *Dracula* (1958), Christopher Lee noiselessly descends the stairs of his decaying castle to greet Jonathan Harker, and by direct implication the audience, in a tight and threatening close-up that gathers force as it extends out in the space of the auditorium. Later in the film, Dracula advances up a flight of stairs in a Victorian residence in search of a new victim; again, we are shown the "gaze of bloodlust" as the vampire's gaze meets that of our own. As far back as F. W. Murnau's *Nosferatu* (1922) this strategy of interlocking gazes had been profitably employed. Dracula seeks to literally hypnotize his victims into a helpless stupor. It is not too much to suggest that this gaze penetrates into the space between the screen and the spectator, lulling us into fatal inactivity as we witness the spectacle before us.

Marilyn Monroe meets the gaze of the viewer in Henry Hathaway's *Niagara* (1953) by putting on her best defensive smile. Marilyn's career is an entire construct of seeing and being seen, extending into the Warhol silkscreens that immortalized her studio-manufactured image while simultaneously assuring her remoteness from genuine human contact. Every aspect of her body language is a pose. One foot covers the other, with the ankle slightly thrust forward; her body is tilted to the right as she hugs the stone wall behind her; her hands grip the wall for support, but her chest is prominently displayed for the gaze of the male fetishist. Only in her face can we see the enormous amount of effort Monroe

FIGURE 19. "The rule of the look and nothing else:" Jason Robards as
Al Capone in *The St. Valentine's Day Massacre* (1966).

FIGURE 20. The gaze of bloodlust in Terence Fisher's *Horror of Dracula*. (Courtesy of Jerry Ohlinger.)

FIGURE 21. Marilyn Monroe confronts the viewer in *Niagara*. (Courtesy of Jerry Ohlinger.)

expends in this seemingly innocuous photograph. Her smile is perfectly chiseled, her teeth white, her eyes gazing straight through the lens into the eyes of the presumably male viewer.

Monroe's exploitation as the commodification of male desire in the 1950s and early 1960s is one of the saddest chronicles of the overall metanarrative viewer gift-exchange employed by the patriarchal cinema in 1950s Hollywood. It is little wonder that, as she grew more assured, Monroe sought roles that would bring her some measure of respect and deflect the attention of the purely sexual gaze she had long subjected herself to at the behest of promoters. In George Marshall's *Houdini* (1953), Tony Curtis and Janet Leigh address the audience witnessing Houdini's act. The smiles, the costumes, the fabrication of event within the film and the imagistic constructs that film traffics in all suggest the hallmark of 1950s Hollywood cinema practice at its most unsettling; breaking through the fourth wall without really challenging and/or confronting the spectator, as questioning his/her (but mostly his) desires. In all of these films, whether we wish to be or not, we are complicitous in the spectacle being presented, at one with the world which we only seek to visit. These films view us and expect us to engage in an exchange of surveilling glances.

In the courtroom sequence of Sam Newfield's *I Accuse My Parents* (1944), the judge who condemns a mother and father for leading their son into "juvenile delinquency" redirects his gaze from them to us, admonishing us to be careful in the nurturing and guidance of contemporary youth. In Freddie Francis's *Paranoiac* (1962), when nurse Liliane Brousse is drowned by sociopath Oliver Reed, we are drowned along with her, and view her demise from her point-of-view, staring up with her at the maniacal face of her murderer. In Lindsay Shonteff's *Curse of the Voodoo* (1965), obnoxiously racist

> game hunter Bryant Halliday is cursed by Chief M'Gobo when he kills a sacred lion [while on safari in Africa]. Back in England, he suffers physical and mental anguish, hallucinates, and is constantly feverish. He returns to Africa [with the aid of his ultra-colonialist assistant, played by Dennis Price] and runs over M'Gobo with a jeep, ending the curse. (Weldon, 150)

FIGURE 22. Tony Curtis and Janet Leigh address the audience in *Houdini*. (Courtesy of Jerry Ohlinger.)

FIGURE 23. The authoritarian gaze of the judge in *I Accuse My Parents*. (Courtesy of Wheeler Winston Dixon.)

Throughout the film, we are led to identify with Halliday alone; the camera tracks with him when he stalks the plains of Africa; in his sickbed in England, he remains resolutely at the center of the frame. None of the Africans in the film (or British Africans, for that matter) are given any sort of an identity—it is only through the obliteration of one race by another that Halliday is permitted to survive.

In Marco Brambilla's *Demolition Man* (1993), the fraudulently benevolent Dr. Raymond Cocteau (Nigel Hawthorne) presides over a futuristic Los Angeles, another Dystopian nightmare landscape that hides repression and thought control behind a mask of peace and social contentment. The "oldies" stations play commercials from the 1970s and 1980s, rather than pop songs; the only restaurant that has been allowed to survive in this new society is an omnipresently franchised Taco Bell. The inevitable underground rebels who oppose this surface society, led by subterranean commando Edgar Friendly (Denis Leary) remind one of the workers in Fritz Lang's *Metropolis*, or the denizens of the working-class hell in Paul Verhoeven's *Total Recall* (1991). The city itself is redolent in the placid vistas envisioned in Michael Anderson's *Logan's Run* (1976), a location of contemporary telematiculture and judiciously employed matte paintings to suggest the massive skyscrapers of 2032. The nominal plot follows the attempts of "San Angeles" cop John Spartan (Sylvester Stallone) to capture sociopath Simon Phoenix (Wesley Snipes), a socially disruptive figure too violent for the pacific San Angeles police to cope with.

Sporting a blond Billy Idol haircut, Snipes shoots and maims his way through the inequitable fabric of San Angelean society until, in the climax of the film, he "thaws out" his fellow criminals from the "cryoprison" they have been entombed in; sadly and predictably, the vast majority of these murderers, rapists, and muggers are African-American. Indeed, the scene in which Phoenix rallies his troops to murder Spartan reminds one of nothing so much as the menacingly macho tableaux featured in many of the more violent "blaxploitation" films of the 1970s; in this instance, however, Phoenix's compatriots will be denied even a small measure of disruptive control, as they are ritualistically eliminated shortly after their reanimation. Despite the fringe presences of street-smart African-American police officer Zachary Lamb (played as a young man by Grand L. Bush, and as an older man by Bill Cobbs and sympathetic Latino police officer Alfredo Garcia [Benjamin Bratt]), it is Snipes who dominates the film. Snipe's climactic moment occurs as he contemplates thawing out a cryogenically imprisoned Jeffrey Dahmer to assist him in his lawless pursuits. Scanning a list of prisoners from whom he may choose his fellow assassins, Snipes comes across Dahmer's name. "Jeffrey Dahmer!" he exclaims. "I *love* this guy!"

The film is a panopticonic surveillance project of massive proportions, in which one is constantly monitored by hidden microphones that censor both speech and action. Contact is achieved through video monitors; conferences consist of monitors gazing at other monitors in an otherwise empty boardroom, devoid of any authentic human presence. Computers, not surprisingly, operate the entire electronic nerve system of the city; the exchange of the commodity of the look is thus managed through the medium of the cathode ray tube alone. Sex has also been outlawed; John Spartan is surprised when his futurist partner, Lieutenant Lenina Huxley (Sandra Bullock) directly offers to "have sex" with him. Lieutenant Huxley, however, means telepathic/electronically mediated "sex," rather than "sex" as a construct of physical contact—a notion she finds disgusting.

The poster for *Demolition Man* presents Stallone and Snipes facing off in a tight close-up, confronting each other with the power of their returned gaze. The tag line of the film encapsulates the entire polemic implicit within the project: "the future isn't big enough for both of them." Leaving aside the one-dimensional parodic intent of many of the protagonists' names within the film ("Spartan" as the indomitable cop; the ever-resilient "Phoenix" as his adversary; the self-reflexive and insulting Latino stereotype "Alfredo Garcia" [after Sam Peckinpah's film of the same title] as Spartan's nominal sidekick, "Raymond Cocteau" [a conflation of Raymond Radiguet and Jean Cocteau] as the corrupt intellectual who rules San Angeles) *Demolition Man* is yet another film that seemingly challenges the dominant order while actually seeking to reinforce it. The San Angelean police of 2032 are seen as hypocritical, effete, and useless; the halcyon future offered by Cocteau's regime is viewed as a repressive construct that must be overthrown at all costs. The dreams of social equity, peace, and coexistence are viewed by *Demolition Man* as intrinsically impossible to attain without social oppression; one's natural instinct is shown as being rooted in violence. Spartan alone can rescue the members of this Edenic society from the twin threats of Cocteau and Phoenix.

Thus *Demolition Man* advises us to stop seeking peace, and accept, even embrace, violence as the only social order with any basis in cultural reality. The metanarrative of the film is clear; society is surveilling you and will continue to surveill you—we offer you the illusion of an escape. And yet it is the construct of the film itself that watches us, draws us into a world of hyperreal perceived homogeneity, offering us a means of figuration in the reconstitutive description of overdetermined subjective malaise. Spartan and Phoenix function as figures of discursive transgression and reterritorialization—to reclaim the future for us from those who would transform it into an alternative heterotopia.

In Jack Sher's *Kathy O* (1958), Patty McCormack, attempting to rupture the public's perception of her as the murderous protagonist of Mervyn LeRoy's *The Bad Seed* (1956), played the role of a spoiled yet essentially misunderstood child star, who ceases to be a problem for her studio and (it is implied) herself when she accepts the familiar warmth offered by the heterotopic couple of Dan Duryea and Jan Sterling. The poster for the film is dominated by an oversize "decapitated" head of Patty McCormack staring blankly into the face of the spectator, her teeth drawn back in a feral grin of demand, her blue eyes glistening with the frenzied energy of public appeal. *Kathy O*, the poster tells us, is "the picture that likes people!"—the film that, to paraphrase Jed Leland in *Citizen Kane* (1941), "likes you so much that you've got to like it back." The visual plea implicit in McCormack's gaze is a desire to be reinscribed on the consciousness of the public, to alter their perceptions of her as an unrepentant child psychopath. These two transgressive figures cannot be allowed to coexist within the same social structure; the present "isn't big enough for both of them."

In Edward L. Cahn's *The Four Skulls of Jonathan Drake* (1958), Eduard Franz, as Professor Jonathan Drake, must combat a racial construct in the supposed person of Dr. Emil Zurich

(Henry Daniell), who is in reality only the *head* of Dr. Zurich, sewn on to the body of a "dead jungle Indian more than two centuries ago." Drake's ancestors, involved in the colonization of South America for profit, massacred the members of an entire native tribe in retaliation for the death of one of their expedition's members. Only the tribal witch doctor escaped the onslaught of violence inflicted by the colonists; now, through the agency of the reconstituted Dr. Zurich, he seeks to behead every male descendant of the Drake family, and after decapitating their corpses, shrink their heads as trophies. Again, Drake's colonial and patriarchal victory over his nemesis can only be complete when "the white head is separated from the brown body . . . all that will be destroyed is evil." In the past, the present, and the future, then, there is only room for one "survivor," one determinant force, one defining social order, one system of beliefs at the expense (and elimination) of any competing methodology of oppositional discourse.

THE GIFT-EXCHANGE OF THE LOOK BACK

The control of gift-exchange in imagistic construction, the Althusserian discourse implicit in the gendered specificity of desire contained within these films, the lack of dialectical transcendence offered to us as an audience deprived of what Colin Wilson has described as "duo-consciousness"—the ability to participate within the construct of a work and yet remain outside it—is not confined to the cinema. Even such a seemingly benign volume as Dorothy Kuhnhardt's pioneering hypertext *Pat the Bunny* (first issued in 1942), in which the child/reader/construct is directed to "pat the bunny," whose tail is made of actual cotton, or "feel daddy's beard," which is constructed of sandpaper. As the text nears its conclusion, the child is told to look into a mirror and behold itself. What kind of a mirror are we being offered in these, and other texts, that confront us with a gaze of their own creation, or inflict our own inquisitive glance back at us, questioning and confirming our roles as spectators/participants within the fictive domain of popular entertainment?

Mary Lambert, the director of *Pet Sematary* (1989), may offer us one less violent mode of territorial countertransgression in her interactive CD-ROM video film *Double Switch* (1993), produced by Digital Motion Pictures. Scripted by Christian Williams and James Reilly, the film centers around a scenario involving a posh hotel which contains, in its secret interior, an Egyptian pyramid. Players/viewers will then be invited to enter or not to enter certain chambers, doorways, hiding places, and secret/revealed passages as the film/game progresses, but without the heavy quotient of violent play acting contained within the metanarrative of *Ground Zero Texas*. Another Digital Motion Pictures production, *Prize Fighter*, directed by Ronald Stein (a second-unit director on Martin Scorsese's *Raging Bull* [1980]), is distinctly less interesting; the viewer/participant adopts the point-of-view of a boxer in the ring, and must ritualistically slug it out with an interminable succession of opponents.

One can acknowledge the returned gaze in the media directly, by incorporating the gaze-within-the-gaze, as Federico Fellini did in *Juliet of the Spirits* (1965), in which all of the television sets viewed within the film feature men and women staring directly at us (and *past* the protagonists within the film, who seem not to notice the baleful surveillance of their televisual coinhabitants). In Agnes Varda's *Vagabond* (1985), the various people along the road who briefly befriend the young woman Mona (Sandrine Bonnaire) continually break through the enforced prison of the narrativistic construct to speak directly to us through the medium/focalizer of the camera lens. What is present in all these instances is the desire to break free of the gaze that controls us, and an admission of the power of that gaze. But as Stuart Hall notes:

As soon as you say "hegemony," people see marching boots, rolling tanks, censorship, people being locked away. What they cannot understand is, the one thing we need to understand in societies like ours, which is how people can be constrained while walking free; being utterly subject to determinations that make you apparently free to say what you like. (Hall, 61)

FIGURE 24. In this actual Sega CD screen output from Digital Pictures' live-action interactive movie, *Double Switch*, Eddie, played by actor Corey Haim, gets zapped and trapped. (Courtesy of Digital Pictures, Inc., © 1993.)

FIGURE 25. The Grads try to help Jeff as he struggles on the teeter tooter trap in this actual Sega CD screen output from Digital Pictures' live-action interactive movie, *Double Switch*. (Courtesy of Digital Pictures, Inc., © 1993).

And so it is with these films, these performative, taxonomic countertestimonies that seek to dominate and inscribe the sign of the dominant culture on the mimetic constructedness of the body dispossessed.

In an illustration in *Discipline and Punish* (plate 8, following page 169), Michel Foucault reprints an illustration depicting a "lecture on the evils of alcoholism in the auditorium of Fresnes prison." The inmates are locked in boxes, with only a narrow space at the top so that they may gaze up on the lecturer who confronts them. The boxes, and the prisoners, are arranged in tiers, as in a conventional theatre, but through the very design of the auditorium's apparatus, the prisoners/viewers cannot look at each other or to the back in the auditorium. They are *forced* to look straight ahead, to be confronted by the gaze of the lecturer, to contemplate their separation from external society, and from the society of the prison, as the members of this audience have been individuated into a series of zones of discipline. Looking at this picture reminded me most forcefully of Peter Kubelka's design for the old Anthology Cinema Archives (as installed in the Public Shakespeare Theatre complex on Lafayette Street in New York City), in which each viewer was forced to inhabit a black velvet box that insulated the viewers from any contact with each other, and forced their attention on the brightly lit screen before them. As if to underscore the dominance of the returned gaze of the screen in this design, Kubelka instructed that before each performance of a film, the screen, flawlessly white, glass-beaded for maximum reflectivity, and lit with dazzling brilliance, should be exhibited to the viewer for a period of several uninterrupted minutes. This gesture in itself is a direct acknowledgment and confirmation of the power of the look back of the screen surface, and of the subtextual surfaces contained within this surface, as configured within the constructed narrativistic mimesis of the cinematic apparatus.

PURE LIGHT

How can we, as an audience, effectively combat the all-entrancing power of this returned gaze from the screen, this vision-without-a-vision that emanates even from the blank receptacle/filter of the screen, devoid of any image other than the significator of light itself? Tony Conrad's *The Flicker* (1966), consisting as it does of "bright blank frames interspersed with solid black frames that more and more recur and recur" (*Time* magazine, as cited in *FMC Catalogue No. 6*, 56), and Takahiko Iimura's *Timing Reels No. 1 and No. 2* (1972), composed of "counting, 1 to 100, or Xs," that is, serial repetitions of the numbering/framing process (*FMC Catalogue No. 6*, 130), reinforce the notion of the cinematic apparatus as a reciprocal projection mechanism, in which projection occurs from *both sides* of the screen. Writing on *The Flicker*, an anonymous spokesperson for the New York Filmmakers' Cinématheque noted that

> This is a film of light . . . white light itself is articulated with such subtle symmetry, such logical development, such absolute proportion as to make almost all other cinema seem formally primitive. The formality of *Flicker* is fused with unparalleled physical power, as the screen radiates tidal waves of light to lap over the audience, and whirlpools of energy spin like sunspots up close. *Flicker* is a tremendous harnessing of cosmic energy by modern art, and a transmission of this energy to the spectator. (*FMC Catalogue No. 6*, 56)

Critic Richard Preston, writing in *The East Village Other*, reported:

> By the [end], one's senses are completely disoriented. . . . The screen appears to have moved forward several yards . . . the walls of the cinema seem to move in and at the same time have a transparent quality . . . the people walking out look rather like ghosts. (*FMC Catalogue No. 6*, 56)

What Conrad performed in *The Flicker* is nothing less than a full-scale confirmation of the returned gaze phenomenon from the cinema screen, using the raw fabric of filmic language, an interplay of white and black frames. Contemporary criticism claimed:

The screen for the first time is used not simply to reflect but to generate light . . . transforms the flat and traditionally non-assertive screen-surface into a pounding dynamo of light. Light engulfs the audience in physically shaking tidal waves, breaks on the retina into hallucinatory color. (Janus Film Society, as cited in *FMC Catalogue No. 6*, 56)

But in fact Conrad's film was more accurately a foregrounding of a process that had been in place for some time. The screen has never been "non-assertive"; it has always been used "not simply to reflect but to generate light." Conrad's *excessive* manipulation of the retinal sensory system reminds one of Antonin Artaud's Theatre of Cruelty, in that it offers the viewer/viewed no escape, and confronts the spectator/participant with the mechanics of spectacle, of theatrical presentation, of the unspoken reciprocal contract between image (live or recorded) and auditor (see Artaud 84-104). Certainly we are aware that performers within a staged construct are aware of the members of the audience; we take as an a priori assumption the phantom existence of the fourth wall, even as we strive (both actor and auditor) to breach it. The video/film camera is merely a filter in this process and does not remove us from the power of the "look back" of performer, screen space, or the screen itself as a "generator" of light. When we enter the theatrical arena, we subject ourselves to control, surveillance, and the power of the gaze no matter what medium the fictive construct we witness employs. Conrad's film is simply a restatement of a process we have long been aware of; the screen, the projection light and the projection apparatus act *upon* us and incorporate us into a reciprocal discourse that is both confrontational and playful. How can we "shake off" the power of this surveillance? Is such a thing possible at all?

HORIZONS OF THE RETURNED GAZE

In this volume, I have considered a number of coefficients of the returned gaze in video/cinema practice. These processes include the Bentham/Foucault panopticon implicit in all video/cinema production/reproduction; the aspect of surveillance inherent in the production of imagistic constructs within the public sphere; the use of surveillance cameras in banks and restaurants; *Cops* and other TV shows that return the voyeur's gaze; the construction of the gaze as part of the hyperreal in Baudrillard in which we work in concert with the film to cocreate the look that controls; the vision of television as a "carrier" wave of electron beams; and the TV without an image as corpse, or corrupted electronic hearth. While the "look back" is currently shaped by the patriarchal control exerted within cinema practice, there exists today a vast and growing number of films that question and undermine this existing order, in the films of Sally Potter, Su Friedrich, Gunvor Nelson, Tamra Davis, Barbara Hammer, Julie Dash, and in the gay films of Terence Davies, the late Derek Jarman, and many others; these films and their creators have been offered as an alternative vision to patriarchal cinema practice.

I have examined the mechanics of pornography, as considered in the writings of Willemen and Prince, among others; the question of what constitutes "pornographic practice," the idea of "the forbidden look returned" when we gaze upon spectacles partitioned off from us within contemporary society; the male and female gaze returned, the straight and gay/lesbian gaze returned within the construct of the "film of desire," the work of Chantal Akerman in *Je Tu Il Elle* and other films, which explicitly and without judgment record and re-represent sexual practices (straight and/or lesbian/gay) for the viewer, in shots of long duration, which returned the gaze of shared sexual desire from the screen.

In *Dreams of the State*, I examined how the control of the returned look in popular entertainment, specifically in films designed solely for exhibition to large commercial audiences serves primarily the interests of the state, and yet how within each of these films there lurks a series of subversive codes, which in turn are either undermined or valorized as the filmmakers (in the context of their work as artists-for-hire) grapple with the limits of representational freedom and/or enslavement within the construct of genre in their application of "the look back." As I noted and documented, many of these films are dystopian science fiction films, in which the state is portrayed as both an inescapable master and a malevolent figure of panopticonic determinism.

These films control our emotions through music cues, shock edits, stock characters, a series of instantly read icons and the like. In this "control project" the films are assisted by focus groups where galvanic skin response and retinal focusing devices simplify and intensify the returned gaze at the most primal level, by seeking out the lowest common denominator members of the audience, and lulling them into an induced trance state of "gaze reciprocity," so that we become "the audience as victim," as in Freddie Francis's *Paranoiac* (1962).

There is also the very real question of what exactly the future of film will be, in terms of image storage and retrieval machinery, and the manner in which the images that comprise an imagistic construct will be created and inscribed for later reproduction. The computer-generated digital dinosaurs in *Jurassic Park*, in the words of media critic Daniel Todd, "may have sounded the death knell for many proven mechanical and optical techniques (Todd 60). Pioneering digital imagists Scott and Minky Billups created the sets for an entire television series, *Wild Space*, using "100 percent digitally composited" sets. Even the "extras" in the series are digitally composited, leaving only the lead actors as actual people being photographed (Todd 58). Already this technique of human replication has been extensively used in television commercials, to recreate portions of a crowd to clone a larger throng. The Billups recently completed a digital production of Roger Corman's production of *The Fantastic Four* (1994) an ambitious science fiction film that had been in production limbo for a number of years because it would have been prohibitively expensive to produce using conventional technology. The Billups "cranked out an astounding 157 effects shots [for the film] on an unheard of budget of $200,000 . . . less than the catering bill on most movies" (Todd 58). The characters in the film are photographed against a blue screen and then composited with props and settings to taste, all at a fraction of the cost of building the usual sets, costuming extras, creating artificial trees, forests, castles, and the like, and the end result is so life-like that it is often hard to tell the difference between the real and the computer-generated. (However, at the last minute, it was decided to scrap Corman's version of *The Fan-*

FIGURE 26. Victim's point-of-view shared by the audience in *Paranoiac*. (Courtesy of Jerry Ohlinger.)

tastic Four for a bigger-budgeted film to be directed by Chris Columbus. "Trailers," or coming attractions sequences of the Corman *Fantastic Four* can, however, still be seen on video rental tapes of the Corman production *Carnosaur* [1994]).

Virtual reality goggles, offering the viewer a primitive simulation of an alternative mode of vision, have recently come into their own at various science and technology fairs, and although they are in the "magic lantern" stage at the moment, the time may soon come when virtual reality image delivery supplants the traditional cinema/video projection arena. Virtual reality goggles will lock our gaze impenetrably into that of the construct or person whom we view, and who can be certain that this "person" we view is, in fact, a human entity. As in Michael Crichton's *Looker* (1981), what we see may well have been constructed specifically with a control objective in mind—an image that seeks to dominate and exploit us without our being aware of the fact. Indeed, such a construct would wish to erase all traces of its origin, so that its operations might be seamless and invisible to all but the technicians who informed its creation. The interactive entertainment industry is already a bigger portion of the recreational market than the rental, sale, production, and/or distribution of motion pictures, and the processes described in this volume will shortly seem quaint precursors of an all-out attack upon the consciousness of the viewer, for the possession of the mind and money of the willing viewer/viewed. Sega, the industry leader in interactive television video games is of this writing (and copartners with Digital Pictures on the *Ground Zero Texas* and *Double Switch* projects) is now worth $3.6 billion and expanding. The bewildering merger of cable and telephone systems in recent months prefigures an enormous interactive web of imagistic exchange that will inevitably seek to control the consumer who views its product, and simultaneously to eliminate all competition. We are entering the age of conglomerate visual control upon the viewer/subject, and what we have seen so far in cinema and video history is only the beginning of a metanarrative exchange which will continue to resonate and reconfigure itself in the years to come, at a pace of such intense hyperacceleration that we will have little choice but to subscribe to the panoply of "services," or "surveillances," offered.

In the face of all this, how can we respond to and shake off the returned gaze? Can the development of "duo-consciousness" (in the words of Colin Wilson) be an effective countermeasure against the embrace of the "gaze that controls"? Can distanciation from the image be achieved when one extricates one's self from the narrative line exclusively and begins to follow, simultaneously, the physical and syntactical construction of the film? If the "look back" is an implicit part of current cinema practice, as I have argued, and an insidiously ignored coefficient of this practice, in the service of political control of the viewer/viewed, then how can we hope to escape its control? Is all spectacle pornographic, in the final analysis? Has the repetitious consumption of (generally useless) goods replaced the creation of narrative as the new commodity exchange agreement between viewer/viewed and the creators of spectacle?

THE COMMODITY OF SPECTACLE

An Associated Press story from October 30, 1993, would seem to suggest that long-form commercials ("interactive" tools of audience manipulation and control) may well be replacing even the most marginal forms of televised entertainment. In a brief essay, Associated Press announced:

> The syndicated *Joan Rivers Show* will end its five-year run on New Year's Eve, replaced Jan. 3 by *Can We Shop?* a daily, dirt-dishing, celebrity-filled home-shopping hour starring you-know-who. "We're going to see everything that I have always done. . . . And we're also going to be selling, because that's what everybody's doing now," Rivers disclosed Friday on *CBS This Morning. Can We Shop?* will be a joint venture of Rivers, Tribune Entertainment Co., QVC Network and Regal Communications, a leading producer of infomercials. ("Joan Rivers Switching Shows," 3)

Thus advertisements—direct appeals to viewer response—have replaced scripted, or even spontaneous, unrehearsed narrative discourse. The "sponsor" has subsumed the space formerly occupied by narrative—advertisements have become programming because they acknowledge and enunciate the metanarrative gift-exchange between viewer/viewed and performer/merchandiser. The "look back," the controlling gaze of the television screen, has become the true interchange of taxonomic fetishistic textuality in commercial imagistic discourse.

In her essay "(Male) Desire and (Female) Disgust: Reading *Hustler*," Laura Kipnis asks, "Is pornography, in fact, so obviously and so simply a discourse about gender?" (221). In many ways, it *is* about the construct gender, of "bringing issues of class into the porn debates [to break] down the theoretical monolith of misogyny" (Kipnis, 222), to explore the reasons why "the repressive apparatuses of the dominant social order return so invariably to the body and to somatic symbols" (Kipnis, 224). It is also about commerce, and the structure of the media webs that seek to, and do, control a good portion of our existence through an epistomological exchange of "somatic symbols." The oppositional discourse inherent in the viewing of, and the act of being viewed by, the dispossessed body of cinema/video discourse, is a means of figuration in which the causal concept of the viewing/viewed process if the reterritorialization of the domestic sphere into an arena of continuous, inexhaustible, and self-reflexive consumption. The QVC and Home Shopping Networks (HSN) are the logical extension of a medium massaged by commerce and created for gain, rather than the dissemination of information. QVC and HSN seek to control, to dominate, to create artificial hegemonic moments based solely on the exchange of the promise of payment. Thus reconstitutive description of cinema/video practice leaves little doubt as to the future of cinema/video practice; we now "pay doubly" for television programming (viewing ads on cable systems that charge us for the privilege of watching those advertisements), and we are required to pay "premium" prices for cable services that exist beyond the zone of advertorial interruption—the so-called "premium cable services." This heightens the distance between the spectator and the filmic/video body, whether in commercial television practice, or in the metanarrative structure of a film like *Bad Lieutenant* (1992), which simultaneously distances and beckons its intended audience.

FIGURE 27. Harvey Keitel in Abel Ferrara's *Bad Lieutenant* (1992); the distance between performer and the audience. (Courtesy of Jerry Ohlinger.)

The gendered specificity of desire posited by Kipnis in relation to pornographic practice obtains as well in the world of the
Home Shopping Network, a world based upon the commercial
triangulation of unsatiated desire. The subjective malaise of the
viewer is eradicated by the desire to obtain; the agential theory in
operation is one of quasi-pathological stimulus and spectatorial
overdetermination. In her book *Taylored Lives*, Martha Banta
documented the ways in which the American worker was acted
upon by the time/motion studies of Frederick Winslow Taylor, as
implemented by Henry Ford and other mass-production indus-
trialists who sought to reduce the individual to machine status,
capable of only simple, repetitive tasks, devoid of waste motion,
designed to fit a rigidly circumscribed location within the
workspace of the corporation.

What the "look back" has done to us, a viewing audience, is
much the same; it has drawn us into a connection with the
video/film image that has been implicit and trans/genderally
implemented since the inception of the cinematograph and the
television cathode ray tube. This returned look instructs, admonishes, takes us into its confidence, and allows us to enter into
the spectacle being created as a participant—coequal, superior, or
as a figure to be acted upon and dominated for commercial/polit-
ical gain. As the various matrices of imagistic commerce gather
themselves into a single conglomerate, it is this last model which
seems to be taking precedence over more altruistic methodologies
of reciprocally acknowledged audience participation. The "look
back" urges us, in fact, to look behind us. Someone is there,
watching. The figure in front of us sees us as well. We can turn
the image on, or we can shut it off, but perhaps the Orwellian
millennium is approaching in which it will be impossible to
avoid the gaze that controls—not because of a governmental law
mandating interactive surveillance models within every home
(and not just those of "criminals"). Rather, the flow of information contained within the fibre optic system, capable of carrying
500 televisual channels where before only thirty or forty could be
accommodated, will become so much a part of our social contract
with the state (banking, voting, car registration, income tax filing,
shopping for groceries, school registration, property tax assess-
ment—the possibilities are unhappily endless) that we will be

practically obliged to hook into the system, to subject ourselves to the gaze that controls, in order to remain in contact with the authorities who seek to control and govern our actions for political or financial gain.

We can resist the domination of these images through an understanding of the countertransgressive discourses—syntactical, iconic, metanarrative—that generate the images which seek to command our collective attention. We can see how this process has developed and expanded from an insidious and occasionally employed coefficient of the film/video viewing experience into an integral function of contemporary telecultural discourse. And yet, in the face of this "division of desire"—the separation of genres, sports, products, and other cultural commodities into individual streams of imagistic commerce—can we long maintain the integrity of consciousness the resistant and truly responsive viewer/subject so perilously requires? The reciprocal exchange of the gaze from the screen, once employed with discretion and a certain selective dis-ease, has now become the foregrounded and central component of the television, and the images speak directly to us; the "fourth wall" has vanished. We go to the cinema, and a series of trailers, commercials, and advertisements (prefigured by the relatively innocuous "movie clocks" used in drive-in theatres in the 1940s and 50s) address us individually, telling us what to do, and what not to do. The armed response is a reality: we can *resist* these images that seek to control. But can we hold out forever? The new image conglomerates—corporate monoliths that vertical integrationist Adolph Zukor could never have envisioned in his most ambitious dreams of empire—continue to expand. As we regard the services and narrative structures these new telephone/cable/direct satellite/interactive film/video constructs provide for our entertainment and/or exploitation, the confluent figures of cultural slippage and libidinal economy inherent in the diegesis of the metacorporational structure may be correctly perceived as a series of troubling incarnationist tropes.

This vision that returns on our vision will return to us again, until, like James Woods in *Videodrome*, we are so connected to the flow of images that comfort us that we have no desire to disengage from the ongoing reciprocal discourse. The

moment signaling the impossibility of any rupture of this reciprocal engagement may, indeed, have already arrived. Comfortably nestled in our armchairs, huddled in a shelter seeking
warmth, riding on an airplane and seeking relief from the tedium
of travel, we may have already inexorably surrendered to the gaze
that controls. The electronic cinematic hearth has become the
new focal point of our narrative, and corporeal existence; we gaze
at it, and it returns our look, staring through the filter of the
lens, inviting us to dream, participate, and/or accept its domination.

BIBLIOGRAPHY

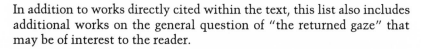

In addition to works directly cited within the text, this list also includes additional works on the general question of "the returned gaze" that may be of interest to the reader.

Abel, Richard. "The 'Blank Screen of Reception' in Early French Cinema." *Iris* 11 (Summer 1990): 27-48.

Albrecht, Thomas. "Sauve qui peut (l'image): Reading for a Double Life." *Cinema Journal* 30.2 (Winter 1991): 61-73.

Allen, Richard. "Brushing Classical Hollywood Narrative Against the Grain of History." *Camera Obscura: A Journal of Feminism and Film Theory* 18 (September 1988): 137-145.

———. "Representation, Illusion and the Cinema." *Cinema Journal* 32.2 (Winter 1993): 21-48.

Altman, Rick. "Television/Sound." *Studies in Entertainment: Critical Approaches to Mass Culture.* Ed. Tania Modleski. Bloomington: Indiana UP, 1986. 39-54.

Anderson, J. L. "Spoken Silents in the Japanese Cinema; or, Talking to Pictures: Essaying the *Katsuben,* Contexturalizing the Texts." Ed. Arthur Nolletti Jr. and David Desser. *Reframing Japanese Cinema: Authorship, Genre, History.* Bloomington: Indiana UP, 1992. 259-310.

Andrew, Dudley. "The Unauthorized Auteur Today." *Film Theory Goes to the Movies.* Ed. Jim Collins, Hilary Radner, and Ava Preacher Collins. New York: Routledge, 1993. 77-85.

Ang, Ien. *Watching Dallas: Soap Opera and the Melodramatic Imagination*. Trans. Della Couling. London: Methuen, 1985.

Armstrong, Nancy. "The Rise of Feminine Authority in the Novel." *Novel* 15.2 (Winter 1982): 127-145.

Armstrong, Paul B. "Play and Cultural Differences." *The Kenyon Review* 13.1 (Winter 1991): 157-171.

Artaud, Antonin. *The Theatre and Its Double*. Trans. Mary Caroline Richards. New York: Grove Press, 1958.

Aspinall, Sue. "The Space for Innovation and Experiment." *Screen* 25.6 (November-December 1984): 73-87.

Auty, Martyn, and Nick Roddick. *British Cinema Now*. London: BFI Publishing, 1985.

Bakhtin, M. M. *The Dialogic Imagination*. Trans. Caryl Emerson and Michael Holquist. Ed. Michael Holquist. Austin: U of Texas P, 1981.

Barnard, Tim, ed. *Argentine Cinema*. Toronto: Nightwood, 1986.

Banta, Martha. *Taylored Lives: Narrative Productions in the Age of Taylor, Veblen and Ford*. Chicago: U of Chicago P, 1993.

Barthes, Roland. *S/Z*. Trans. Richard Miller. New York: Hill and Wang, 1974.

Bates, Robin. "Holes in the Sausage of History: May '68 as Absent Center in Three European Films." *Cinema Journal* 24.3 (Spring 1985): 24-42.

Baudrillard, Jean. "The Precession of Simulacra." *Art After Modernism: Rethinking Representation*. Ed. Brian Wallace. New York: The New Museum of Contemporary Art, 1984, 253-282.

Baudry, Jean-Louis. "The Apparatus: Metapsychological Approaches to the Impression of Reality in Cinema." *Narrative, Apparatus, Ideology: A Film Theory Reader*. Ed. Philip Rosen. New York: Columbia UP, 1986, 299-318.

——— . "Ideological Effects of the Basic Cinematic Apparatus." *Narrative, Apparatus, Ideology: A Film Theory Reader*. Ed. Philip Rosen. New York: Columbia UP, 1986. 286-298.

Bauman, Zygmunt. *Intimations of Postmodernity*. London: Routledge, 1992.

Bazin, André. *French Cinema of the Occupation and Resistance: The Birth of a Critical Esthetic*. Trans. Stanley Hochman. New York: Ungar, 1981.

Becker, Lee B., and Klaus Schoenbach. "When Media Content Diversifies: Anticipating Audience Behaviors." *Audience Responses to Media Diversification: Coping with Plenty*. Ed. Lee B. Becker and Klaus Schoenbach. Hillsdale, NJ: Lawrence Erlbaum, 1989. 1-28.

Bellour, Raymond. "Believing in the Cinema." *Psychoanalysis and Cinema*. Trans. Dana Polan. Ed. E. Ann Kaplan. New York: Routledge, 1990, 98-109.

––––––. "Segments/Analyzing." *Narrative, Apparatus, Ideology*. Ed. Philip Rosen. New York: Columbia UP, 1986. 286-298.

Belton, John. "CinemaScope and Historical Methodology." *Cinema Journal* 28.1 (Fall 1998): 22-44.

Berleant, Arnold. "Toward a Phenomenological Aesthetics of Environment." *Descriptions*. Ed. Don Ihde and Hugh J. Silverman. Albany: State U of New York P, 1985, 112-128.

Bhabha, Homi K. "Race and the Humanities: The 'Ends' of Modernity?" *Public Culture* 4.2 (Spring 1992): 81-88.

Bick, Ilsa J. "The Look Back in *E.T.*" *Cinema Journal* 31.4 (Summer 1992): 25-41.

Blomberg, Thomas G., Gordon P. Waldo, and Lisa C. Burcoff. "Home Confinement and Electronic Surveillance." *Intermediate Punishments: Intensive Supervision, Home Confinement and Electronic Surveillance*. Ed. Blinda R. McCarthy. Monsey, NY: Criminal Justice P, 1987. 169-180.

Boltz, Marilyn. "Temporal Accent Structure and the Remembering of Filmed Narratives." *Journal of Experimental Psychology: Human Perception and Performance* 18.1 (1992): 90-105.

Bordwell, David. "ApProppriations and ImPropprieties: Problems in the Morphology of Film Narrative." *Cinema Journal* 27.3 (Spring 1988): 5-20.

———— . "A Cinema of Flourishes: Japanese Decorative Classicism of the Prewar Era." *Reframing Japanese Cinema: Authorship, Genre, History.* Ed. Arthur Nolletti Jr., and David Desser. Bloomington: Indiana UP, 1992. 327-346.

———— . "Classical Hollywood Cinema: Narrational Principles and Procedures." *Narrative, Apparatus, Ideology.* Ed. Philip Rosen. New York: Columbia UP, 1986. 17-34.

———— . *Making Meaning: Inference and Rhetoric in the Interpretation of the Cinema.* Cambridge: Harvard UP, 1989.

Bordwell, David, and Kristin Thompson. *Film Art: An Introduction.* 2nd ed. New York: Knopf, 1986.

Borges, Jorge Luis. "Borges on Film." Trans. Ronald Christ and Gloria Waldman. *Argentine Cinema.* Ed. Tim Barnard. Toronto: Nightwood, 1986. 127-135.

Bouillin-Dartvelle, Roselyne. "Belgium: Language Division Internationalized." *Audience Responses to Media Diversification: Coping with Plenty.* Ed. Lee B. Becker and Klaus Schoenbach. Hillsdale, NJ: Lawrence Erlbaum, 1989. 51-70.

Bourdon, David. *Warhol.* New York: Abrams, 1989.

Boyd, Douglas A. *Broadcasting in the Arab World: A Survey of Electronic Media in the Middle East.* Ames: Iowa State UP, 1993.

Boyle, Deirdre. "From Portapak to Camcorder: A Brief History of Guerrilla Television." *Journal of Film and Video* 44.1/2 (Spring-Summer 1992): 67-79.

The Boys' and Girls' Cinema Club Annual. Vol. 1. London: Juvenile Productions, 1949.

Branigan, Edward. *Point of View in the Cinema: A Theory of Narration and Subjectivity in Classical Film.* Berlin: Mouton, 1984.

Bresson, Robert. *Notes on Cinematography.* Trans. Jonathan Griffin. New York: Urizen, 1977.

Brunette, Peter. "Rossellini and Cinematic Realism." *Cinema Journal* 25.1 (Fall 1985): 34-49.

Bruno, Giuliana. "Heresies: The Body of Pasolini's Semiotics." *Cinema Journal* 30.3 (Spring 1991): 29-42.

————. *Streetwalking on a Ruined Map: Cultural Theory and the City Films of Elvira Notari*. Princeton: Princeton UP, 1993.

Burgoyne, Robert. "The Cinematic Narrator: The Logic and Pragmatics of Impersonal Narration." *Journal of Film and Video* 42.1 (Spring 1990): 3-16.

Butler, Judith. "Sexual Inversions," *Foucault and the Critique of Institutions*. Ed. John Caputo and Mark Yount. University Park: Pennsylvania State UP, 81-99.

————. *Gender Trouble: Feminism and the Subversion of Identity*. New York: Routledge, 1990.

Camper, Fred. "*Remedial Reading Comprehension* by George Landow." *Film Culture* 52 (Spring 1971): 73-77.

Canyon Cinema Catalogue No. 7. San Francisco: Canyon Cinema, 1992.

Certeau, Michel de. *The Practice of Everyday Life*. Trans. Steven F. Rendall. Berkeley: U of California P, 1984.

Chakrabarty, Dipesh. "The Death of History? Historical Consciousness and the Culture of Late Capitalism." *Public Culture* 4.2 (Spring 1992): 47-66.

Chen, Xiaomei. "Occidentalism as Counterdiscourse: 'He Shang' in Post-Mao China." *Critical Inquiry* 18.4 (Summer 1992): 686-712.

Chenail, Ronald J. *Medical Discourse and Systemic Frames of Comprehension*. Norwood, NJ: Ablex, 1991.

Cixous, Hélène. "The Laugh of the Medusa." *Signs* 14 (Summer 1979): 875-899.

Clark, Katerina, and Michael Holquist. *Mikhail Bakhtin*. Cambridge: Harvard UP, 1984.

Clear, Todd R., Suzanne Flynn, and Carol Shapiro. "Intensive Supervision in Probation: A Comparison of Three Projects." *Intermediate Punishments: Intensive Supervision, Home Confinement and Electronic Surveillance*. Ed. Belinda R. McCarthy. Monsey, NY: Criminal Justice P, 1987. 31-50.

Clover, Carol J. *Men, Women, and Chainsaws: Gender in the Modern Horror Film*. Princeton: Princeton UP, 1992.

Cocteau, Jean. *Cocteau on the Film*. Recorded by André Fraigneau: Trans. Vera Traill. New York: Dover, 1972.

Collins, Ava Preacher. "Loose Canons: Constructing Cultural Traditions Inside and Outside the Academy." *Film Theory Goes to the Movies*. Ed. Jim Collins, Hilary Radner, and Ava Preacher Collins. New York: Routledge, 1993. 86-102.

Conover, Ted. "Trucking Through the AIDS Belt." *The New Yorker* (August 16, 1993): 57-75.

Coover, Robert. "Hyperfiction: Novels for the Computer." *The New York Times Book Review* (August 29, 1993): 1, 8-12.

Copjec, Joan. "Vampires, Breast-Feeding and Anxiety." *October* 58 (Fall 1991): 24-43.

Crafton, Donald. "Audienceship in Early Cinema." *Iris* 11 (Summer 1990): 1-12.

Crawford, Larry. "Looking, Film, Painting: The Trickster's In Site/In Sight/Insight/Incite." *Wide Angle* 5.3 (1983): 64-69.

Culler, Jonathan. "Warwick Studies in Philosophy and Literature: Political Criticism." *Writing the Future*. Ed. David Wood and Emmanuel Levinas. London: Routledge, 1990. 192-204.

Cvetkovich, Ann. "The Powers of Seeing and Being Seen: *Truth or Dare* and *Paris Is Burning*." *Film Theory Goes to the Movies*. Ed. Jim Collins, Hilary Radner, and Ava Preacher Collins. New York: Routledge, 1993. 155-169.

Dagrada, Elena. "Through the Keyhole: Spectators and Matte Shots in Early Cinema." *Iris* 11 (Summer 1990): 95-106.

Daly, Ann. "Dance History and Feminist Theory: Reconsidering Isadora Duncan and the Male Gaze." *Gender in Performance: The Presentation of Difference in the Performing Arts*. Ed. Laurence Senelick. Hanover, NH: UP of New England, 1992. 239-259.

Dasenbrock, Reed Way. "Word-World Relations: The Work of Charles Altieri and Edward Said." *New Orleans Review* 12.1 (Spring 1985): 92-96.

Dasgupta, Gautam. "*The Mahabharata*: Peter Brooks' 'Orientalism.'" *Performing Arts Journal* 10.3 (1987): 9-16.

Davis, Robert Con. "Theorizing Opposition: Aristotle, Greimas, Jameson, Said." *L'Esprit Createur* 27.2 (Summer 1987): 5-18.

De Lauretis, Teresa. *Technologies of Gender: Essays on Theory, Film and Fiction*. Bloomington: Indiana UP, 1987.

DeLoughry, Thomas T. "State of the Art Courtroom Unveiled at William and Mary." *The Chronicle of Higher Education* 40.5 (September 22, 1993): A22, A25.

Deming, Robert H. "The Television Spectator-Subject." *Journal of Film and Video* 37.3 (Summer 1985): 49-63.

Denzin, Norman K. *Images of Postmodern Society: Social Theory and Contemporary Cinema*. London: Sage, 1991.

Derrida, Jacques. *The Ear of the Other: Otobiography, Transference, Translation*. Ed. Christie McDonald. Trans. Peggy Kamuf. Lincoln: U of Nebraska P, 1985.

———. Lecture at the University of Nebraska, Lincoln, on "The Phantom Authority of the Police." April 19, 1990.

———. "The Other Heading: Memories, Responses, and Responsibilities," *PMLA* 108.1 (January 1993): 89-93.

Diawara, Manthia. *African Cinema: Politics and Culture*. Bloomington: Indiana UP, 1992.

Dixon, Wheeler Winston. "Alice Guy: Forgotten Pioneer of the Narrative Cinema," *New Orleans Review* 19.3/4 (Summer 1992): 7-15.

———. "*Boys in Brown*: Montgomery Tully and the Independent Frame Method." *Film Criticism* 16.1/2 (Fall-Winter, 1991-92): 18-32.

———. "The Camera Vision: Narrativity and Film." *New Orleans Review* 12.2 (Summer 1985): 57-61.

———. *The Charm of Evil: The Life and Films of Terence Fisher*. Metuchen, NJ: Scarecrow, 1992.

———. "The Child as Demon Since 1961 in Films." *Films in Review* 37.2 (February 1986): 78-83.

———. *The Cinematic Vision of F. Scott Fitzgerald*. Ann Arbor: UMI, 1986.

——— . "The Doubled Image: Montgomery Tully's *Boys in Brown* and the Independent Frame Process." *Film Criticism* 16.1/2 (Fall-Winter 1991-92): 18-32.

——— . "Dystopian Science Fiction: Notes for a Series of Films at the National Film Theatre, London." *NFT Monthly* (April 1992): 8-13.

——— . *The Early Film Criticism of François Truffaut.* Bloomington: Indiana UP, 1993.

——— . "The Early Films of Andy Warhol." *Classic Images* 214 (April 1993): 38-40.

——— . "Film and Literature: The Narrative Connection." *Thousand Oaks Journal* 1.1 (Fall 1987): 35-38.

——— . *The Films of Freddie Francis.* Metuchen, NJ: Scarecrow, 1991.

——— . "François Truffaut: A Life In Film." *Films in Review* 36.6/7 (June-July 1986): 331-336; 36.8/9 (August-September 1985): 413-417.

——— . "An Interview with Roger Corman." *Post Script* 8.1 (Fall 1988): 2-15.

——— . "It Looks at You: Notes on the 'Look Back' in Cinema." *Post Script* 13.1 (Fall 1993): 77-87.

——— . "In Defense of Roger Corman." *The Velvet Light Trap* 16 (Fall 1976): 11-15.

——— . "*The Long Day Closes*: An Interview with Terence Davies." *Cinéaste* 19.2/3 (1992): 20-23.

——— . "The Marginalized Vision of Montgomery Tully." *Classic Images* 224 (February 1994): C8-10, 12, 56-57; 225 (March 1994): 52-56.

——— . "William Inge as Walter Gage: *Bus Riley's Back in Town*." *Literature Film Quarterly* 16.2 (Spring 1988): 101-106.

Doane, Mary Ann. "The Clinical Eye: Medical Discourses in the 'Woman's Film' of Western Culture." Ed. Susan Rubin Suleiman. Cambridge: Harvard UP, 1986, 152-174.

——— . *The Desire to Desire: The Woman's Film in the 1940s.* Bloomington: Indiana UP, 1987.

——— . "The Economy of Desire: The Commodity Form in/of the Cinema." *Quarterly Review of Film and Video* 11.1 (1989): 23-34.

——— . "The Voice in the Cinema: The Articulation of Body and Space." *Narrative, Apparatus, Ideology: A Film Theory Reader.* Ed. Philip Rosen. New York: Columbia UP, 1986. 335-348.

Dollimore, Jonathan. "The Dominant and the Deviant: A Violent Dialectic." *Critical Quarterly* 28.1/2 (Spring-Summer 1986): 179-182.

——— . *Sexual Dissidence: Augustine to Wilde, Freud to Foucault.* Oxford: Clarendon Press, 1991.

Dyer, Richard. *Now You See It: Studies on Lesbian and Gay Film.* London: Routledge, 1990.

Eisner, Lotte H. *Fritz Lang.* Ed. David Robinson. New York: Oxford UP, 1977.

El-Dib, Ali Yehia. "Alternative Methods of the Production Process of Independent Narrative Films: A Descriptive Analytic Approach." *Dissertation Abstracts International* 49.11 (May 1989): 3187A.

Erwin, Timothy. "Modern Iconology, Postmodern Iconologies." *Image and Ideology in Modern/PostModern Discourse.* Ed. David B. Downing and Susan Bazargan. Albany: SUNY P, 1991, 309-320.

Fanon, Frantz. *The Wretched of the Earth.* Trans. Constance Farrington. New York: Grove, 1968.

Faulkner, Christopher. *The Social Cinema of Jean Renoir.* Princeton: Princeton UP, 1986.

Ferguson, Frances. "Sade and the Pornographic Legacy." *Representations* 36 (Fall 1991): 1-21.

Filmmakers' Cooperative Catalogue No. 7. New York: New American Cinema Group, 1989.

Filmmakers' Cooperative Catalogue No. 6. New York: New American Cinema Group, 1975.

Filmmakers' Cooperative Catalogue No. 4. New York: New American Cinema Group, 1967.

Finney, Brian. "Suture in Literary Analysis." *Lit: Literature Interpretation Theory* 2.2 (November 1992): 131-144.

Fischer, Lucy. *Shot/Countershot: Film Tradition and Women's Cinema*. Princeton: Princeton UP, 1989.

Fish, Stanley. "The Young and the Restless," *The New Historicism*. Ed. H. Aram Veeser. New York: Routledge, 1989, 303-316.

Fish, Stanley, Walter Jackson, and Edward Said. "Profession Despise Thyself: Fear and Self-Loathing in Literary Studies." *Critical Inquiry* 10.2 (December 1983): 349-373.

Foucault, Michel. *Discipline and Punish: The Birth of the Prison*. Trans. Alan Sheridan. New York: Vintage, 1979.

Gallagher, Catherine. "Marxism and the New Historicism." *The New Historicism*. Ed. H. Aram Vesser. New York: Routledge, 1989.

———. "Politics, the Profession, and the Critic." *Diacritics: A Review of Contemporary Criticism* 15.2 (Summer 1985): 37-43.

Gaudréault, André. "Narration and Monstration in the Cinema." *Journal of Film and Video* 39.2 (Spring 1987): 29-36.

Gendron, Bernard. "Theodor Adorno Meets the Cadillacs." *Studies in Entertainment: Critical Approaches to Mass Culture*. Ed. Tania Modleski. Bloomington: Indiana UP, 1986. 18-36.

Gerson, Robert. "Captive Light. Seeing the Movies in Prison." *The Antioch Review* 50.3 (Summer 1992): 538-550.

Getino, Octavio. "Some Notes on the Concept of a "Third Cinema." *Argentine Cinema*. Ed. Tim Barnard. Toronto: Nightwood, 1986. 99-108.

Gidal, Peter. "Against Sexual Representation in Film." *Screen* 25.6 (November-December 1984): 24-30.

———. "The Anti-Narrative (1978)." *Screen* 20.2 (Summer 1979): 73-93.

———. *Materialist Film*. London: Routledge, 1989.

Gifford, Denis. *British Cinema: An Illustrated Guide*. London: A. Zwemmer, 1968.

———. *The British Film Catalogue 1895-1970; A Reference Guide*. New York: McGraw-Hill, 1973.

———. *The Illustrared Who's Who in British Films*. London: B. T. Batsford, 1978.

Giles, Dennis. "Television Reception." *Journal of Film and Video* 37.3 (Summer 1985): 12-25.

Godard, Jean-Luc. *Godard on Godard*. Trans. and ed. Tom Milne. New York: Da Capo, 1986.

Goldberg, Marianne. "The Body, Discourse, and *The Man Who Envied Women*." *Women and Performance: A Journal of Feminist Theory* 3.2 (1987-88): 97-102.

Goulding, Daniel J., ed. *Post New Wave Cinema in the Soviet Union and Eastern Europe*. Bloomington: Indiana UP, 1989.

Graham, Peter. *The New Wave*. New York: Viking, 1968.

Grant, Barry Keith. *Voyages of Discovery: The Cinema of Frederick Wiseman*. Urbana: U of Illinois P, 1992.

Gray, Herman. "Recodings: Possibilities and Limitations in Commercial Television Representations of African American Culture." *Quarterly Review of Film and Video* 13.3/4 (May 1991): 117-130.

Hall, Stuart. "The Toad in the Garden: Thatcherism Among the Theorists." *Marxism and the Interpretation of Culture*. Ed. Cary Nelson and Lawrence Grossberg. Chicago: U of Illinois P, 1988. 35-57.

Hardt, Michael. *Gilles Deleuze: An Apprenticeship in Philosophy*. Minneapolis: U of Minnesota P, 1993.

Harvey, Robert. "Sartre/Cinema: Spectator/Art That is Not One." *Cinema Journal* 30.3 (Spring 1991): 43-59.

Heath, Stephen. *Questions of Cinema*. Bloomington: Indiana UP, 1981.

Heath, Stephen, and Gillian Skirrow. "An Interview with Raymond Williams." *Studies in Entertainment: Critical Approaches to Mass Culture*. Ed. Tania Modleski. Bloomington: Indiana UP, 1986. 3-17.

Hedges, Inez. *Breaking the Frame: Film Language and the Experience of Limits*. Bloomington: Indiana UP, 1991.

Heider, Karl G. *Indonesian Cinema: National Culture on Screen*. Honolulu: U of Hawaii P, 1991.

Helt, Richard C., and Marie E. Helt. *West German Cinema: 1985-1990. A Reference Handbook*. Metuchen, NJ: Scarecrow, 1992.

Hill, Jerome. "Brakhage's *Eyes.*" *Film Culture* 52 (Spring 1972): 43-46.

Hill, John. *Sex, Class and Realism: British Cinema 1956-1963.* London: BFI Publishing, 1986.

Hollinger, Karen. "Listening to the Female Voice in the Woman's Film." *Film Criticism* 16.3 (Spring 1992): 34-52.

Holloway, Ronald. "Bulgaria: The Cinema of Poetics." *Post New Wave Cinema in the Soviet Union and Eastern Europe.* Ed. Daniel J. Goulding. Bloomington: Indiana UP, 1989. 215-247.

Holmlund, Christine Anne. "Displacing Limits of Difference: Gender, Race and Colonialism in Edward Said and Homi Bhabha's Theoretical Models and Marguerute Duras's Experimental Films." *Quarterly Review of Film and Video* 13.3/4 (May 1991): 1-22.

Hondo, Med. "Cinémas africains, écrans colonisés." *Le Monde* (January 21, 1982): 12.

hooks, bell. *Black Looks: Race and Representation.* Boston: South End P, 1992.

Hull, David Stewart. *Film in the Third Reich: A Study of the German Cinema 1933-1945.* Berkeley: U of California P, 1969.

Hunter, Dianne. "Interview with Jean Baudrillard." *Image and Ideology in Modern/PostModern Discourse.* Ed. David B. Downing and Susan Bazargan. Albany: SUNY P, 1991. 287-292.

Husserl, Edmund. *Cartesian Medians.* Trans. Dorion Cairns. The Hague: Nijhoff, 1973.

Indiana, Gary. "A Day at the Sex Factory." *The Village Voice* 38.34 (August 24, 1993): 26-28, 30, 33-37.

Issari, Mohammad Ali. *Cinema in Iran, 1900-1979.* Metuchen, NJ: Scarecrow, 1989.

Ivens, Joris. *The Camera And I.* New York: International Publishers, 1969.

Jameson, Fredric. "Modernism and Imperialism." *Nationalism, Colonialism and Literature.* Ed. Terry Eagleton, Frederick Jameson, and Edward W. Said. Minneapolis: U of Minnesota P, 1990. 43-66.

――― . *The Political Unconscious.* Ithaca: Cornell UP, 1981.

————. *Signatures of the Visible*. New York: Routledge, 1990.

Jarman, Derek. *Queer Edward II*. London: BFI Publishing, 1991.

"Joan Rivers Switching Shows." *The Lincoln Journal-Star* (October 30, 1993): 3.

Johnson, Douglas, and Madeleine Johnson. *The Age of Illusion: Art and Politics in France 1918-1940*. New York: Rizzoli, 1987.

Johnson, Kenneth. "The Point of View of the Wandering Camera." *Cinema Journal* 32.2 (Winter 1993): 49-56.

Kapsis, Robert E. "The Historical Reception of Hitchcock's *Marnie*." *Journal of Film and Video* 40.3 (Summer 1988): 46-63.

Katzman, Lisa. "The Women of Porn: They're not in it for the Money Shot." *The Village Voice* 38.34 (August 24, 1993): 31-33.

Keil, Charles. "The Story of Uncle Josh Told: Spectatorship and Apparatus in Early American Cinema." *Iris* 11 (Summer 1990): 63-76.

Kepley, Vance, Jr. "Spatial Articulation in the Classical Cinema: A Scene from *His Girl Friday*." *Wide Angle* 5.3 (1983): 50-58.

Kipnis, Laura. *Ecstasy Unlimited: On Sex, Capital, Gender and Aesthetics*. Foreword by Paul Smith. Minneapolis: U of Minnesota P, 1993.

Kirby, Lynn. "The Urban Spectator and the Crowd in Early American Train Films." *Iris* 11 (Summer 1990): 49-62.

Klein, Gilbert. "Tout va Bien." *Film Quarterly* 26.4 (Summer 1973): 39.

Kozloff, Max. *The Privileged Eye: Essays on Photography*. Albuquerque: U of New Mexico P, 1987.

Kramer, Lloyd S. "Literature and Historical Imagination." *The New Cultural History*. Ed. Lynn Hunt. Berkeley: U of California P, 1989. 97-128.

Kristeva, Julia. "The Adolescent Novel." *Abjection, Melancholia and Love: The Work of Julia Kristeva*. Ed. John Fletcher and Andrew Benjamin. New York: Routledge, 1990. 8-23.

————. "Ellipsis on Dread and the Specular Seduction." *Narrative, Apparatus, Ideology: A Film Theory Reader*. Ed. Philip Rosen. New York: Columbia UP, 1986. 236-243.

———. *Language: The Unknown: An Initiation into Linguistics*. Trans. Anne M. Menke. New York: Columbia UP, 1989.

———. *Powers of Horror: An Essay on Abjection*. Trans. Leon S. Roudiez. New York: Columbia UP, 1982.

———. *La Révolution du langage poétique*. Paris: Sevil, 1974.

Kroker, Arthur, and David Cook. *The Postmodern Scene: Excremental Culture and Hyper-Aesthetics*. New York: St. Martin's Press, 1986.

Kunhardt, Dorothy. *Pat the Bunny*. Racine, WI: Golden Press, 1942.

Lacan, Jacques. *Television: A Challenge to the Psychoanalytical Establishment*. Trans. Denis Hollier, Rosalind Krauss, Annette Michelson, and Jeffrey Mehlman. Ed. Joan Copjec. New York: Norton, 1990.

Landy, Marcia. *British Genres: Cinema and Society, 1930-1960*. Princeton: Princeton UP, 1991.

Laqueur, Thomas. *Making Sex: Body and Gender from the Greeks to Freud*. Cambridge: Harvard UP, 1990.

Larsen, Egon. *Spotlight on Films*. London: Max Parrish, 1950.

Lawton, Anna. "Toward a New Openness in Soviet Cinema, 1976-1987." *Post New Wave Cinema in the Soviet Union and Eastern Europe*. Ed. Daniel J. Goulding. Bloomington: Indiana UP, 1989. 1-50.

Lehman, Peter. "Looking at Ivy Looking at Us Looking at Her." *Wide Angle* 5.3. (1983): 59-63.

Lent, John A. *The Asian Film Industry*. Austin: U of Texas P, 1990.

Lent, John A., George S. Semsel, Keiko McDonald, and Manjunath Pendakur. *The Asian Film Industry*. Austin: U of Texas P, 1990.

Leonhard, Sigrun D. "Testing the Borders: East German Film Between Individualism and Social Commitment." *Post New Wave Cinema in the Soviet Union and Eastern Europe*. Ed. Daniel J. Goulding. Bloomington: Indiana UP, 1989. 51-101.

Levinson, Jerrold. "Seeing, Imaginarily, at the Movies." *The Philosophical Quarterly* 43.170 (January 1993): 70-79.

Levy, Mark R., and Sven Windahl. "The Concept of Audience Activity." *Media Gratifications Research: Current Perspectives*. Ed. Karl Erik Rosengren, Lawrence A. Wenner, and Philip Palmgreen. Beverly Hills: Sage, 1985. 109-122.

Lyotard, Jean-François. *The Postmodern Condition: A Report on Knowledge*. Trans. Geoff Bennington and Brian Massumi. Minneapolis: U of Minnesota P, 1984.

Macaskill, Brian. "Figuring Rupture: Iconology, Politics, and the Image." *Image and Ideology in Modern/PostModern Discourse*. Ed. David B. Downing and Susan Bazargan. Albany: SUNY P, 1991. 249-272.

MacCabe, Colin. *Tracking the Signifier: Theoretical Essays; Film, Linguistics, Literature*. Minneapolis: U of Minnesota P, 1985.

MacDonald, Scott. "Avant-Garde Film: Cinema as Discourse." *Journal of Film and Video* 40.2 (Spring 1988): 33-42.

———. "From Zygote to Global Cinema via Su Friedrich's Films." *Journal of Film and Video* 44.1/2 (Spring-Summer 1992): 30-41.

MacDougall, David. "When Less is Less—The Long Take in Documentary." *Film Quarterly* 46.2 (Winter 1992-93): 36-46.

Mandelbaum, Howard, and Eric Myers. *Forties Screen Style: A Celebration of High Pastiche in Hollywood*. New York: St. Martin's P, 1989.

———. *Screen Deco*. New York: St. Martin's P, 1985.

Marchetti, Gina. "Ethnicity, the Cinema, and Cultural Studies." *Unspeakable Images: Ethnicity and the American Cinema*. Ed. Lester D. Friedman. Urbana: U of Illinois P, 1991. 277-307.

McShine, Kynaston. *Andy Warhol: A Retrospective*. New York: Museum of Modern Art, 1989.

Mellencamp, Patricia. "Situation and Simulation." *Screen* 26.2 (March-April 1985): 30-41.

Merleau-Ponty, Maurice. "Introduction to *Signs*." *Phenomenology, Language and Sociology: Selected Essays of Maurice Merleau-Ponty*. Ed. John O'Neill. London: Heinemann, 1974.

Metz, Christian. "Current Problems of Film Theory: Christian Metz on Jean Mitry's *L'Esthétique et Psychologie du Cinéma*. Vol. 2." Trans. Diana Matias. *Screen* 14.1/2 (Spring-Summer 1973): 40-87.

——. "On the Impression of Reality in the Cinema." *Film Language: A Semiotics of the Cinema*. New York: Oxford UP, 1974. 3-15.

——. "Problems of Denotation in the Fiction Film." *Narrative, Apparatus, Ideology*. Ed. Philip Rosen. New York: Columbia UP, 1986. 35-65.

Michelson, Annette. "'Where Is Your Rupture?': Mass Culture and *Gesamtkunstwerk*." *October* 56 (Spring 1991): 42-63.

Miller, Debra. *Billy Name: Stills From the Warhol Films*. Munich: Prestel, 1994.

Miller, Jane. *Seductions: Studies in Reading and Culture*. Cambridge: Harvard UP, 1990.

Minh-ha, Trinh T. "All-Owning Spectatorship." *Quarterly Review of Film and Video* 13.3/4 (May 1991): 189-204.

——. *Framer Framed*. New York: Routledge, 1992.

Mitchell, William J. *The Reconfigured Eye: Visual Truth in the Post-Photographic Era*. Cambridge: MIT P, 1992.

Mitchell, W.J.T. "Iconology and Ideology: Panofsky, Althusser, and the Scene of Recognition." *Image and Ideology in Modern/PostModern Discourse*. Ed. David B. Downing and Susan Bazargan. Albany: SUNY P, 1991. 321-329.

Modleski, Tania. *Feminism Without Women: Culture and Criticism in a 'Postfeminist' Age*. New York: Routledge, 1991.

——. "The Terror of Pleasure: The Contemporary Horror Film and Postmodern Theory." *Studies in Entertainment: Critical Approaches to Mass Culture*. Ed. Tania Modleski. Bloomington: Indiana UP, 1986. 155-166.

Mohanty, Chandra Talpade. "Under Western Eyes: Feminist Scholarship and Colonial Discourses." *Boundary* 2.12 (1984): 336.

Moi, Toril. *Sexual/Textual Politics: Feminist Literary Theory*. London: Routledge, 1985.

Mora, Carl J. *Mexican Cinema: Reflections of A Society 1896-1988*. Berkeley: U of California P, 1989.

Morrison, Toni. *Playing in the Dark*. Cambridge: Harvard UP, 1992.

Morse, Margaret. "Talk, Talk, Talk—The Space of Discourse in Television." *Screen* 26.2 (March-April 1985): 2-17.

Mulvey, Laura. "Changes." *Discourse: Journal for Theoretical Studies in Media and Culture* 7 (Fall 1985): 11-30.

Nadel, Alan. "God's Law and the Wide Screen: *The Ten Commandments* as Cold War Epic," *PMLA* 108.3 (May 1993): 415-430.

Newman, Beth. "'The Situation of the Looker-On': Gender, Narration and Gaze in *Wuthering Heights*." *PMLA* 105.5 (October 1980): 1029-1041.

Newton, Judith Lowter. "History as Usual? Feminism and the 'New Historicism.'" *The New Historicism*. Ed. H. Aram Veeser. New York: Routledge, 1989. 152-167.

Nietzche, Friedrich. *Twilight of the Idols and The Anti-Christ*. Trans. R. J. Hollingdale. Harmondsworth: Penguin, 1968.

Nixon, Sean. "Have You Got the Look? Masculinites and Shopping Spectacle." *Lifestyle Shopping: The Subject of Consumption*. London: Routledge, 1992. 149-169.

Nygren, Scott. "New Narrative Film in Japan: Stress Fractures in Cross-Cultural Postmodernism." *Post Script* 11.1 (Fall 1991): 48-56.

Olderaan, Frank, and Nick Jankowski. "The Netherlands: The Cable Replaces the Cinema." *Audience Responses to Media Diversification: Coping with Plenty*. Ed. Lee B. Becker and Klaus Schoenbach. Hillsdale, NJ: Lawrence Erlbaum, 1989. 29-50.

Paik, Nam June. "Adios 20th Century." *Point of Contact* 3.3 (April 1993): 104-109.

Pêcheux, Michel. "Discourse: Structure or Event?" *Marxism and the Interpretation of Culture*. Ed. Cary Nelson and Lawrence Grossberg. Urbana: U of Illinois P, 1988. 633-650.

Pendergrast, Mark. "A Brief History of Coca-Colonization." *The New York Times*, August 19, 1993, C: 13.

——— . *For God, Country and Coca-Cola*. New York: Scribner's, 1993.

Perlmutter, Ruth. "Lizzie Borden: An Interview." *Post Script* 6.2 (Winter 1987): 2-11.

———. "Peter Greenaway: An Inter-Review." *Post Script* 8.2 (Winter 1989): 56-63.

Perry, George. *The Great British Picture Show: From the 90s to the 70s*. New York: Hill and Wang, 1974.

Petley, Julia. "The Lost Continent." *All Our Yesterdays*. Ed. Charles Barr. London: BFI Publishing, 1986.

Pirie, David. *A Heritage of Horror: The English Gothic Cinema 1946-1972*. London: Gordon Fraser, 1978. New York: Avon, 1974.

Polan, Dana. *Power and Paranoia: History, Narrative and the American Cinema 1940-1950*. New York: Columbia UP, 1986.

Poulet, Georges. "Criticism and the Experience of Interiority." *Reader-Response Criticism: From Formalism to Post-Structualism*. Trans. Catherine Macksey. Ed. Jane P. Tompkins. Baltimore: Johns Hopkins UP, 1980.

Preston, John. "The Theatre of Sexual Initiation," *Gender in Performance: The Presentation of Difference in the Performing Arts*. Ed. Laurencd Senelick. Hanover, NH: UP of New England, 1992. 324-335.

Prince, Stephen. "The Pornographic Image and the Practice of Film Theory." *Cinema Journal* 27.2 (Winter 1988): 27-39.

Quilligan, Maureen. *The Allegory of Female Authority: Christine de Pizan's* Cité Des Dames. Ithaca: Cornell UP, 1991.

Rainer, Yvonne. "Narrative in the (Dis)Service of Identity: Fragments Toward a Performed Lecture Dealing with Menopause, Race, Gender and Other Uneasy Bedfellows in the Cinematic Sheets; Or, How Do You Begin to Think of Yourself as Lesbian." *Review of Japanese Culture and Society* 4 (December 1991): 46-52.

Renoir, Jean. *Renoir on Renoir: Interviews, Essays and Remarks*. Trans. Carol Volk. Cambridge: Cambridge UP, 1989.

Rhodes, Anthony. *Propaganda: The Art of Persuasion [in] World War II*. Secaucus, NJ: Wellfleet, 1987.

Richie, Donald. "The Inn Sequence in Ozu's *Late Autumn.*" Ed. Arthur Nolletti Jr. and David Desser. *Reframing Japanese Cinema: Authorship, Genre, History.* Bloomington: Indiana UP, 1992. 113-125.

Rodowick, D. N. *The Difficulty of Difference: Psychoanalysis, Sexual Difference and Film Theory.* New York: Routledge, 1991.

Ronell, Avital. *The Telephone Book.* Lincoln: U of Nebraska P, 1989.

Roud, Richard. *Jean-Marie Straub.* New York: Viking, 1972.

Roudiez, Léon S. Introduction, *Desire in Language: A Semiotic Approach to Literature and Art.* By Julia Kristeva, Oxford: Blackwell. 1-20.

Ruby, Jay. "Speaking For, Speaking About, Speaking With, or Speaking Alongside: An Anthropological and Documentary Dilemma." *Journal of Film and Video* 44.1/2 (Spring-Summer 1992): 42-66.

Ruoff, Jeffrey K. "Movies of the Avant-Garde: Jonas Mekas and the New York Art World." *Cinema Journal* 30.3 (Spring 1991): 6-28.

Said, Edward W. *Culture and Imperialism.* New York: Knopf, 1993.

———. "Foucault and the Imagination of Power." *Foucault: A Critical Reader.* Ed. David Couzens Hoy. Oxford: Blackwell, 1986. 149-155.

———. *Orientalism.* New York: Pantheon, 1978.

———. "The Politics of Knowledge." *Raritan: A Quarterly Review* 11.1 (Summer 1991): 17-31.

Scarry, Elaine. *The Body in Pain: The Making and Unmaking of the World.* New York: Oxford UP, 1985.

Schmutzler, Robert. *Art Nouveau.* New York: Abrams, 1962.

Schnitman, Jorge A. *Film Industries in Latin America: Dependency and Development.* Norwood, NJ: Ablex, 1984.

Schultz, Victoria. "Interview with Roberto Rossellini." *Film Culture* 52 (Spring 1971): 1-42.

Sconce, Jeffrey. "Spectacles of Death: Identification, Reflexivity, and Contemporary Horror." *Film Theory Goes to the Movies.* Ed. Jim

Collins, Hilary Radner, and Ava Preacher Collins. New York: Routledge, 1993. 103-119.

"Selection from *De la Séduction.*" *Image and Ideology in Modern/Post-Modern Discourse.* Trans. Dianne Hunter. Ed. David B. Downing and Susan Bazargan. Albany: SUNY P, 1991. 293-298.

Seltzer, Mark. *Bodies and Machines.* New York: Routledge, 1992.

Sherman, Eric, and Martin Rubin. *The Director's Event.* New York: Signet, 1969.

Shields, Rob. "Spaces for the Subject of Consumption." *Lifestyle Shopping: The Subject of Consumption.* London: Routledge, 1992. 1-20.

Shohat, Ella. "Ethnicities-in-Relation: Toward a Multicultural Reading of American Cinema." *Unspeakable Images: Ethnicity and the American Cinema.* Ed. Lester D. Friedman. Urbana: U of Illinois P, 1991. 215-250.

Sholle, David. "Reading the Audience, Reading Resistance: Prospects and Problems." *Journal of Film and Video* 43.1/2 (Spring-Summer 1991): 80-89.

"Shooting Script for Christmas Time Home Movies." *Better Homes and Gardens* (December 1960): 26.

Shuster, Mel. *The Contemporary Greek Cinema.* Metuchen, NJ: Scarecrow, 1979.

Siegel, Joel E. *Val Lewton: The Reality of Terror.* New York: Viking, 1973.

Silverman, Kaja. "Fragments of A Fashionable Discourse." *Studies in Entertainment: Critical Approaches to Mass Culture.* Ed. Tania Modleski. Bloomington: Indiana UP, 1986. 139-152.

——— . *Male Subjectivity at the Margins.* New York: Routledge, 1992.

——— . "Suture" (excerpts). *Narrative, Apparatus, Ideology: A Film Theory Reader.* Ed. Philip Rosen. New York: Columbia UP, 1986. 219-235.

Singer, Ben. "Film, Photography, Fetish: The Analyses of Christian Metz." *Cinema Journal* 27.4 (Summer 1988): 4-22.

Snider, Mike. "Video Game Ratings Present a New Difficulty Level." *USA Today*, March 3, 1994, 4D.

Snow, Michael. *"La Région centrale." Film Culture* 52 (Spring 1971): 58-63. Transcribed and edited by Charlotte Townsend.

Sobchack, Vivian. *The Address of the Eye: A Phenomenology of Film Experience*. Princeton: Princeton UP, 1992.

———. "Postmodern Modes of Ethnicity." *Unspeakable Images: Ethnicity and the American Cinema*. Ed. Lester D. Friedman. Urbana: U of Illinois P, 1991. 329-352.

Sparkes, Vernon M., and Jeffrey P. Delbel. "United States: Changing Perceptions of Television." *Audience Responses to Media Diversification: Coping with Plenty*. Ed. Lee B. Becker and Klaus Schoenbach. Hillsdale, NJ: Lawrence Erlbaum, 1989. 333-352.

Spivak, Gayatri Chakravorty. "The New Historicism: Political Comment and the Postmodern Critic." *The New Historicism*. Ed. H. Aram Veeser. New York: Routledge, 1989. 277-292.

Squire, Corrine. "Toute une Heure—An Interview with Chantal Akerman." *Screen* 25.6 (November-December 1984): 67-72.

Staiger, Janet. "Class, Ethnicity and Gender: Explaining the Development of Early American Film Narrative." *Iris* 11 (Summer 1990): 13-26.

Stam, Robert. "Bakhtin, Polyphony and Ethnic/Racial Representation." *Unspeakable Images: Ethnicity and the American Cinema*. Ed. Lester D. Friedman. Urbana: U of Illinois P, 1991. 251-276.

———. "Eurocentrism, Afrocentrism, Polycentrism: Theories of Third Cinema." *Quarterly Review of Film and Video* 13.3/4 (May 1991): 217-238.

———. *Reflexivity in Film and Literature: From Don Quixote to Jean-Luc Godard*. Ann Arbor: UMI Research Press, 1985.

Stam, Robert, Robert Burgoyne, and Sandy Flitterman-Lewis, eds. *New Vocabularies in Film Semiotics: Structuralism, Post-Structuralism and Beyond*. London: Routledge, 1992.

Steinman, Clay. "Reception Theory: Film/Television Studies and the Frankfurt School." *Journal of Film and Video* 40.2 (Spring 1988): 4-19.

Stewart, Lucy Ann Liggett. *Ida Lupino as Film Director, 1949-1953: An Auteur Approach.* New York: Arno, 1980.

Straub, Kristina. "Feminist Politics and Postmodernist Style." *Image and Ideology in Modern/PostModern Discourse.* Ed. David B. Downing and Susan Bazargan. Albany: SUNY P, 1991. 273-286.

Tafler, David. "The Circular Text: Interactive Video, Reception, and Viewer Participation." *Journal of Film and Video* 40.3 (Summer 1988): 27-45.

Tagg, John. *The Burden of Respresentation: Essays on Photographies and Histories.* Amherst: U of Massachusetts P, 1988.

Taubin, Amy. "Mirror, Mirror." *The Village Voice* 38.29 (July 20, 1993): 57.

Taussig, Michael. "The Magic of the State." *Public Culture* 5.1 (Fall 1992): 63-66.

Telotte, J. P. "Film and/as Technology: An Introduction." *Post Script* 10.1 (Fall 1990): 3-8.

"The Photography of the Month." *American Cinematographer* 22.5 (May 1941): 222.

Thompson, Kristin, and David Bordwell. "Linearity, Materialism and the Study of Early American Cinema." *Wide Angle* 5.3 (1983): 4-15.

Tierney, John. "Movies That Push Buttons." *The New York Times,* October 3, 1993, B:1, B:26-27.

Todd, Daniel. "Directors of Digital Production." *Wired* 1.6 (December 1993): 58-60.

Tomasulo, Frank P. "The Text-in-the-Spectator: The Role of Phenomenology in an Eclectic Theoretical Methodology." *Journal of Film and Video* 40.2 (Spring 1988): 20-32.

Trouillot, Michel-Rolph. "The Vulgarity of Power." *Public Culture* 5.1 (Fall 1992): 75-82.

Vaughn, Joseph B. "Planning for Change: The Use of Electronic Monitoring as a Correctional Alternative." *Intermediate Punishments: Intensive Supervision, Home Confinement and Electronic Surveil-*

lance. Ed. Belinda R. McCarthy. Monsey, NY: Criminal Justice P, 1987. 169-180.

Vernet, Marc. "The Look at the Camera." *Cinema Journal* 28.2 (Winter 1989): 48-63. Trans. of "Le regard à la camèra: figures de l'absence," by Dana Polan. *Iris* 1.2 (1983): 31-45.

Walsh, Michael. "The Perfect Alibi of Images." *Image and Ideology in Modern/PostModern Discourse.* Ed. David B. Downing and Susan Bazargan. Albany: SUNY P, 1991. 299-308.

Wang, Ban. "'I' on the Run: Crisis of Identity in Mrs. Dalloway." *Modern Fiction Studies* 38.1 (Spring 1992): 177-192.

Watney, Simon. "Never-Never Land: An Examination of the Case for the Impossibility of Children's Fiction." *Screen* 26.1 (January-February 1985): 86-89.

Watson, Julia, and Sidonie Smith. "Introduction: De/Colonization and the Politics of Discourse in Women's Autobiographical Practices." *De/Colonizing the Subject: The Politics of Gender in Women's Autobiography.* Ed. Julia Watson and Sidonie Smith. Minneapolis: U of Minnesota P, 1992. xiii-xxxi.

Weiss, Allen S. "Poetic Justice: Formations of Subjectivity and Sexual Identity." *Cinema Journal* 28.1 (Fall 1988): 45-64.

Weldon, Michael. *The Psychotronic Encyclopedia of Film.* New York: Ballantine, 1983.

Willemen, Paul. "Letter to John." *Screen* 21.2 (Summer 1980): 53-66.

Willemen, Paul, and Jim Pines. *Questions of Third Cinema.* London: BFI Publishing, 1989.

Williams, Linda. *Hard Core: Power, Pleasure, and the "Frenzy of the Visible."* Berkeley: U of California P, 1989.

Williamson, Judith. "Woman Is an Island: Femininity and Colonization." *Studies in Entertainment: Critical Approaches to Mass Culture.* Ed. Tania Modleski. Bloomington: Indiana UP, 1986. 99-118.

Wilson, Colin. *Poetry and Mysticism.* San Francisco: City Lights, 1969.

Wober, Joseph Mallory. "The U.K.: The Constancy of Audience Behavior." *Audience Responses to Media Diversification: Coping with*

Plenty. Ed. Lee B. Becker and Klaus Schoenbach. Hillsdale, NJ: Lawrence Erlbaum, 1989. 91-108.

Wollen, Peter. "Baroque and Neo-Baroque in the Society of the Spectacle." *Point of Contact* 3.3 (April 1993): 8-21.

——— . *Signs and Meaning in the Cinema.* Bloomington: Indiana UP, 1969.

Wurzer, Wilhelm S. *Filming and Judgment: Between Heidegger and Adorno.* Atlantic Highlands, NJ: Humanities Press International, 1990.

Young, Iris M. "Pregnant Subjectivity and the Limits of Existential Phenomenology." *Descriptions.* Ed. Don Ihde and Hugh J. Silverman. Albany: SUNY P, 1985. 25-34.

Zavarzadeh, Mas'ud. Letter to the author, dated July 20, 1993.

——— . *Seeing Films Politically.* Albany: SUNY P, 1991.

Zillman, Dolf. "The Experimental Exploration of Gratifications from Media Entertainment." *Media Gratifications Research: Current Perspectives.* Ed. Karl Erik Rosengren, Lawrence A. Wenner, and Philip Palmgreen. Beverly Hills: Sage, 1985. 225-240.

Zimmerman, Patricia R. "Hollywood, Home Movies, and Common Sense: Amateur Film as Aesthetic Dissemination and Social Control, 1950-1962." *Cinema Journal* 27.4 (Summer 1988): 23-44.

INDEX